CCCC STUDIES IN WRITING & RHETORIC

Edited by Victor Villanueva, Washington State University

The aim of the CCCC Studies in Writing & Rhetoric Series is to influence how we think about language in action and especially how writing gets taught at the college level. The methods of studies vary from the critical to historical to linguistic to ethnographic, and their authors draw on work in various fields that inform composition—including rhetoric, communication, education, discourse analysis, psychology, cultural studies, and literature. Their focuses are similarly diverse—ranging from individual writers and teachers, to work on classrooms and communities and curricula, to analyses of the social, political, and material contexts of writing and its teaching.

SWR was one of the first scholarly book series to focus on the teaching of writing. It was established in 1980 by the Conference on College Composition and Communication (CCCC) in order to promote research in the emerging field of writing studies. As our field has grown, the research sponsored by SWR has continued to articulate the commitment of CCCC to supporting the work of writing teachers as reflective practitioners and intellectuals.

We are eager to identify influential work in writing and rhetoric as it emerges. We thus ask authors to send us project proposals that clearly situate their work in the field and show how they aim to redirect our ongoing conversations about writing and its teaching. Proposals should include an overview of the project, a brief annotated table of contents, and a sample chapter. They should not exceed 10,000 words.

To submit a proposal, please register as an author at www.editorial manager.com/nctebp. Once registered, follow the steps to submit a proposal (be sure to choose SWR Book Proposal from the drop-down list of article submission types).

ASSEMBLING COMPOSITION

Edited by

Kathleen Blake Yancey
Florida State University

Stephen J. McElroy
Florida State University

Conference on College
Composition and
Communication

National Council of
Teachers of English

Staff Editor: Bonny Graham
Series Editor: Victor Villanueva
Interior Design: Mary Rohrer
Cover Design: Mary Rohrer, Lynn Weckhorst, and Stephen J. McElroy

NCTE Stock Number: 01988; eStock Number: 01995
ISBN 978-0-8141-0198-8; eISBN 978-0-8141-0199-5

It is the policy of NCTE in its journals and other publications to provide a forum for the open discussion of ideas concerning the content and the teaching of English and the language arts. Publicity accorded to any particular point of view does not imply endorsement by the Executive Committee, the Board of Directors, or the membership at large, except in announcements of policy, where such endorsement is clearly specified.

NCTE provides equal employment opportunity (EEO) to all staff members and applicants for employment without regard to race, color, religion, sex, national origin, age, physical, mental or perceived handicap/disability, sexual orientation including gender identity or expression, ancestry, genetic information, marital status, military status, unfavorable discharge from military service, pregnancy, citizenship status, personal appearance, matriculation or political affiliation, or any other protected status under applicable federal, state, and local laws.

Every effort has been made to provide current URLs and email addresses, but because of the rapidly changing nature of the Web, some sites and addresses may no longer be accessible.

Publication partially funded by a subvention grant from the Conference on College Composition and Communication of the National Council of Teachers of English.

Library of Congress Cataloging-in-Publication Data

Names: Yancey, Kathleen Blake, 1950–
Title: Assembling composition / edited by Kathleen Blake Yancey, Stephen J. McElroy
Description: Urbana, IL : National Council of Teachers of English, 2017 | Series: Studies in writing & rhetoric | Includes bibliographical references and index.
Identifiers: LCCN 2016041837 (print) | LCCN 2016043728 (ebook) | ISBN 9780814101988 (pbk.) | ISBN 9780814101995
Subjects: LCSH: English language—Composition and exercises—Study and teaching (Higher)
Classification: LCC PE1404 .A77 2017 (print) | LCC PE1404 (ebook) | DDC 808/.0420711—dc23
LC record available at https://lccn.loc.gov/2016041837

CONTENTS

ACKNOWLEDGMENTS

TOGETHER, KATHLEEN (KATHI) AND STEPHEN thank Victor Villanueva for his guidance throughout the processes of submission, revision, and publication: his consistent encouragement was always welcome, and his contributions have enhanced *Assembling Composition*. We likewise thank two anonymous reviewers, who enabled us to see the project through new eyes and whose recommendations informed our revisions, as well as Bonny Graham for her publication assistance. We thank as well several in the field who have responded so generously to this project, including Jackie Preston and Derek Owens. We also thank our many current and former students and colleagues at Florida State University, among them Travis Maynard, Rory Lee, Matt Davis, Heather Lang, Joe Cirio, Michael Neal, Rachel Efstathion, and Christina Giarrusso: their input and feedback have contributed to our ever-evolving understanding of assemblage and the ways it functions in composition theory and practice.

In addition, Stephen thanks his wife, Gloria, for her continuing steadfast support and their new daughter, Viola, whose smile is a vector of inspiration. He also thanks Heather Johnson and the other wonderful people at the Curt Teich Postcard Archives for the lines of flight they have generated in his scholarship.

And kathi thanks David, Genevieve, Sui, Calder, Matt, and Kelly for the assemblages of experiences, occasions, and stories always informing, animating, and giving life to her work.

I   IN THEORY

1

Assembling Composition: An Introduction

Kathleen Blake Yancey and Stephen J. McElroy

ASSEMBLAGE—A THEORY AND PRACTICE LOCATED IN media, contexts, and combinations—has been cited by several scholars in rhetoric and composition as providing a new and helpful way of understanding composing, especially in an era marked by postmodernism and postpedagogy. In their 2006 article "Plagiarism, Originality, Assemblage," for example, Johndan Johnson-Eilola and Stuart Selber famously defined assemblage as "texts built primarily and explicitly from existing texts in order to solve a writing or communication problem in a new context" (381) and urged that the assemblage composing practices characterizing the workplace also characterize school-based composing. Byron Hawk's 2007 award-winning *Counter-History of Composition: Toward Methodologies of Complexity* linked assemblage to invention, arguing that "a new paradigm built around complexity could produce a postdialectical understanding of contemporary pedagogies of invention for the emerging scene produced by digital technology" (7), an understanding enacted through assemblages formed by students, teachers, classrooms, and curricula in academic spaces. More recent scholarship has charted other paths. In his 2016 *Assembling Arguments*, for instance, Jonathan Buehl has recast assemblage as "rhetorical assembly," which he defines as a fundamental composing practice for multimodal writing in the sciences. Focusing on what he calls the transformative quality of assemblage, Dustin Edwards, in a 2016 *Computers and Composition* article, sees in its transformative nature both an extension and an adaptation of classical imitation. And not least, in her 2015 *College Composition and Communication* article Jacqueline Preston understands assemblage as the centerpiece of a new radical pedagogy, one in which previously transgressive textual practices are the norm. In these efforts, as we explain below, assemblage refers to and sanctions the makingness that textuality affords and its use, reuse, and repurposing of materials, especially chunks of texts, in order to make something new.

In their definitions and understandings of assemblage, this recent scholarship in rhetoric and composition is, as the authors often make clear, indebted to earlier work on assemblage occurring both in art and in critical theory: the thinking about assemblage in these two contexts thus provides a starting point for this chapter. We then turn to the ways that scholars in rhetoric and composition have approached assemblage, tracing similarities and differences and sounding themes across them so as to provide a background for the essays making up this volume. We then conclude the chapter by introducing the remaining chapters, suggesting how they provide continuation with and adaptations of earlier work on assemblage as they raise new questions guiding future theory and practice.

ASSEMBLAGE IN ART

In 1961 the Museum of Modern Art (MoMA), under the direction of the associate curator William Seitz, opened an exhibition called "The Art of Assemblage." Although the word *assemblage* had been in use for centuries, as the OED suggests,[1] the definition of assemblage was nonetheless sufficiently unfamiliar that it led MoMA's press release announcing the event.

> Assemblage, a method initiated by major artists early in this century, which has been increasingly practiced by young artists here and abroad since World War II, is the subject of a major exhibition The Art of Assemblage at the Museum of Modern Art from October 4 through November 12. . . . An "assemblage" (a more inclusive term than the familiar "collage") is a work of art made by fastening together cut or torn pieces of paper, clippings from newspapers, photographs, bits of cloth, fragments of wood, metal or other such materials, shells or stones, or even objects such as knives and forks,

chairs and tables, parts of dolls and mannequins, and automobile fenders. The symbolic meaning of these objects, not originally intended as art materials, can be as important as their realistic aspects. (1)

As Seitz explains, assemblage in the world of art is a practice bringing together everyday materials to create a new text, a text emerging from and bearing traces of a mix of connotations and contexts that also has symbolic import:

When paper is soiled or lacerated, when cloth is worn, stained or torn, when wood is split, weathered or patterned with peeling coats of paint, when metal is bent or rusted, they gain connotations which unmarked materials lack. More specific associations are denoted when an object can be identified as the sleeve of a shirt, a dinner fork, the leg of a rococo chair, a doll's eye or hand, an automobile bumper or a social security card. (84)

In other words, it is precisely in the mix of "disparate elements," each of which has its own resonances and traces, that the new and the symbolic of assemblage are made, elements that, according to the UK's Tate gallery, are sometimes "scavenged," other times "bought specially."

Pablo Picasso is often identified as the originary composer of assemblage, particularly in his more sculptural works like *Still Life* (1914), "made from scraps of wood and a length of tablecloth fringing, glued together and painted" (Tate), and indeed his works were among those included in MoMA's "Art of Assemblage" exhibition, in part because of his attention to the tools he did not need, in part because of the diverse materials he combined. As Ann Temkin and Anne Umland explain, Picasso's "breakthrough came with the realization that he did not need particular tools or difficult-to-manipulate materials in order to work sculpturally" (15), that he could "cobble together," or assemble, many materials and many different *kinds* of materials, especially those of the everyday, into a single composition: "String, wire, pieces of paper and cardboard, wood scraps, and tin cans were cut, folded, glued, stitched, or otherwise assembled. The results were musical instruments and other still life subjects of an unprecedented sort" (15). Materiality, everydayness, and cobbling together thus defined Picasso's early assemblages and forecast his continuing interest in this artistic practice.

But another, contemporaneous artist, one with a somewhat different motivation if a similar practice, had an entire gallery in the MoMA exhibition dedicated to his compositions: Kurt Schwitters. A German painter born toward the end of the nineteenth century, Schwitters found in the assemblage of everyday materials—"bus and train tickets, stamps, wrappers, newsprint, buttons and other refuse which he collected in his pockets as he walked in the streets" (MoMA)—a response to a specific cultural and historical moment, that of the Weimar Republic in the aftermath of World War I. As art critic Alan G. Artner observes, this moment was one of crisis for Schwitters: "The Weimar Republic had been proclaimed in Germany; the old order had broken down. Schwitters thought 'new things had to be made from fragments.' The pictures he created with found objects and detritus were, as he said, 'new art forms out of the remains of a former culture.'" In other words, it was the collapse of the old culture that motivated a new artistic exploration, one that understood the "choosing, distributing and reshaping" of everyday materials as an assemblage practice equal in value to painting, as Schwitters himself explains:

> Merz paintings [Schwitters's term for his assemblages] are abstract works of art. The word "Merz" essentially means the totality of all imaginable materials that can be used for artistic purposes and technically the principle that all of these individual materials have equal value. Merz art makes use not just of paint and canvas, brush and palette, but all the materials visible to the eye and all tools needed . . . the wheel off a pram, wire mesh, string and cotton balls—these are factors of equal value to paints. The artist creates by choosing, distributing and reshaping the materials. (91)

The artist, in Schwitters's terms, thus creates compositions via an assemblage practice employing everyday materials, one that in his case provided a mechanism for responding to the collapse of an old cultural order. To make the new, fragments of the old were used, but specifically to transform them into the new. Art, in this view, thus taps the material of the everyday to provide a corrective new composition for responding to the moral collapse of the old culture.

ASSEMBLAGE IN CRITICAL THEORY

Drawing from critical theory, two competing scholarly definitions for assemblage are helpful, especially given our interest in the role of assemblage in writing contexts. In the first sense, as defined in the work of Gilles Deleuze and Félix Guattari, an assemblage is "a multiplicity which is made up of many heterogeneous terms and which establishes liaisons, relations between them across ages, sexes and reigns—different natures. Thus, the assemblage's only unity is that of co-functioning: it is a symbiosis, a 'sympathy'" (Deleuze and Parnet, qtd. in Anderson et al. 177). Here, the heterogeneous terms at work in any given act of composing co-function in a specific combination, an assemblage: the writer, her pen and paper, her ideas, her purpose, her audience; the Web designer, his markup languages, his editing program, his browser; the advertising executive, her products, her medium, her market. The constituents in each of these assemblages *unite*, relate, and produce. This first sense of *assemblage* thus allows us also to see composing as proceeding from interrelated combinations of bodies, concepts, and ideas: approaching composing in this light allows us to see and trace the assembled components and to map out how they work together, how they are related, to generate a particular composition. The second sense of *assemblage* refers to any text resulting from such a constellation, with text being understood metaphorically.

In the context of writing, however, it's worth noting that a text isn't only the composition a student writes in class: such a text, which we understand as synonymous with *composition*, could be a book, an image, a postcard, an album, and so on. Such a capacious definition, influenced by the works of Gunther Kress and D. F. McKenzie, is directly related to assemblage. Kress, drawing our attention to the multimodality of all texts, calls an ensemble of modes that is "semiotically and communicationally complete" a text (149); a multimodal ensemble, in its provisionality and contingency, is assemblage-like. Similarly, McKenzie's definition of *text* underscores the role of the materiality of texts. As Jerome McGann observes, McKenzie's text "is meaning-constitutive not simply in its 'contained' or delivered message, but in every dimension of its material existence" (20). In other words, for both Kress and McKenzie, meaning is made and shared through engagement with materials, a feature of assemblage shared with art.

At the same time, citing John Phillips's article in the May 2006 issue of *Theory, Culture & Society*, both Stephen McElroy and Jonathan Buehl observe that there is some confusion around the term *assemblage* as it is commonly used in critical theory. Phillips claims that the confusion is basically a translation issue: Deleuze and Guattari, writing in French, never used the word *assemblage* in a philosophical sense. Instead, the attribution of that term is the result of a 1981 translation of their article "Rhizome" by Paul Foss and Paul Patton. Rather than *assemblage,* the common French term used by Deleuze and Guattari is *agencement,* which has "the senses of either 'arrangement,' 'fitting' or 'fixing'" (108). Phillips describes the Deleuzian usage of *agencement* as conveying "an event, a becoming, a compositional unity," making a tidy connection to composition (109). Bruce Braun, after Phillips, elaborates on the term's meaning, also pointing to what he calls the "inadequate" translation of *agencement* to *assemblage* in a 2008 issue of *Progress in Human Geography*:

> Deleuze and Guattari's concept relates and combines two different ideas: the idea of a "layout" or a "coming together" of disparate elements, and the idea of "agency" or the capacity to produce an effect. . . . Hence, agencement neatly relates the *capacity to act* with the *coming together of things* that is a necessary and prior condition for any action to occur, including the actions of humans. (671, emphasis in original)

Agencement thus has a connotative power that *assemblage* lacks in that it incorporates the notion of agency and conditions for action

—or conditions for composition. Phillips notes that most but not all scholars writing in English have followed Foss and Patton's translation, a practice that scholars in rhetoric and composition likewise followed. Thus, given the asserted inadequacy of the translation from Deleuze and Guattari, and considering the fact that both of these conceptualizations of assemblage are applicable and valuable, it would make sense to use (1) the original *agencement* when referring to the configuration of bodies, machines, conditions, techniques, and so on, that bring about and participate in the production of a text; and (2) *assemblage* to describe assembled texts, that is, texts that are composed after and with other texts. However, given that the field has not ordinarily made this distinction, the essays here employ *assemblage* as a single term to refer to both configurations and texts. Not least, an important implication of this critical-theory view of assemblage, as outlined by Alex Reid in the next chapter in referring to Jody Shipka's conception, is that assemblage has the potential "to put the natural and social, the nonhuman and the human, realms back together," especially, Reid notes, given the ubiquity of digital technologies and their networking capacities. From the perspective of critical theory, then, assemblage allows us to articulate the ensembles creating texts, the texts themselves, and the complementary roles that both human and nonhuman participants play in a material, multimodal composing process.

ASSEMBLAGE IN RHETORIC AND COMPOSITION

Scholarship on assemblage composing has emphasized different dimensions of the practice, as we explain below. Among these are its explicit use of texts for social effects, its material and multimodal quality, its transformational power, and its pedagogical value.

One of the most cited sources for assemblage in rhetoric and composition is the 2007 Johndan Johnson-Eilola and Stuart Selber *Computers and Composition* article "Plagiarism, Originality, Assemblage." Johnson-Eilola and Selber invoke assemblage to describe a practice of composing with "original and existing fragments," one intermingling new and borrowed texts—such combinations and interminglings a primary characteristic, they claim, of most texts, especially those oriented to "social effects":

What if the "final" product a student produces—a text—is not concerned with original words or images on a page or screen but concerned primarily with assemblages of parts? Importantly, in this reconception, the assemblages do not distinguish primarily between which parts are supposed to be original and which have been found and gathered from someplace else; assemblages are interested in what works, what has social effects. The distinction between original and existing fragments in a text is, if not meaningless, at least secondary. In essence, we are arguing for a reorganization that is actually implied if not valued in many rubrics for assessing writing used by teachers who take a social approach: Rhetorical purposes can be addressed in context by either original or borrowed/quoted texts without a hierarchy of distinction between the two. (380)

In this case, of course, Johnson-Eilola and Selber, interested in how we assess student writing, argue that originality as it has historically been construed isn't a salient feature or criterion for today's composition. With no hierarchy between original and assembled texts, what matters isn't the ontological status of each, but rather the "social effects" of the text as a completed whole.

Johnson-Eilola and Selber thus do not define assemblage in the Deleuze-Guattarian sense of agencement regarding the collection/connection of people, technologies, events, intentions, and so on from which a text emerges; instead, Johnson-Eilola and Selber's definition aligns with that in art, where in art, as in writing, assemblage refers to "texts built primarily and explicitly from existing texts in order to solve a writing or communication problem in a new context" (381). As we investigate the nature of composing, thinking of texts as assemblages in Johnson-Eilola and Selber's sense of the term is useful because it explicates the fact that all texts emerge from contexts already saturated with other texts: textual production is necessarily informed and influenced, either directly or indirectly, by the texts that came before it. Moreover, such borrowing is multimodal in character as well: composers borrow words and passages; they borrow fonts, color palettes, images, and patterns. There are no texts that are absolutely original (though their assemblage may be), and naming texts as assemblages acknowledges that. It also articulates the collaborative nature of composing, pointing us to the various producers whose work contributes to a final product.

In *Assembling Arguments: Multimodal Rhetoric and Scientific Discourse,* Jonathan Buehl focuses our attention on a specific variant of discourse, scientific discourse, one defined by multimodality, especially by a multimodal verbal-visual textual relationship and by the materiality of composing itself and of the production, distribution, and circulation of texts. Drawing on two examples four hundred years apart to demonstrate the need to consider visual texts as the important counterpart to verbal texts (rather than as some afterthought or decoration), Buehl summarizes the verbal-visual nature of scientific text and points to both its potential and its challenges.

> Both groups faced rhetorical tasks requiring combinations of images and text, and their rhetorical performances were both enabled and constrained by available technologies of observation and reproduction. . . . As these cases . . . demonstrate, visualization offers creators of scientific discourse immense rhetorical potential and introduces equally significant rhetorical problems; however, a comprehensive rhetorical account of multimodal scientific argumentation has yet to emerge. (6–7)

To provide a framework for this account, Buehl turns to three "interdependent rhetorical processes, the conception, assembly, and circulation of rhetorical artifacts—in relation to three overlapping domains of human experience, the cognitive, the material, and the social" (20). These three concepts—conception, assembly, and circulation—collectively "provide a set of screens that can disclose features of rhetorical performance in multimodal texts that might otherwise pass unnoticed" (23). Here, borrowing from critical theory, a rhetorical artifact is theorized as a *rhetorical assembly,* "best characterized as an emerging form that temporarily fixes a diverse range of relations among concepts, institutions, symbol systems, and media" (24). More generally, in this effort, Buehl is specifically interested in multimodality in assemblaged rhetorical artifacts, and, like others

—he cites Rebecca Howard's concept of patchwriting and Joseph Bizzup's curricular BEAM research model (in its categorizing of sources)—Buehl is "attempt[ing] to reposition composition as a process of assembly" (250–51).

Two aspects of Buehl's project are especially important for scholars interested in assemblage composing. First is his attention to materiality, an approach resembling that of the art world's that specifically addresses verbal-visual multimodality: it includes the physical materials of composing at the same time that it provides for an embodied physical articulation. Material elements, Buehl says, "are the resources and constraints related to the existence and movement of physical structures: space, time, substance, and so on. They include the properties of objects—such as paper and ink and pixels—but they also include the properties of physical bodies: for example, people with larger frames may be able to project sound with greater volume" (21).

Second is Buehl's reconception of assemblage as rhetorical assembly, a reconceptualization with two motives. First, as Buehl observes and as we have seen above, *assemblage* as a term is used inconsistently, even in the same field; thus in Buehl's view it isn't helpful in the way a central term needs to be. Second, citing Johnson-Eilola and Selber's definition of assemblage as too narrow, Buehl reaches for what he understands as a wider construct, one including both "prior" texts and originary ones: "The crucial difference between this assemblage [as defined by Johnson-Eilola and Selber] and a broader rhetorical assembly as I use the term is that the latter does not restrict the assembled material to preexisting text, thereby leaving room for both 'original' and 'recycled' material" (27). It's accurate, of course, to note that the Johnson-Eilola and Selber assemblage emphasizes the use of what they call existing fragments, but this emphasis needs to be fully contextualized. Johnson-Eilola and Selber are clear, for instance, that in their view such a distinction—that is, between original and reused texts—is "if not meaningless, at least secondary"; "assemblages are interested in what works, what has social effects" (380). In other words, Buehl and Johnson-Eilola and Selber here seem to be theorizing composi-

tion somewhat differently; the social and its effects governing composing for Johnson-Eilola and Selber play a lesser role in Buehl's
formation. But in another way, these scholars seem to understand
assemblage very similarly. Buehl wants it to include both prior texts
and new material, while Johnson-Eilola and Selber seem to provide for both kinds of texts: assemblage, they say, includes "texts
built primarily and explicitly from existing texts in order to solve
a writing or communication problem in a new context." The key
word here seems to be *primarily*: assemblages built primarily, but
not exclusively, from existing texts. Their model thus does allow for
the inclusion of both past and new texts that Buehl advocates and
provides a warrant for our use of the term *assemblage* here. In sum,
Buehl's attention to verbal-visual multimodality and its role in assemblage is useful for composing: it reminds us that the verbal and
the visual are modes equal in value and even more valuable when
used together. Likewise, Buehl's attention to materiality comple-
ments his interest in multimodality and links us to the work on
assemblage developed in art.

In his 2016 *Computers and Composition* article, "Framing Remix
Rhetorically: Toward a Typology of Transformative Work," Dustin
Edwards emphasizes another dimension of assemblage: its transformative capacity. Like Buehl, Edwards is concerned about the
ambiguity surrounding assemblage; his remedy shifts the focus to
an overarching concept, remix, locating a typology of what he calls
remix practices, including assemblage. More specifically, the four-
part typology, including assemblage, reappropriation, redistribution, and genre play, operates heuristically to "foster intentionality"
(46). Moreover, as Edwards explains, such a typology has the potential of "reconcil[ing] the sprawling posture of remix in writing
practice":

> If we are to accept remix as a valid and important composing
> practice, one that has the potential to teach a wealth of rhe-
> torical knowledge for a digital age, we need to further develop
> and refine approaches to discuss the many nuances involved
> in transforming already existing material. A possible way to
> reconcile the sprawling posture of remix in writing practice is

to develop a typology that begins to delineate the rhetorical distinctions among types of remixed compositions. Here, I work toward such a typology by outlining four varieties of re-mix—assemblage, reappropriation, redistribution, and genre play—in an effort to alleviate confusion about a term encumbered with excessive meaning. (43)

Like Johnson-Eilola and Selber and like Buehl, Edwards thus intends to authorize new composing practices that are now possible, and increasingly frequent, given digital technology.

Edwards situates his concept of assemblage within ideas of rhetorical imitation, invention, and community, which allows him to consider the ethical use of material as well. As he notes, imitation in classical rhetoric "was deeply connected to invention, style, memory, ethics, and being" (44): imitation as a frame contextualizes remix as rhetorical. Moreover, given rhetorical topoi as inventional devices, this frame "celebrates a sort of community stockpile from which composers can continuously invent and reinvent"[2] at the same time that it demonstrates that composing, inherently communal, is a textual process of building from other texts. Not least, such a framework includes an ethical dimension:

> Finally, to position remix within a revived frame of imitation encourages a sense of ethical mindfulness. It positions remix writers as producers, evaluators, and collaborators, and thereby demonstrates that responsible textual production matters, that the materials of remixes have histories, and that remixed texts might themselves be repurposed. In other words, it positions remix as a process whereby rhetors are productively and ethically—not haphazardly—working with other texts, communities, and people. (44)

In defining assemblage, Edwards echoes Johnson-Eilola and Selber (whom he also cites): "Assemblage is a method of composing wherein a composer builds a new text by gathering, repurposing, and redeploying a combination of already-existing texts," and he links this practice to a definition of remix provided by Henry Jenkins: "'[the] creative juxtaposition of materials that otherwise occupy very different cultural niches'" (57). Assemblage composing thus creatively juxtaposes chunks of text emerging from very different contexts into a new text, much as is done in art. "Importantly," Edwards notes, "Jenkins mentioned that materials may be—and are very likely to be—disparate" (47). Through Edwards, then, assemblage is established as a creative method of invention with ethical implications, one with antecedents in artistic practice.

Finally, Jacqueline Preston, in a 2015 issue of *College Composition and Communication*, employs assemblage to provide a more robust and satisfying pedagogy of composition than other post-process approaches have provided.[3] In "Project(ing) Literacy: Writing to Assemble in a Postcomposition FYW Classroom," Preston makes three arguments in support of this aim. First, like Edwards, she emphasizes the living quality of assemblage writing: "To regard writing as an assemblage," she says, "is to insist that what is important about writing is not its capacity to represent ideas but, rather, what writing does, from whence it comes, and how it reproduces. Writing always and already functions with and connects with other assemblages—other writings, histories, memories, places, people, ideas, events, and so forth" (39). It is thus assemblage's capacity to bring together diverse, sometimes dissonant multiples—texts, fragments of texts, and intangibles; *other writings, histories, memories, places, people, ideas, events, and so forth*—that makes it such a generative means of composing. Second, quoting Deleuze and Guattari's *A Thousand Plateaus*, Preston emphasizes the becomingness of assemblage composing, which contrasts with a more conventional view of writing located in what she calls representation:

> Critical beyond the mechanics and organization underscored in theories of writing as primarily representation is writing's complexity, its relevancy, its contingency, and, of particular importance, its *becoming* (Deleuze and Guattari 272). To speak of *becoming* is to highlight writing's protean quality. *Becoming* underscores change, flight, and movement. In *becoming*, one piece of the assemblage is knitted into the landscape of another piece, changing its value as an element and bringing about a new kind of unity. (39)

Third, and not least, citing Victor Villanueva's 2013 appeal for more productive curricular approaches to basic writing and first-year writing (FYW) in "Toward a Political Economy of Basic Writing Programs," Preston both argues that assemblage composing is useful for college writers and shows us how it is so:

> To approach writing as an assemblage in the FYW classroom is to move away from a notion of writing as a set of discrete skills and processes and rather to draw attention to the heterogeneous components that go into the production or genesis of the writing. Herein, the writer is faced with writing's complexity, the diverse and overlapping experiences, and competing ideas that meet in and contribute to the writing space. The process of writing is one of removing a piece of writing, an event, an experience, or a memory, from its original function to bring about a new one. (40)

The writing space here resembles Johnson-Eilola and Selber's conception of composing, with Preston's "removal" of text from one context so as to use it in another also echoing Edwards's invocation of Jenkins's creative juxtaposition by means of shifts in cultural niches. Assemblage writing, for Preston, is thus a multicontextual practice of borrowing and arranging as a mechanism for creating a new text, much as defined by Kurt Schwitters.

EXPLORING COMPOSITION VIA ASSEMBLAGE THEORY AND PRACTICE

Assemblage has, as outlined here, looked somewhat different in different contexts: taken together, it is itself an assemblage, though always interested in media, combinations, and contexts. The artistic practice of collecting, combining, and reshaping older materials for a new composition is translated into two activities in critical theory, the textual assemblage itself and the agencement/assemblage of human beings, materials, and technologies from which it emerges. In rhetoric and composition, these antecedents in art and critical theory situate new emphases in assemblage for writing, among them assemblage's explicit reuse of texts for social effects, its material and multimodal quality, its transformational power, and its pedagogical value. Taking such observations as a point of departure, this collection of essays continues to explore assemblage for multiple purposes, among them to retheorize writing, especially given current interest in materiality and technology; to "field test" such reconceptualizations for the classroom; and to consider what such reconceptualizations might help us understand about writing in the world. More specifically, this collection speaks to four dimensions of assemblage in particular: (1) ways that theories of writing, especially multimodal theories of writing informed by assemblage are especially suited to our current digital and material composing practices, as suggested by Buehl and Johnson-Eilola and Selber; (2) ways that introducing students to assemblage composing as theory and practice might help them better understand what Preston calls the aliveness of writing; (3) ways that we can trace earlier composing practices in the world as variants of assemblage, thus providing a fuller history of assemblage and composing; and (4) ways that, as Edwards suggests, we can begin to interrogate assemblage as an ethical practice.

In the book's first section, "In Theory," Alex Reid, Jeff Rice, and James Kalmbach provide a vocabulary and a theory for thinking about assemblage, especially the ways it changes in a world infused with digital technologies. Explicitly concerned with how the concept of assemblage can help us theorize and adapt to the changing landscape of digital technology and writing, they approach composing through the lenses, respectively, of big data, aggregation, and engagements.

Alex Reid offers the first word in this section: in "Big-Data Assemblies: Composing's Nonhuman Ecology," he provides a theoretical treatment of assemblage informed especially by Manuel DeLanda and by Gilles Deleuze, in partnership with Félix Guattari. Framing assemblage theory as offering a "nonhuman conception of cognition, agency, and expression," Reid argues that such a conception allows us to see the ways in which technology and media participate in the act of composition, which is itself an exercise of rhetorical practice. Digital networks have made the nonhuman dimensions of rhetorical-compositional activity more visible, Reid claims, but our conventional rhetorical approaches struggle to account for technology, except as an extension or limitation of human agency or as a tool for some ideological end. Reid's approach, in contrast, considers how "big-data" analysis, combined with assemblage theory, might reframe our understanding of composing, helping us see human activity as participating in a larger media ecology.

Jeff Rice, in the third chapter, takes up the question of the relationship(s) between assemblage, aggregation, and response on social-media platforms such as Facebook. In "They Eat Horses, Don't They?" Rice argues that aggregation is a means of assemblage, and more specifically that aggregation, as compiled on the Web through RSS and social-media feeds, constitutes a kind of just-in-time assemblage of different and disparate perspectives collected and displayed in one place on the screen. Moreover, as Rice demonstrates, the aggregated response that happens on a particular platform, Facebook, where users share opinions, images, videos, links to articles, and so on, has the capacity and often the tendency, because of the sheer volume of activity and the speed of the response potential, to occlude context—in this case, the intention of the original message—and, as important, to confirm preconceptions already available. As a consequence, Rice recommends caution in interpreting such assemblages: he encourages us to explore the implications of this type of assemblage given its tendency to separate and distort the relationship between prior understandings, circulated messages, and a "given state of affairs."

What technology—digital and otherwise—means in assemblage composing, for James Kalmbach, can be summed up in a single term: engagements. In "Beyond the Object to the Making of the Object: Understanding the Process of Multimodal Composition as Assemblage," Kalmbach focuses on the scene of writing, a kind of agencement defined by an *assemblage of engagements* involving multiple participants, including a composer, technologies, interfaces, templates, and content. For Kalmbach, as for Reid, multimodal composing involves both the human and the nonhuman.

Composers are tasked not only with participating in these engagements, Kalmbach says, but also with negotiating between and among such engagements. Interested as well in how students conduct these engagements and negotiations, Kalmbach observes that interacting with students as they think about and critically discuss their processes of negotiation poses a difficult but promising challenge. In addition, as a means of demonstrating what this looks like for students, Kalmbach describes different assignment sets that he has used in his classes over the years as technologies and their accompanying engagements have shifted—thus providing a metanarrative about his own engagement as an instructor—and calls on the work of students to illustrate his argument.

The next three chapters, which constitute the section "In the Classroom/On Campus," draw on the assemblage thinking presented in the first section as they turn our attention to the role that assemblage plays or might play in the classroom, in a kind of "field test"—for undergraduate students working in both print and digital contexts and for graduate students assembling electronic portfolios. Beginning this section with his "Assemblage Composing, Reconsidered," Michael J. Michaud starts by revisiting his earlier concerns about assemblage-as-plagiarism—a composing imported from workplace to classroom—in light of more recent thinking on assemblage-as-composition, focusing on assemblage as a naturalized composing practice for many students, especially those who bring workplace assemblage-composing (back) into school with them. Michaud then situates such practices within rhetoric and composition as a context for arguing that given the nature of today's composing and our own theories, it's not a question of whether assemblage should be allowed, but rather of how we can teach it as a composing process. Two genres in particular, Michaud claims, are hospitable for assemblage, a print white paper and a multimodal electronic blog, and he provides information about how in using assemblage theory we can teach these as specific genres whose composition can help students both practice composing and understand it.

Like Michaud, Stephen J. McElroy and Travis Maynard are interested in the potential of assemblage for teaching, in their case in a specific course, first-year composition (FYC), where for them assemblage provides the key concept explicitly anchoring the course. Echoing Edwards's interest in assemblage as transformation, McElroy and Maynard, in "Copy, Combine, Transform: Assemblage in First-Year Composition," first explain the rationale for making assemblage the centerpiece of FYC. "[W]e began to see assemblage as something more central to the work of composing than previously understood," they tell us, "as a concept and practice that, in combination with multimodality, should be made more explicit for our students. Thus, in putting assemblage at the center of the course and in helping students to 'see, think, and do' assemblage, we hoped that students would become more experienced with the work of composing writ large." Given this commitment, McElroy and Maynard design such a course and teach it, here detailing its components, its outcomes, and its benefits: students understood and used assemblage as a heuristic for invention, appreciated the difference between plagiarism and effective quotation, and transferred rhetorical thinking into new contexts and for new audiences.

Completing the set of chapters articulating curricular and pedagogical applications of assemblage is Kristine L. Blair's "ePortfolio Artifacts as Graduate Student Multimodal Identity Assemblages." Here Blair defines ePortfolios as assemblages of digital multimodal artifacts, networked spaces, and student identities, but focuses on the role ePortfolios play in fostering graduate-student identity. Like Michaud, Blair links genre and assemblage, attending, in her case, to the two genres of the literacy narrative and the teaching philosophy statement as valuable in supporting graduate-student identity developed in ePortfolios. In highlighting these genres, Blair demonstrates that the play and experimentation they encourage contribute both to portfolios and to identities graduate students create and represent in these portfolios. The ePortfolios themselves are thus positioned as sites of assemblage welcoming an openness and flexibility, much as Preston claims, that academic professionalism requires.

This third section, "In the World," considers how assemblage can help us understand composing more broadly, in the world at large, especially as a material, multimodal practice with ethical implications. In the eighth chapter, Jody Shipka's "To Gather, Assemble and Display: Composition as [Re]Collection," we are introduced to assemblage-as-collection as a very specific kind of composing, one emerging from various practices of material collecting. More specifically, Shipka attends to the materiality of assemblage as she offers a collection-based framework that positions composers as collectors of different elements—materials, ideas, quotations, and so on. Here, Shipka's intent is to encourage the development of "more robust notions of meaning-making practices" that, in accord with Reid's conception explained in Chapter 2, take into account the roles that humans and nonhumans play in the composing process. To illustrate directions we might take as instructors, Shipka draws on her experiences with an "Evocative Objects Workshop" she has conducted at conferences. Such collection-based composing activities, Shipka suggests, allow for the imagining of new combinations, new possibilities, and new assemblages.

In Chapter 9, Stephen J. McElroy provides another account of production and composition outside the academy, that employed to create a vernacular genre: the postcard. In "Assemblages of Asbury Park: The Persistent Legacy of the Large-Letter Postcard," McElroy begins by explaining the origins of the large-letter postcard genre in the early twentieth century. Then, exploring the modes and methods of their production-qua-assemblage, McElroy demonstrates the ways in which these assembled designs have resonated across the decades as they have circulated in a diverse array of textual instantiations. He argues that tracing these instantiations genealogically allows us to see two aspects of assemblage previously undocumented: the ways in which assemblages respond to contexts, and the ways that they shape the contexts for future acts of composition, including in political life.

Kathleen Blake Yancey pursues another site of assemblage composing in "Multimodal Assemblage, Compositions, and Composing: The Corresponding Cases of Emigrant Cemetery Tombstones and 'A Line for Wendy.'" Identifying memorial texts as sites especially hospitable to assemblage, Yancey begins with cemeteries and traces the kinds of borrowing informing tombstones, demonstrating that, like Buehl's multimodal science writing, the borrowing on tombstones is a historical verbal and visual practice, in this case one providing for multiple identities. Yancey is also interested in the processes of assemblage a print composer engages in when creating memorial texts, a question introduced in McElroy's chapter on postcard production, taken up by Kalmbach, and forecast by Schwitters in his three-part conception of composing: "choosing, distributing and reshaping the materials." To explore assemblage composing in the context of creating a unique text, Yancey documents composing decisions—especially those involving layout, arrangement, and authorship—contributing, through fragments of texts authored by colleagues and friends, to the assembled "A Line for Wendy" memorializing Wendy Bishop.

Chapter 11 provides an evaluative perspective on assemblage: Kristin L. Arola and Adam Arola's consideration of both the practices and the ethics of assemblage-borrowing from First Nations materials. Arola and Arola's "An Ethics of Assemblage: Creative Repetition and the 'Electric Pow Wow'" returns to the work of Deleuze as a context for examining First Nation electronic music and detailing the implications of appropriating it, in the process suggesting that Deleuzian assemblage can help us reconsider the issue of cultural authenticity as it appears in new assemblages. Equally important, in a particularly valuable contribution, Arola and Arola begin to take up the necessary task of distinguishing between "good" and "bad" assemblages. Drawing on the assembled music of A Tribe Called Red as exemplar, Arola and Arola argue, first, that we can distinguish between good and bad assemblages; and second, that good assemblages are marked by four characteristics: they are responsive, they productively introduce novelty, they allow us to see something new, and they attend to their own effect.

Bringing tentative closure to this larger assemblage of texts as they compose their own assemblaged text, Johndan Johnson-Eilola and Stuart Selber identify and comment on four themes emerging from this collective composing. In "Conclusion: Reterritorialization," they speak to "assemblage as connection with other peoples and times, assemblage as material object, assemblage as performance, and assemblage as pedagogy." In their processes of considering and composing, Johnson-Eilola and Selber raise many questions useful for guiding our thinking going forward. As they note, their questions "do not have a stable answer," but are rather provocative and inventive, leading to "a constant performance: disassemblage and reassemblage, call and response, writing and rewriting."

Or: assemblage.

NOTES

1. The earliest recorded instances of *assemblage* provide interesting antecedents for later conceptualizations: the first two instances include the idea of coming together—in 1717, in Elijah Fenton's *Poems on Several Occasions*: "In sweet assemblage, ev'ry blooming grace Fix love's bright throne in Teraminta's face" (205)—and the joining together of two things, in 1728, in Ephraim Chambers's *Cyclopaedia* (at cited word): "The Assemblage of two Bones for Motion, is called Articulation." See the entry for "assemblage, n." in the *OED Online*.

2. Given the link between imitation and assemblage that Edwards makes, it would also be worth exploring other genres hosting other assemblages, among them commonplace books (see the Harvard University Library's digitized collection at <http://ocp.hul.harvard.edu/reading/commonplace.html>) and scrapbooks.

3. There is other scholarship in composition employing assemblage: see, for example, Christy Desmet, Deborah Miller, Elizabeth Davis, Ron Balthazor, and Beth Beggs's discussion of electronic portfolios as multimodal assemblages and Jeff Rice's discussion of networked assessment.

WORKS CITED

Anderson, Ben, Matthew Kearnes, Colin McFarlane, and Dan Swanton. "On Assemblages and Geography." *Dialogues in Human Geography* 2.2 (2012): 171–89. doi:10.1177/2043820612449261.

Artner, Alan G. "New Things Had to Be Made from Fragments: Kurt Schwitters Created Enduring Artworks from Some of the World's Most Perishable Materials." *Chicago Tribune* 15 Jan. 1995: n. pag. Web. 10 Sep. 2016.

"Assemblage, n." *OED Online*. Oxford UP, 2016. Web. 12 Sep. 2016.

Braun, Bruce. "Environmental Issues: Inventive Life." *Progress in Human Geography* 32.5 (2008): 667–79. doi: 10.1177/0309132507088030.

Buehl, Jonathan. *Assembling Arguments: Multimodal Rhetoric and Scientific Discourse*. Columbia: U of South Carolina P, 2016. Print.

Deleuze, Gilles, and Claire Parnet. *Dialogues*. Trans. Hugh Tomlinson and Barbara Habberjam. New York: Columbia UP, 1987. Print. European Perspectives.

Deleuze, Gilles, and Félix Guattari. *A Thousand Plateaus*. Trans. Brian Massumi. Minneapolis: U of Minnesota P, 1987. Print. Vol. 2 of *Capitalism and Schizophrenia*. 2 vols. 1972–80.

Desmet, Christy, Deborah Miller, Elizabeth Davis, Ron Balthazor, and Beth Beggs. "Artifacts, Interface, and Links: Electronic Portfolios as Multimodal Practice." Computers and Writing Conference: Mechanization and Writing, Frostburg State U, 7 June 2013. Panel.

Edwards, Dustin W. "Framing Remix Rhetorically: Toward a Typology of Transformative Work." *Computers and Composition* 39 (2016): 41–54. http://dx.doi.org/10.1016/j.compcom.2015.11.007.

Hawk, Byron. *A Counter-History of Composition: Toward Methodologies of Complexity*. Pittsburgh: U of Pittsburgh P, 2007. Print.

Jenkins, Henry. *Confronting the Challenges of Participatory Culture: Media Education for the Twenty-first Century*. Cambridge: MIT P, 2009.

Johnson-Eilola, Johndan, and Stuart A. Selber. "Plagiarism, Originality, Assemblage." *Computers and Composition* 24.4 (2007): 375–403. http://dx.doi.org/10.1016/j.compcom.2015.11.007.

Kress, Gunther. *Multimodality: A Social Semiotic Approach to Contemporary Communication*. New York: Routledge, 2010. Print.

McElroy, Stephen J. "Assembling Postcards: The Multimodal Production of Curt Teich & Company." Diss. Florida State U, 2014. Print.

McGann, Jerome. "Theory of Texts." *London Review of Books* 18 Feb. 1988: 20–21. Web. 10 Sep. 2016.

Museum of Modern Art. "The Art of Assemblage." Press release. 4 Oct. 1961. Web. 12 Sep. 2016.

Phillips, John. "Agencement/Assemblage." *Theory, Culture & Society* 23.2–3 (2006): 108–09. doi:10.1177/026327640602300219.

Preston, Jacqueline. "Project(ing) Literacy: Writing to Assemble in a Postcomposition FYW Classroom." *College Composition and Communication* 67.1 (2015): 35–63. Print.

Rice, Jeff. "Networked Assessment." *Computers and Composition* 28.1 (2011): 28–39. http://dx.doi.org/10.1016/j.compcom.2010.09.007.

Schwitters, Kurt. "Merz Painting." *I Is Style*. Ed. Rudi Fuchs. Amsterdam: Stedelijk Museum; Rotterdam: NAi, 2000. 91. Print.

Seitz, William Chapin. *The Art of Assemblage*. New York: Museum of Modern Art, 1961. Print.

Tate. "Assemblage." *Glossary of Art Terms*. *Tate.org.uk*, n.d. Web. 12 Sep. 2016.

Temkin, Ann, and Anne Umland. "Picasso Sculpture: An Introduction." *Picasso Sculpture*. Ed. Temkin and Umland. New York: Museum of Modern Art, 2015. Print.

2

Big-Data Assemblies: Composing's Nonhuman Ecology

Alex Reid

IN THIS CHAPTER I INVESTIGATE ASSEMBLAGE THEORY, as articulated in the work of Gilles Deleuze and Félix Guattari and later developed by Manuel DeLanda and others, as it pertains to the investigation of digital composing. Assemblage theory proposes an ontology that is fundamentally different from the anthropocentric view of symbolic action that has largely shaped rhetoric and composition, offering in its stead a nonhuman conception of cognition, agency, and expression that investigates rhetoric as an activity that precedes and exceeds human beings. Digital networks have made the nonhuman dimensions of rhetorical-compositional activity more visible, but our conventional rhetorical approaches struggle to account for technology, except as an extension or limitation of human agency or as a tool for some ideological end. Here, then, I consider how "big-data" analysis, combined with assemblage theory, might reframe our understanding of composing and help us see human activity as participating in a larger media ecology.

⌒

For the most part, the focus of composition studies has been on the social, cultural, and ideological operation of writing. One can view the cultural emphasis of postprocess composition specifically as a response to postmodern theories, but the articulation of language as a cultural and human, rather than natural or nonhuman, activity has a deeper history. As Bruno Latour has argued, European modernism, beginning with the development of the scientific method and Enlightenment philosophy in the seventeenth century, divided the world into two distinct realms: one natural and one social. In the modern view, the natural world operates by immutable laws, but true knowledge of the natural world is forever unavailable to us. The social-human realm, on the other hand, is an immanent (and thus changeable) space that permits thought and agency. For the Moderns, language—all symbolic behavior really—is a part of this social world. In this system, due to their access to the symbolic, social world, humans acquire an exceptional ontological status, separating them in kind from all other beings. At one point, we might have explained this human exceptionality in terms of a divine gift, and many today still hold to this belief. Academically, at least within our field, that exceptionality is explained by our evolved and epigenetic capacity for symbolic behavior: it is our capacity for language that distinguishes us from other animals (as Kenneth Burke would tell us), allows for the creation of societies, and produces our capacity for thought beyond the instinctual behaviors of others. In short, we assert that language is *for us*. Language enables and circumscribes both our capacity to produce knowledge about the natural world and our ability to create our sociocultural world. Aside from some brief forays into animal rhetoric (e.g., Kennedy), even debates over how "big" rhetoric should get remain limited to human symbolic behavior (Schiappa).

Assemblage theory, however, as Jody Shipka argues in this volume, puts the natural and the social, the nonhuman and the human, realms back together. In connecting humans and nonhuman objects within a common ontological space, assemblage theory articulates language and symbolic behavior as a relational capacity that emerges within a network of human and nonhuman objects. Language and symbolic behavior are not things "we" do, but are instead things with which we relate and activities in which we participate. Language is no longer "for us." This philosophical move thus uniquely situates assemblage theory to address the role of technologies and other nonhuman entities in our shifting digital compositional context because it does not articulate language as an inherent human-cultural characteristic, but rather as a nonhuman participant in a larger communicational network. To this point, my chapter provides a heuristic exploration of this supposition. It asks, first, if we conceive of composing as a process involving the participation of human and nonhuman objects rather than one located strictly within human beings (or human beings and some amorphous "culture"), what might we learn? And second, and more important, how might such a supposition shift and expand our conception of what is possible?

As the chapter title indicates, I am particularly interested in "big-data assemblies." By now, *big data* is a familiar term that stretches across disciplines and industries. It begins with recognizing the massive amounts of data that are produced and stored across digital networks at a rate that astronomically exceeds the data produced in print in the last century. Big data also includes an understanding of the computational power required to process that data, resulting in a wide range of analytical and interpretive possibilities. How do these matters interest rhetoric and composition? Since the early days of the Internet, the attention of computers and writing has mostly turned toward digital multimodal composing, to the creation of webpages with hyperlinks and images, and then later with video, animation, and so on. While the variety of media has enlarged, an expanded multimodality has framed our approach to digital rhetoric, perhaps in part because it articulates a digital composing practice that remains manageable by a single author or a small group of collaborators within the confines of a college course. In this respect multimodal composition is teachable in a way that resonates with twentieth-century pedagogies. It permits us to hold on to a more anthropocentric rhetorical practice among digital networks. However, this version of multimodality, with its focus on the combination of media types that mostly precede the digital era (e.g., photographs, videos, graphics, audio recordings, and, of course, text), proves to be limited as a conceptual approach for understanding the breadth of digital rhetoric. As the concept of big data suggests, digital rhetoric runs from the binary realm, expressed in voltage across a circuit, through the proliferating media forms of various proprietary systems, each with its own unique capacities, to the common media and information types of the Web, which allow humans but also machines to communicate with one another. In short, big-data assemblies open new avenues for investigation that do not put individual human beings (or human beings at all) at the center of rhetorical practice. Such investigations are not simply adjacent to more anthropocentric concerns as a separate form of research; they instead transform our understanding of the role humans play in composing.

AN ASSEMBLAGE-THEORY PRIMER

Assemblage theory offers a method for investigating these questions by establishing an ontology that focuses on the external relations among objects rather than on presupposing that objects are predefined by essential, internal qualities. In short, rather than beginning with the ontological premise that symbolic behavior is an intrinsic quality of being human, assemblage theory allows one to investigate symbolic behaviors as emerging from the external relations among humans and nonhumans. Here, I examine assemblage theory as it begins in the work of Deleuze and Guattari and is further developed by DeLanda. Appropriately for our interests, Deleuze and Guattari introduce the concept of assemblage in *A Thousand Plateaus* in the context of discussing the composition of the book. "In a book, as in all things, there are lines of articulation or segmentarity, strata and territories; but also lines of flight, movements of deterritorialization and destratification. Comparative rates of flow on these lines produce phenomena of relative slowness and viscosity, or, on the contrary, of acceleration and rupture. All this, lines and measurable speeds, constitutes an *assemblage*" (3–4). *Assemblage* becomes a central term in the book, but given the nature of Deleuze and Guattari's style it isn't possible to give a complete, authoritative definition. However, they do draw some "general conclusions about assemblages" (88).

On a first, horizontal, axis, an assemblage comprises two segments, one of content, the other of expression. On the one hand it is a machinic assemblage of bodies, of actions and passions, an intermingling of bodies reacting to one another; on the other hand it is a collective assemblage of enunciation, of acts and statements, of incorporeal transformations attributed to bodies. Then on a vertical axis, the assemblage has both territorial sides, or reterritorialized sides, which stabilize it, and cutting edges of deterritorialization, which carry it away. (88)

Admittedly, at this level of generality, assemblages appear inscrutably abstract, an unavoidable result of attempting to describe a concept that accounts for how being happens. Nonetheless: an assemblage has two axes. The first axis has objects, actions, and relations on one end, and on the other end what might be loosely termed expressions. Though these are diagrammatically separated, they make up a single axis. Any object—a bichon, a city bus, Derek Jeter, an electron—comprises these elements: physical, material elements as well as expressive elements. The first axis has two general tendencies registered on the second axis: one tendency is cybernetic and homeostatic; the other is mutative or destructive. In order to understand the expressive role of assemblages, it is necessary to set aside considerations of self-awareness and intentionality. That is, one can assert that a river can express something without making an argument that it is conscious and self-aware. For example, one might think of the way an ecosystem might develop around the expression of a river: its speed and slowness, its cycle of flooding, and so on. The river isn't just the water flowing downhill. It is also the geology it traverses and slowly transforms and the rain, lakes, and springs that feed it. That's an assemblage. So, to return to the general description of an assemblage, a river has an intermingling of bodies, such as the water molecules, the soil and rocks of the riverbed, and the geologic contours of the terrain. It also has enunciations and incorporeal transformations: it marks a boundary between nations; it shapes the movements of animals that drink and feed at its shores; it defines an ecosystem that differs from the upper reaches of the hills that surround it. It has a tendency toward territorialization: over time, it wears a consistent path through the land. It also has a tendency toward deterritorialization: it can dry up; it can be diverted for irrigation; the damage caused by a sudden flood might forever alter its path. The key point here is that the river emerges as an assemblage among these external relations. The material objects that interrelate to create the river, the expressions of the river, its tendency to stay the same or change: these are all products of external relations, not intrinsic characteristics of some essential "riverness" (a point that is central to the argument for assemblage as creative repetition articulated by Kristin Arola and Adam Arola in this volume).

The theory of assemblage I am working with here is founded on Deleuze and Guattari's work, but with one key modification developed by DeLanda. In *A New Philosophy of Society,* DeLanda describes an assemblage with "an extra axis defining processes in which specialized expressive media intervene, processes which consolidate and rigidify the identity of the assemblage or, on the contrary, allow the assemblage a certain latitude for more flexible operation while benefiting from genetic or linguistic resources (processes of coding and decoding)" (19). This departure from Deleuze and Guattari's approach allows DeLanda to investigate social processes of organizing and communicating.

Within this concept of assemblage, DeLanda distinguishes between properties and capacities, which provide terminology for understanding how the relations within and among assemblages produce new possibilities for action. One of the challenging parts of this concept is that assemblages are composed of other assemblages. There is no essential, primary unit (e.g., an atom) from which all assemblages are composed. To borrow from a familiar phrase, it's assemblages all the way down. Any assemblage, once composed, will have properties, which are a denumerable list of characteristics. To draw on an example DeLanda employs, one might say that a knife, as an assemblage, exhibits the property of sharpness. A knife may be sharp or not, but its degree of sharpness is always present. In addition, assemblages also have capacities, which emerge in their relations with other assemblages. An assemblage has an open, indeterminate number of capacities as those capacities are only limited by the number of relations into which an assemblage enters. De-Landa offers the knife's *capacity* to cut as an example. "In fact, the capacity to cut may never be actual if the knife is never used. And when that capacity is actualized it is always as a double event: to cut—to be cut. In other words, when a knife exercises its capacity to cut it is by interacting with a different entity that has the capacity to be cut" ("Emergence" 385). That is, capacities cannot be internal. They require some external relationship in order to become real. One cannot act without someone or something to act upon.

How might we employ the concept of assemblage to understand the conventional composition classroom? We could begin with the variety of objects in the room—desks, lights, windows, chalkboards, screens, data projectors, etc. All of these objects exert some physical presence in the room; they have size and shape, for example. They also have an expressive force: the hardness of the seats, the dull hum of the fluorescent lights, or the dustiness of the chalk. They have a collective enunciation as a classroom, assigning roles to the people who also participate in the classroom assemblage as students and faculty. The classroom has certain properties: a particular number of desks, for example. It is worth noting that the number of desks can change without the classroom ceasing to be a classroom, just as a knife that is dull is still a knife. The classroom also has capacities. For example, the chairs have the capacity to offer seating, but only in relation to people who can sit in them. Recognizing this, we include special desks for students who do not relate to the standard desk by sitting at it (e.g., students in wheelchairs). There are tendencies toward territorialization and the regular behavior of those people: students sit in one area and the professor stands in another. The class might sit in a circle, but one cannot erase the roles of student and professor so easily. There are also deterritorializing tendencies—broken chairs, missing chalk, flickering lights—that disrupt the assemblage's regular function. In every instance a classroom will have material content and expressions. It will have properties that are always present and capacities that might emerge depending on who or what else is in the room. The classroom has a tendency to remain a classroom and the potential to become something else.

To these dimensions, DeLanda adds the third axis of expressive media and symbolic behavior, which introduces specific discourses into the classroom. The assemblage of the room is transformed depending on whether its inhabitants are members of a student club, a graduate course, a first-year composition class, etc. We might say that as a professor, I have the capacity to teach students, but that capacity can only be activated within the assemblage of a classroom (or some other pedagogical/curricular space) and only when I encounter other people who have the capacity to serve the role of students in the same classroom assemblage. That is, they must be people who are enrolled as students in my class. I might have the capacity to teach other people in other situations, but not as a professor teaching students, which requires participation in a particular assemblage. This would be one of the "incorporeal transformations" of the classroom assemblage. It turns people into students and professors, just as the same people in a courtroom become jurors, witnesses, and defendants. When the objects that participate in the assemblage change, for example when one introduces new media technologies, the capacities of the students and faculty change as well.

If we can imagine the assemblages of the objects participating in the composing of an essay or an online comment, we can also follow many other assemblages: the genres to which these texts belong, the technological networks on which they are communicated, the communities of authors and readers sharing these messages, the institutions these communications support, and so on. Assemblage theory situates human actors among nonhuman actors in these compositional processes and offers a way to understand the roles of human beings in larger assemblages. What we can see from De-Landa is that agency isn't located inside a human author, and it isn't located in some idealist realm. Agency emerges in and among us, human beings and nonhuman alike: just as a knife's capacity to cut becomes real only when it comes into relationship with another object that has the capacity to be cut, a human being's ability to write only becomes real within a network of actors that facilitate writing.

Moreover, the emergence of digital media networks has altered the assemblages of human communication by shifting the properties and capacities of the coded dimension. The capacity to post to a blog rather than submit an article to a journal, the capacity to share video or images, the capacity for real-time interaction over a distance: these all alter our compositional assemblages as surely as the laptops with a wi-fi connection open on students' desks alter their experience of the classroom in which they sit. When our discipline approaches these situations from more conventional perspectives, the new technologies are viewed as either enhancing or inhibiting an inherent, human, agential property for symbolic behavior. That is, either the technology helps us to write or it gets in the way. If one views symbolic behavior as an emergent capacity of an assemblage, however, one sees that different technologies activate different capacities for communication. It is not easy to map capacities. We cannot simply say that a smartphone inhibits essay writing, for example. Instead, we can say that the assemblages in which we participate have tendencies toward territorialization and deterritorialization that result in the development and mutation of genres and other symbolic behaviors. In the last part of this chapter, I will turn in particular to sites of "big data" as an example of these shifts.

BIG DATA

While *big data* is a term widely in use, its meaning is elusive. *Big*, obviously, is a relative term. What is big for Google or the NSA is different from what is big for NIH or NSF projects or for the student-data needs of a large university. In composition, one might consider the thirty million words students produce each year in a composition program of a size similar to the one I oversee as big. Or maybe we'd consider the tens of billions of words produced nationally in first-year writing programs as big. Moving in a different and even larger vein, the vast social-media networks in which our students might participate—Facebook, Twitter, Instagram, etc.— constitute a series of big-data sets. By employing DeLanda's theory of assemblage, it is possible to analyze both homogeneous and heterogeneous collections of data. So we might think of those sets of data that have been collected and processed as part of a research project as homogeneous. In terms of assemblages, this would represent the exertion of a strong territorializing force, complemented by an equally strong coding force. One can trace the servers, networks, monetary investments, coding standards, offices, and people involved in creating such assemblages. They are valuable and often proprietary because they do not happen accidentally. Indeed, we might say that the value of a company like Facebook is represented in its proprietary data set. On the other hand, we might also speak of looser, more deterritorialized and decoded data sets such as the set of all HTML websites or all the videos available online. At its most expansive, these heterogeneous assemblages might be understood as forming the media-data ecologies within which the more homogeneous data assemblages operate, just as the more homogeneous Facebook or YouTube operate within the larger ecology of the Web. Media and information types, often defined by file type, find themselves interacting, expanding or dying off, reproducing, and generating new types within these ecologies.

Put into the context of the composition classroom, assemblage theory gives us a different way of understanding the various activities that over the years we have called "inventing the university," joining discourse communities, learning *the* writing process, and so on. Our twentieth-century approaches to composing, while quite diverse in many respects, shared a common participation in an assemblage of print-based media. The material and expressive capacities of paper, ink, typewriters, books, journals, and libraries exerted strong territorializing forces on composing. A writer's access, particularly a student writer's access, to information, colleagues, and an audience was severely limited in comparison to the situation today. Institutional practices, such as regulations regarding intellectual property and plagiarism, built up around these contexts, as did market forces like the publishing industry, which took advantage of the bottleneck in the publication and distribution of compositions. As a consequence, today I compose in much the same way as a scholar from the last century: alone with a keyboard and texts. I could be composing in a different way, but the institutional practices surrounding tenure might not value that work. They insist that I work in a relatively solitary way, or at least they often do in English departments (though less so in other disciplines where collaboration is more common). Those scholarly composing assemblages work their way down to the undergraduate level and into first-year composition, where we insist that students compose in similar ways. However, just as the wi-fi and cellular phone signals penetrating the traditional classroom serve to deterritorialize and mutate many of our conventional pedagogies, the big-data assemblies of social media and Internet databases are shifting the way we compose. So while it may appear that my compositional practices echo those of the last century, closer inspection demonstrates that those practices are mutating. Perhaps the shifts appear subtle. For example, twenty years ago, in order to write this chapter, I would have driven to the library, searched a print index (or a non-networked database), found some articles, made photocopies, driven home, read the articles, and then quoted and cited them. Today, I accomplish the same thing in minutes with a Google search. The resulting essay might appear the same to the reader, but the process is very different.

Twentieth-century academic essays were part of a disciplinary field; they shared genre conventions and methodological paradigms; they cited one another; they shared an audience. Again, on the surface, the digital version of this essay might appear the same. It will not even break the surface conventions of print by incorporating video or Web links, but it has moved into an entirely different media ecology. Like the digital photograph, which once printed and framed on one's wall might appear indiscernible from a non-digital photograph but when posted to Instagram is entirely different, the digital version of the essay acquires new capacities quite different from a printed version of itself. The humanities have only begun to explore what is possible when text is approached as data. From tracing citation patterns to topic modeling, maps of conversations and discourse communities take on new shapes. In short, this essay becomes part of a big-data assemblage. While on the one hand it remains a discrete chapter in a specific essay collection, once it appears online in PDF or HTML format it becomes available for a vastly greater number of connections, audiences, and purposes. How does this change alter our understanding of rhetorical and compositional practices? If we begin with the accepted premise that composing is shaped by one's participation in a discourse community and genre, how does the mutation of the legacy, print-age concepts of community and genre into the concept of a big-data assemblage shift our understanding of composing and authorship?

A detailed answer to that question will require extensive research, but my short, provisional answer offered here is that the role of nonhumans, as well as humans, in composing will need to be reevaluated. One probable result is that academic writers (if writer is still the correct term) will find themselves in a period of greater heterogeneity in terms of composing. That is, it is likely that at some future moment, the current rapid churn of technological innovation will settle, and genre communities will regularize and reterritorialize. Some scholarly genres that will function in a way analogous to the articles and monographs of the last century will develop. Until then, scholars and their students find themselves in a more fluid situation. In rhetoric and composition, the history of the journal *Kairos* is a good example of this, as it has identified itself as a site for such scholarly experimentation. As such, it represents a kind of mutative edge of the assemblage of scholarly publication. However, it is not an edge that has to date interested itself much in the particular mutative potential of big data. Indeed, where big data has entered into the digital humanities, it has remained largely insulated as an analytical method rather than as a compositional tool (e.g., Derek Mueller's analysis of citations over twenty-five years of publications in the journal *College Composition and Communication*). That is, one might perform a computational analysis on a large set of texts and perhaps produce some data visualization of those texts, but the resulting scholarship is no more shaped by big data in terms of its genre or composition than is this essay.

One place where we might begin to see big-data scholarly compositional assemblages is in the Digital Humanities Now project, which aggregates the blogging and other online contributions of a large group of scholars loosely affiliated under the rubric of digital humanities. Here it is not the individual contributions that are of interest, but rather their combination. And this is the key point: I can't compose a "big-data assemblage" in the way I can compose a blog or an article or a monograph. My role as an author and my particular thoughts or intentions are not the issue except inasmuch as they become part of a larger mosaic. Digital Humanities Now is a relatively small set of data, but it is already more than any single person is likely to consume. So how do I understand my activity then? How do I make rhetorical and compositional decisions if I view my purpose as operating within a big-data assemblage rather than authoring a unique message? Is my objective to trend like a popular hashtag on Twitter or increase my Google PageRank? Perhaps something like Wikipedia is the model for a more homogenized, big-data disciplinary assemblage. At one point there were more than thirty million Wikipedia accounts, though the estimate of 270,000 active users was probably a better measurement of participation ("Wikipedia Community"). It is not so unreasonable to imagine that several thousand scholars in a field could compose on a single platform, that the currently heterogeneous media ecology of the discipline might meld into a more homogeneous environment.

Presented with the thought experiment of imagining composing in such a context, we begin to encounter different rhetorical and compositional pressures, such as the findability and interoperability of one's texts with others. Even though I know this essay will be placed in the context of other essays in a single collection, I have limited means for addressing those possible synergies. In the iterative environment of a big-data assemblage, those connections could grow. Rather than composing a series of stand-alone museum pieces, one might have a more organic approach to scholarship. In other words, we might be surprised to discover that a big-data assembly might feel more like a "human" conversational space than the metaphorical Burkean parlor conversation that is imagined to occur among texts, given that the exchanges could occur in real time and thus allow for the iterative back-and-forth of face-to-face conversation in a way that texts cannot. Unlike the parlor, though, it might feel more like having a conversation in a giant stadium before a concert where the collective result is something more like a buzzing noise than a message. Big-data assemblages compose meaning from what only appears to be noise to the human being who is unable to process what is going on around him or her without developing new analytical tools. In the context of big-data assemblages, as an author I am no longer only "in conversation" via the intertextuality of quotations and other direct citations, nor with a nebulous, imagined, invisible and mute "discourse community" and audience, nor even with the specific editors and readers that engage in the publishing process. I become part of a larger, real-time stream of data for which I must develop new capacities to read and understand.

Big data confronts us with the realization that symbolic behavior is not only for us, that as human beings we have entered into a symbiotic relationship with the enunciative, expressive capacities of assemblages. We become vehicles for expression and in turn put expression to work for ourselves just as we simultaneously make use of and participate in the natural ecologies we encounter. This shift in perspective is more difficult in terms of symbolic behavior because we have always viewed ourselves as the beginning and end of language. Big data bursts that illusion as surely as the telescope burst our illusion that we were at the center of the universe. As vertiginous as this reorientation might be, for rhetoricians it permits new spaces for composing at a time when the traditional, print-based scholarly genres and modes of publication are running out of steam. Multimedia journals and monographs such as those published by *Kairos* and the Computers and Composition Digital Press; more conventionally textual, open-access journals and book publishers, such as the WAC Clearinghouse; subscription-based library databases; and other ebook options from university presses: these all represent efforts to shift from print to digital genres. Along with these shifts within academic publishing, the larger cultural shifts of big data and social and mobile media offer us an opportunity to rethink our anthropocentric prejudices by examining the vast assemblages of rhetorical activity around us. Undoubtedly, the discipline is not in search of a scholarly Facebook or Twitter or even Wikipedia or blogosphere. It is equally difficult to imagine a rhetoric and composition smartphone app. However, once we recognize that it is not the "nature" of intellectual work to be solitary or slow or even written, that such experiences were only the result of the assemblages in which scholars labored, and that there is no necessary moral value to these activities, then new possibilities might emerge. As Ian Bogost argues, "[W]riting is dangerous for philosophy—and for serious scholarly practice in general. It's not because writing breaks from its origins as Plato would have it, but because writing is *only one form* of being. The long-standing assumption that we relate to the world only through language is a particularly fetid, if still bafflingly popular, opinion. But so long as we pay attention only to language, we underwrite our ignorance of everything else" (90). Bogost's point is to propose "carpentry," to suggest that academics might seek to make things in addition to writing about them, a point resonating with Shipka's argument located in a material context. More important, from my view, is his observation of the special role we give to language in our relationship with the world. It is not so much writing itself that is dangerous. It is our fixation upon a particular, print-culture writing practice as a defining, intrinsic activity of being human that must be addressed.

Assemblage theory serves as a tool for tackling this problem and imagining alternative possibilities of rhetorical engagement.

WORKS CITED

Bogost, Ian. *Alien Phenomenology, or What It Is Like to Be a Thing.* Minneapolis: U of Minnesota P, 2012. Print.

DeLanda, Manuel. "Emergence, Causality and Realism." *The Speculative Turn: Continental Materialism and Realism.* Ed. Levi Bryant, Nick Srnicek, and Graham Harman. Melbourne: re:press, 2011. 381–92. Print.

———. *A New Philosophy of Society: Assemblage Theory and Social Complexity.* London: Continuum, 2006. Print.

Deleuze, Gilles, and Félix Guattari. *A Thousand Plateaus.* Trans. Brian Massumi. Minneapolis: U of Minnesota P, 1987. Print. Vol. 2 of *Capitalism and Schizophrenia.* 2 vols. 1972–80.

Kennedy, George A. "A Hoot in the Dark: The Evolution of General Rhetoric." *Philosophy and Rhetoric* 25.1 (1992): 1–21. *JSTOR*. Web. 7 Jan. 2015.

Latour, Bruno. *We Have Never Been Modern*. 1991. Trans. Catherine Porter. Cambridge: Harvard UP, 1993. Print.

Mueller, Derek. "Grasping Rhetoric and Composition by Its Long Tail: What Graphs Can Tell Us about the Field's Changing Shape." *College Composition and Communication* 64.1 (2012): 195–223. *ProQuest*. Web. 22 Oct. 2016.

Schiappa, Edward. "Second Thoughts on the Critiques of Big Rhetoric." *Philosophy and Rhetoric* 34.3 (2001): 260–74. *EBSCOHost*. Web. 9 Sep. 2016.

"Wikipedia Community." *Wikipedia*. Wikimedia Foundation, 25 Apr. 2014. Web. 1 May 2014.

3

They Eat Horses, Don't They?

Jeff Rice

I BEGIN WITH AN ANECDOTE. I FIRST THOUGHT FACEBOOK was stupid and only for teenagers. After joining Facebook in 2007, I realized that the site was not just for teenagers, but for adults as well, adults who consistently share information in order to be engaged. In this anecdote, I discover a moment of response. When I felt Facebook was stupid and for teenagers, I responded to a popular circulation of meaning: Facebook is superficial; Facebook is for kids. I formulated that response from an aggregation of previously exposed moments and ideas—including the site's founding at Harvard University to connect with peers, the site's advertising basis, and the site's connection to silly, time-draining apps and games—that eventually led to an assumption: Facebook is superficial. Responses, such as the one I formed, can be limiting.

My initial response to Facebook does not reflect my current response to Facebook. That current usage is based on a different aggregation (social connectivity, scholarly interest, the sharing of photos of my kids, discussions of food, shared rants, etc.) that has shifted my overall response. Aggregation and assemblage share much in common, particularly how they gather and collect into a space diverse materials, ideas, positions, artifacts, and other items. In this chapter, I use the terms interchangeably in order to understand both as the same process of response. As I write about Facebook, I write about responses. Responses assemble into one space a number of gestures, even when they appear to be individual acts without relationship to other positions. One such gesture, I note, is the anecdote, the narrative of a short yet supposedly memorable event that stands for a larger meaning. To my first anecdote, I join another Facebook anecdote as part of the overall assemblage that begins this chapter.

On November 30, 2011, I posted on my Facebook profile a link from Chowhound.com entitled "They Eat Horses, Don't They?"[1] The short piece outlined the American aversion to eating horses by placing this disgust within the context of an impending congressional bill to ban slaughtering horses for consumption. The piece noted that while horsemeat may seem exotic to many in the United States, even the less-than-exotic Canadians enjoy eating horse. For the Chowhound.com story, perception drives response. As the piece I linked to explained:

> But in Canada, a country rarely considered exotic, you can get raw horse in Vancouver (at Yoshi's, a Japanese restaurant), horse steak in Toronto (at the bistro La Palette), and horse anything in Quebec—even a fast-food chain, the Belgian Frite Alors, sells horse tartare. (Horse is free of tuberculosis and tapeworms, and thus safer than beef to eat raw.) (Day)

My linked Chowhound.com status update's fifteen comments are minor by most posts' standards. The quality or quantity of responses—from angry to humorous—is not what interests me. Instead, I am interested in the *drive to respond* that a status update, among other new-media moments, creates. A status update generates response as readers feel involved enough in a topic that they comment on or share it. A status update about eating horsemeat generates *some* response depending on what the reader assembles/aggregates.

Aggregation response is based on how readers and texts engage the logic of aggregation in order to assemble a variety of commentary, news, websites, personal moments, and other matter into complex bodies of information that are seldom stable. The exigence for this chapter on assemblage and aggregation is a simple Facebook status update I posted about eating horses and why fifteen people responded. The update and the generated responses serve as departure points for a larger discussion of aggregation within social media as a layered system of assemblage-based responses. My purpose is to offer new insight into rhetoric and social media regarding how response is an assemblage based on aggregation.

HORSE RESPONSE

On June 28, 2013, I followed my previous horse update by posting to Facebook a link to a *Business Week* report describing the end of a six-year ban on slaughtering horses for consumption in the United States.[2] Responses followed. In this case, as I did with the Chowhound.com essay, I participated in a common circulation of news and noteworthy items on Facebook. As Facebook users engage with media outside of the platform (Twitter, news sites, blogs), they often feel compelled to share links from such media on Facebook. This sharing allows ideas and events to move through both strong ties (family, friends, co-workers) and weak ties (people one knows only to some extent or only via people one does know). Link-sharing functions as a type of response; I read something, believe it has meaning, and in order to respond to that meaning share the link with others who I believe will find meaning in it as well. The other members within my social network, in turn, may share that link. In doing so, we believe that the pieces of information we engage with are, following Karine Nahon and Jeff Hemsley, *remarkable*. "By this we mean that they exhibit qualities such that people want to make a remark about them" (98). At each moment I shared the two links, I believed that eating horsemeat was a remarkable idea; horse consumption prompts feelings of fascination, disgust, and interest. Discussion of horse consumption almost makes people feel *as if they are involved in eating horse as well.*

These particular links, like other links regarding the consumption of horsemeat that I have posted on Facebook, tend to produce some level of outrage over both the thought of eating a horse and the *desire to inform others* about horse consumption. Yet why does a link to a story about eating horses cause "friends" to become angry, feel troubled, or even want to respond? I was not advocating the consumption of horsemeat nor showing a picture of myself eating horsemeat. I merely shared information. The mere sharing of information produced specific responses because of the way that information was shared within a specific network. Within the various levels of food information distribution that many of us participate in outside of Facebook, horsemeat generates a rhetoric of either exoticism or outrage, and these responses are carried from various media to Facebook interactions. Media share with us the knowledge that some people eat horses in Belgium, Canada, Japan, and elsewhere. Chowhound.com facilitates that knowing, as I indicated with my shared link. In *Strange Foods,* after a historical overview of nations that have eaten horse, Jerry Hopkins facilitates that knowledge by providing a recipe for horse tartare (10), noting that horsemeat "is particularly suited for raw dishes" (12). The Travel Channel circulates this knowledge as well. Andrew Zimmern, host of the popular *Bizarre Foods* television show, makes that knowledge explicit in the show's Toronto episode when he eats horse tartare at the Black Hoof restaurant.

When Zimmern focuses on the consumption of horse, he displays a *remarkable* moment. Viewers are expected to respond to that moment by becoming engaged with it: tweeting it, linking to its hosted YouTube videos, and commenting on Facebook (as I did as well). Remarkable moments are meant to be shared. Remarkable moments, however, are not arbitrarily cast into the ether of social media nor do they form out of a simple moment of fascination or interest. Instead, they are shared with connected groups in order to continue facilitating the specific knowledge at stake when the main channels of media communication (book, website, travel show) cannot on their own facilitate or assemble it. Facebook's Paul Adams writes, "Every one of us uniquely connects multiple groups of people together, so if messages are to spread, they have to pass through the people who connect groups. In other words, the people who spread ideas are just regular people" (47). People who respond are regular people, but when assembled across media spaces, their responses create complex sharing. As one such regular person, I spread an idea about horsemeat consumption because I thought it was remarkable. Others may not have shared this view, but their likes or comments continue the sharing. The remarkability of the idea gains traction because of who shares, and, contrary to Adams's claim, this sharing stems not from "regular people," but from people within specific physical and virtual locations. That is, "regular" is not the clarifying factor; it's rather one's position within a network of aggregated moments that is important.

Horses engage in all kinds of activities, many of which others find remarkable as well. People breed horses, for example, to race around a track for betting or to jump over obstacles for show. The shock of watching horses race around a track, for some, is nowhere near as intense as the shock of a man in a Toronto restaurant eating raw horsemeat chopped fine and mixed with onions. When I posted my link to Facebook, that shock spread. If I am but one person in a network spreading a message, and that message is not about horse racing or equestrian games, why does my response produce more shock than other responses related to horses? What is the location of my response? We live in Lexington, Kentucky, a city known for horse breeding. We also live on the far south side of town, where horse farms are abundant. The animals raised on these farms—humanely or not by well paid or poorly paid immigrants—are raised, not for consumption, but to run fast or to walk elegantly. With that point, I produce a response to the situation I am located within. As I locate my situation geographically (where I live), I note that I am not outraged by Kentucky horse breeding. As I locate my situation in relationship to food (what I eat), I am also not outraged by a news story regarding approval for the slaughter and sale of horses for human consumption. In that same location, I am also not outraged by the slaughter and sale of cows, lambs, goats, pigs, chickens, and other animals for human consumption. The distinction is not that I eat meat or enjoy watching horses run around a track (I do the first, but not the second), but that the assembled positions we form around such subjects when we respond to their presence in our information circles (where we are located), even when contradictions arise (eating is not OK, racing is OK), are the result of response as assemblage and aggregation. With social media, these responses can be more intense than they have been in the age of print culture, even though the same conditions for response have always existed. The invention of the essay, for instance, is based on the logic of response: I read something; I think about it; I respond to it by writing an essay. Social media intensify this rhetorical gesture. With these two brief beginning anecdotes, I find my exigence for this chapter beyond the anecdotes that I started with: how is aggregation the basis of social-media response? What kind of assemblage does aggregation produce when we respond in specifically located social-media spaces?

SOCIAL-MEDIA RESPONSES

I am not advocating the sale of horsemeat or the sale of any animal for consumption. Instead, I am interested in how social-media responses heighten interest, disgust, or celebration in a McLuhanist sense of involvement. When Marshall McLuhan noted that items brushing against other items produce startling and effective results, he spoke to the notion of response that has become highlighted in the age of social media, where remixes, parodies, status updates, tweets, and blog posts frame a digital culture of information brushing up against other information. "We have had to shift our stress of attention from action to reaction," McLuhan noted (*Medium* 68). Observing the effects of television, film, and radio in the 1960s, McLuhan was concerned with juxtaposition among text and image, a basis for assemblage practices (such as in remixes or collage) where the uncanny combination of unlike materials in a textual or media space produces a response. *Understanding Media* posed such juxtapositions in terms of specific media forms (radio, comics, television), but *The Medium Is the Massage* visualized the process as an extended argument about juxtaposition. In one example McLuhan provides in *The Medium Is the Massage*, a Civil Rights protester is arrested under a movie-theater marquee. The startling (and remarkable) result is the overlap of an involved, entertained culture and an age of involved, political turmoil. On one page the marquee reads "Suspense and Excitement!" and when the page is turned the reader sees juxtaposed under the marquee an African American woman being arrested, with a group of other African Americans visible in the background. McLuhan's text reads, "Movies are better than ever! Hollywood is often a fomenter of anti-colonialist revolutions"

(*Medium* 129–31). What does McLuhan suggest is the response? Entertainment responds to political turmoil in its heading, or vice versa? *The Medium Is the Massage* highlights the juxtaposition, for whichever purpose, as the response.

Juxtaposition, however, is not only the visual display of unlike items; it is also part of discursive digital practices as well. Juxtaposition occurs in what Adams calls the conversational aspect of social media, or what Malcolm Gladwell calls "connectors'" "telling," where the types of juxtapositions McLuhan highlighted motivate response as communicative acts occur among shared moments and individuals. These responses are circulated by both weak and strong ties, though, as Jacob Goldenberg, Barak Libai, and Eitan Muller note in their research on social media and advertising, word-of-mouth (conversational) dissemination depends largely on weak ties. "When personal networks are small, weak ties were found to have a stronger impact on information dissemination than strong ties" (219). Among weak ties, status updates brush up against established beliefs in a small personal network (such as my 823 Facebook friends). A series of responses (telling or conversation-based) become a thread on Facebook or on another platform. The exigence I begin with regards weak ties as the basis of response networks assembling across social-media spaces where horse consumption is discussed. Reading about horse consumption, a Facebook user becomes involved. "The perennial quest for involvement, fill-in, takes many forms," McLuhan claims (*Medium* 78). In the rest of this chapter, I sketch out social-media response as a "brushing" in order to situate this process via the specific assemblage practice of aggregation, where juxtaposition (both like and unlike the juxtaposition Yancey traces in this volume) asks readers to fill in and be involved.

AGGREGATION

In social media, aggregation, as assemblage practice, is understood via the RSS (Really Simple Syndication) reader, a platform that pushes websites (via their feeds) to one space in the user's browser where the websites can be organized and read (rather than the reader visiting each site independently). Aggregation juxtaposes like and unlike information from a variety of locations into one location. Aggregation's RSS legacy is present in Facebook feeds, Instagram photographs, and Twitter feeds, all of which work off the principle of the feed, a basic element of aggregation. Aggregation, as an assemblage, is a larger concept than the RSS reader itself. Drawing from Gilles Deleuze, Jane Bennett explains assemblages via an aggregation-style definition, "ad hoc groupings of diverse elements, of vibrant materials of all sorts. Assemblages are living, throbbing confederations that are able to function despite the persistent presence of energies that confound them from within" (23–24). Aggregation compiles in one place a number of perspectives that otherwise would be read or viewed separately. These ad hoc juxtapositions create a body (the entire reader experience) even as the disparate elements function independently (they exist elsewhere in other reader experiences different from my browser's assemblage). Bennett focuses on human and nonhuman interaction (a borrowing from Bruno Latour), where "an assemblage owes its agentic capacity to the vitality of the materials that constitute it" (34). The aggregated materials I assemble for reading thus include the nonhuman (the materials) but also me (the reader). RSS signifies this juxtaposition online, but as my anecdotes briefly demonstrate, Facebook status updates are another space of this activity, albeit in a form that resembles another version of aggregation.

Prior to conventional aggregation tools such as RSS, Vilém Flusser called aggregation the "technical image," which he named "computations of concepts" (10). These computations, picked up within images and by viewers, are mentally constructed to produce ideas and discourse. The computation involves how one might assemble the items—present or absent—within the image or text's location. In every image, Flusser argued, exist previous ideas and concepts the viewer aggregates into the image's present meaning (much as RSS does in a browser). These meanings or technical images are often repeated as viewers take the meanings into future discursive moments. When I posted on Facebook a link to a Chowhound.com or *Business Week* story on horsemeat consumption, the responses were based on how viewers responded to the computations or aggregations occurring in the technical image they encountered and felt engaged with: feelings about horses, representations of horses, beliefs in what kinds of meat are suitable for consumption, etc. The responses presented a grouping of diverse elements. A technical image is any image (literal or figurative) where such groupings occur. My shared link was one type of technical image for those who read it and responded to it.

In "Rhetoric of the Image," Roland Barthes identified how images aggregate a rhetoric based on the ways separate and diverse items are assembled into one space and how the reader of that space engages with the assemblage. Barthes noted that a Panzani advertisement's pairing of colors, a tomato, a package of spaghetti, and an onion into one physical space produces the rhetorical arrangement of what he called "Italianicity," the overall presentation of what constitutes being Italian. As Shipka argues, collections—or in this case aggregations—of objects demonstrate meanings, here being Italian, because of how the human (the recipient/viewer) and the nonhuman (the assembled objects) interact within a media space (advertising). "The perceptual message and the cultural message," Barthes writes of the grouped-together image of Italian objects, are assembled by the viewer of the advertisement so that a sense of what is Italian is understood (36). Italianicity captures the rhetorical feeling of all things Italian by aggregating past activities into one space. "Italianicity is not Italy," Barthes assures us (49). Italianicity is not a representation of Italy. It is an aggregation of a perceived Italy formed from various media interactions. The object, within the viewer's network of perceptions and previous understandings, produces meaning by drawing upon and aggregating previous assumptions, cultural biases, past experiences, reading habits, viewing habits, and other behaviors. If I aggregate the items in the image into the sense of what is Italian, I do so because I have aggregated into my technical image specific associations of what is Italian (eating in an Italian restaurant, visiting Italy, watching a movie set in Italy, purchasing a can of tomatoes in the grocery store). I juxtapose or aggregate these associations into a visual meaning: the advertisement.

This generic sense of "icity" Barthes highlighted is based on a viewer's response to an aggregated set of objects. The objects affect one another within their internal network—in this case, the advertisement—and in this engagement, the objects also affect the viewer's assemblage into something remarkable, such as the sense of what is Italian. In digital platforms, this assemblage of "icity" not only assembles a variety of moments or experiences into an image or idea, but circulates those moments as a technical image. These technical images are sometimes referred to as memes or viruses for the ways they are spread or repeated across media platforms, but they could also be simple status updates or tweets. Barthes did not draw attention to how the "icity" he attributed to the advertisement is disseminated by those who receive it and, consequently, come to believe it as more than an "icity," that is, as a representation of an actual thing or idea. Henry Jenkins, Sam Ford, and Joshua Green call this process spreadable media, when audiences share content across media platforms because of what was shared with them; that is, sharing is a response connecting recipients of content, not just recipients and producers of content. "As people listen, read, or view shared content, they think not only—often, not even primarily—about what the producers might have meant but about what the person who shared it was trying to communicate" (13). Communication (as telling, word of mouth, or some other act) is between social-media aggregators of *remarkable* content. The initial site of content production fades in favor of the spreadability of a message or response among users, and with that process, we encounter remarkability. One might, for instance, respond to McLuhan's sharing of an African American woman's arrest outside a movie theater in the 1960s with outrage. With outrage, one might become involved in the technical meaning (aggregating various unjust arrests and abuses African Americans experienced in the 1960s). This involvement might prompt responses: more protests, op-eds, gatherings, and, for contemporary purposes, likes, retweets, blog posts, and remixes. One contemporary example of this outrage is the set of responses to University of California Davis police officer John Pike's pepper-spraying protesting students.

AGGREGATED RESPONSE

When John Pike pepper-sprayed University of California Davis students participating in a localized version of Occupy Wall Street on November 18, 2011, he would not have guessed that his image would be assembled into a series of circulated photographs passed from content recipient to content recipient. These images, whether critical or parodic, aggregated a number of moments and ideas internalized as technical images. As a technical image, the John Pike event can be located within a collective, aggregated memory of past moments associated with protest and civil rights such as that found within the McLuhan photograph, university protests, a history of protest in California universities, the repeated refrain of "The whole world is watching" at the 1968 Democratic convention in Chicago, 1960s police brutality, and the concept of free speech. These previous cultural images become collectively aggregated by recipients into that of one police officer's usage of force so that an "icity" of outrage is expressed by a number of individuals who responded to the attack. In that expression, digital Facebook became one platform for response as involvement, much as the print advertisement is a platform for Barthes.

We can trace a few of these responses as example. On November 19, 2011, less than a day after the incident, the Facebook group OccupyMARINES posted a picture of John Pike with the statement "He likes to Pepper Spray Kids when they are defenseless and in a sitting position."[3] A few hours later, the Facebook page Being Liberal had reproduced the image of Pike pepper-spraying students with the declaration "This cop is SICK!"[4] A November 19 post of the Pike photograph on Occupy Wall St.'s Facebook page critiqued the act as "horrific crimes against humanity."[5] Occupy Seattle's Facebook page as well responded to the incident and asked that the image be shared so that the "injustice is exposed to everyone."[6] The post earned almost 36,000 likes (see Figure 3.1). These reactions led to the visual responses that quickly followed these textual ones.

With the Pike incident's spread across media platforms by various users of the image (and not by the original photographer), *outragicity* occurred. Response, in the case of the Pike image, becomes

OccupyMARINES · 66,197 like this
November 19, 2011 at 5:18pm ·

🖒 Like

This is Lt. John Pike - He likes to Pepper Spray Kids when they are defenseless and in a sitting position. His information is Public, so Anonymous decided to share it for your enjoyment 😊

Anonymous ● DOX: UC Davis Pepper Spraying officer, Lt. John Pike
anoncentral.tumblr.com

DOX: UC Davis Pepper Spraying officer, Lt. John Pike
http://99anon.tumblr.com/post/130230 61194/d0x-uc-davis-pepper-spraying-officer-lt-john-pike DOX: UC Davis Pepper Spraying officer, Lt. John Pike....

Like · Comment · Share   💬 180

🖒 231 people like this.

💬 View previous comments   48 of 85

Jo Ann Ryan a big fat tub of shit ,maybe he should pass up the donuts and practice self control 😣
November 19, 2011 at 5:48pm · Like · 🖒 1

Aaron Buchanan http://xllnt.com/yunocheckvoicemail.m4a

http://xllnt.com/yunocheckvoicemail.m4a
xllnt.com

November 19, 2011 at 5:49pm · Like · 🖒 1

Greg Seward I emailed him. Thinking of blowing up his phone line come Monday.
November 19, 2011 at 5:49pm via mobile · Like

Figure 3.1. Immediate response to post about John Pike.

a user-generated activity in which each response differs slightly from the others, but all are anchored by the technical image of Pike pepper-spraying students, an image publicly deemed remarkable.[7] Within this technical image, viewers may also find concepts that diverge from the image's projected meaning (i.e., the promise of democracy as opposed to the reality of police brutality) or that merge with the image's other projected meanings (i.e., other canonical moments of campus violence such as Kent State). Nahon and Hemsley trace the assemblage of Pike responses found online to a number of moments of expression, and not to just one circulated photograph. "The incident was not composed of one viral event," they write, "but many viral and non-viral streams of shared content, which, together, formed a viral topic. The topic was made up of videos, photos, blog posts, news articles, and memes" (110–11).

The transmedia storytelling is enacted as multiple media platforms are engaged to tell an aggregated/assembled story of outragicity. Eventually, the outrage expressed via status updates, tweets, and blog posts became assemblages, remixes of the technical image of Pike's act.

Beyond the initial critiques, the dominant images that remain from the Pike incident are the remixes of his pepper-spraying. Limor Shifman divides the complex interaction of Pike remix responses into two forms: the political and popular culture. "These political versions share a clear idea, namely that the officer brutally violated the basic values of justice and freedom as represented by the protestors" (51). In the popular-culture versions of the Pike image, Shifman notes, the rationale is more open-ended, less reliant on outragicity. "Pike is pepper spraying icons such as Snoopy and Marilyn Monroe as well as a battery of stars identified with other Internet memes, such as 'Little Baby Panda' and Keyboard Cat'" (51), creating an "amused and humorous" response, which, I add, could still be based on the overall affect of outrage (53). The story of John Pike, as told through both political commentary and parody, is the reduction of a moment into a series of assembled ideas reposted as remix: Pike pepper-spraying at the signing of the Declaration of Independence, Pike pepper-spraying Pink Floyd's *Dark Side of the Moon* album cover, Pike pepper-spraying at the Last Supper, Pike pepper-spraying at Iwo Jima, etc. This reduction is shared as a series of assembled responses.

With these images, John Pike's image is spreadable, as Jenkins, Ford, and Green argue; spreadable media are the types of response in which audiences

> select material that matters to them from the much broader array of media content. . . . They do not simply pass along static texts; they transform the material through active production processes or through their own critiques and commentary, so that it better serves their own social and expressive needs. (294)

In the case of the Pike image, the aggregation of responses circulated—the digitally altered images of Pike pepper-spraying a smelly bathroom or Paul McCartney on the cover of the *Abbey Road* album—exist because of spreadability's expression of communal social beliefs. Nahon and Hemsley identify this as the result of sharing across interest networks. Those who make the altered images, or who linked to them, or reposted them, or tweeted them, did so because they, too, felt a sense of aggregated outragicity *even if the exact details of what occurred on the UC Davis campus were not known.* The aggregation, after all, does not ask those who share the images under question to also include what occurred before the photograph was taken, after the photograph was taken, on the computer where the photograph was altered, or on the computer where the photograph was viewed. Nor did Barthes's aggregation ask viewers of the advertisement to question where the placed products came from, who consumed them, or what their cultural history is outside of Italy. Response movement depends on the immediate response to the image, which feeds off of communal, aggregated belief (police are brutal, college campuses are sites of legitimate protest) based on communally accepted aggregated meanings assembled in the image (the space of the assemblage). In the aggregation, weak ties connect audiences via a communal network built of response. "Those who find that the content is salient to them," Nahon and Hemsley write,

> resonant with their views, or just *interesting*, share it with others and create an *interest network*. Some will create and share *response content*, most of which will receive little attention, but the few that manage to go viral will add to the evolving narrative of the network as people engage in collective sense-making through the content they share. (13)

Three days after the pepper-spraying incident, Daily Kos contributor Heartland Liberal shared this sentiment when responding to the Pike incident via the hyperbolic declaration (aggregated from other cultural meanings of police actions) that "I only hope this serves as a wake up call to America that we are teetering on the verge of a police state, and I hope people are asking themselves whether this is where we want to go, or if this is what America is all about." The author questioned the value of the many images that had, in three days, been assembled as response. These images, Heartland Liberal noted, anticipate a viewership capable of aggregating the references based on their shared interest. Heartland Liberal, after all, had arrived at a hyperbolic response via such aggregated references. But could others?

> I am old enough I think I got most of the references. But I have to wonder whether teenagers and young twenties will recognize John Lennon and Yoko Ono. If not, that I could understand. Maybe they will recognize the meaning of "Four Dead in Ohio?"

Communal interest does not always equal a shared reference point (Kent State, John Lennon) nor a reality (one police officer pepper-spraying students does not equal "police state"). My links to horsemeat consumption received little attention since my interest network (those interested in horsemeat consumption) is small, and any remarkability or interest is minimal because we do not share reference points (food culture, horses for engagement outside of racing or show). The larger network of weak ties assembled around the Pike image, on the other hand, was vast. Its remarkability spoke to a larger aggregation of meaning and cultural reference than my links did. Its technical image was communal enough that not all reference points needed to be shared for the assemblage to take effect. Outragicity survived on aggregation alone.

CONCLUSION

My horsemeat status update was posted weeks after the John Pike incident went viral. This social-media overlap regarding two distinct and unrelated postings tells another narrative, how one story quickly spreads across media outlets and how one story does not. This overlap tells the story of remarkability, for what is remarkable at the moment (the sudden exclamation regarding horsemeat consumption) is not always as powerful as what is remarkable over time (a history of campus social protest). This overlap is the story of response. The power of aggregation is stronger in the John Pike example than in the horsemeat example because there are more items available over time that can be aggregated and spread. With numerous options, response spreads further and with more impact. As it spreads, the response increases, often shadowing or erasing the original message. Outrage over John Pike has more meaning than the action of John Pike, because of the aggregated response. If I had posted my link in a Facebook group focused on breeding horses for race or for show, I'm sure I would have generated a more substantial response because, like those attracted to the Pike image, my link would have engaged an outragicity based on that specific interest network's aggregations.

My purpose has been to trace response in social-media spaces based on a variety of positions, from my anecdote to more complex variations. In her discussion of digital memes, Shifman calls positioning "the location of a message within social networks and . . . its association with certain actors" (70). While the focus of Shifman's work is memes, we can say the same about social-media-based response. When an item—an image, idea, status update, tweet—is located in a specific space—Facebook page, circulated photo—it motivates the actors to respond. At some point, if the response is circulated, remixed, or linked enough, an aggregated meaning is produced. The implications of this idea involve rethinking our own interactions with circulated ideas so that we pause in our belief that a circulated message, on its own, reflects a given state of affairs; we might instead consider the aggregated moments located within the response itself. To do so, we can assume, would involve a rethinking as well of both practice (reading social-media moments) and ideology (believing in social-media moments).

NOTES

1. https://www.facebook.com/902995400/posts/146791198758878
2. https://www.facebook.com/902995400/posts/10152923717415401
3. https://www.facebook.com/OMCorg/posts/291471277550436
4. https://www.facebook.com/beingliberal.org/posts/108536452595073
5. https://www.facebook.com/OccupyWallSt/posts/179580395465080

6. https://www.facebook.com/OccupySeattle/posts/286973288009
468

7. See the Tumblr devoted to such images of Pike pepper-spraying:
http://peppersprayingcop.tumblr.com/

WORKS CITED

Adams, Paul. *Grouped: How Small Groups of Friends Are the Key to Influence on the Social Web*. Berkeley: New Riders, 2012. Print.

Barthes, Roland. "Rhetoric of the Image." *Image Music Text*. Trans. Stephen Heath. New York: Hill, 1977. 32–51. Print.

Bennett, Jane. *Vibrant Matter: A Political Ecology of Things*. Durham: Duke UP, 2010. Print.

Day, Nicholas. "They Eat Horses, Don't They?" *Chowhound.com*. 17 Nov. 2006. Web. 10 Sep. 2016.

Flusser, Vilém. *Into the Universe of Technical Images*. Trans. Nancy Ann Roth. Minneapolis: U of Minnesota P, 2011. Print.

Gladwell, Malcolm. *The Tipping Point*. Boston: Little, 2000. Print.

Goldenberg, Jacob, Barak Libai, and Eitan Muller. "Talk of the Network: A Complex Systems Look at the Underlying Process of Word-of-Mouth." *Marketing Letters* 12.3 (2001): 211–23. Print.

Heartland Liberal. "UC Davis, John Pike, and the Birth of a Meme." *Daily Kos.com*. Daily Kos, 21 Nov 2011. Web. 13 Sep. 2016.

Hopkins, Jerry. *Strange Foods: Bush Meat, Bats, and Butterflies: An Epicurean Adventure around the World*. Hong Kong: Periplus, 1999. Print.

Jenkins, Henry, Sam Ford, and Joshua Green. *Spreadable Media: Creating Value and Meaning in a Networked Culture*. New York: New York UP, 2013. Print.

McLuhan, Marshall. *Understanding Media: The Extensions of Man*. New York: McGraw, 1964. Print.

McLuhan, Marshall, and Quentin Fiore. *The Medium Is the Massage: An Inventory of Effects*. Prod. Jerome Agel. Corte Madera: Gingko, 2001. Print.

Nahon, Karine, and Jeff Hemsley. *Going Viral*. Cambridge: Polity, 2013. Print.

Shifman, Limor. *Memes in Digital Culture*. Cambridge: MIT P, 2014. Print.

"Toronto: Horse Heart and Flipper Pie." Host Andrew Zimmern. *Bizarre Foods*. Travel Channel, 25 Nov. 2013. Television.

4

Beyond the Object to the Making of the Object: Understanding the Process of Multimodal Composition as Assemblage

James Kalmbach

MY ARGUMENT IN THIS ESSAY IS THAT JOHNDAN Johnson-Eilola and Stuart Selber's notion of "assemblage" as a type of text that is made up of other texts and that has been created in order to solve a real-world problem can also be used to describe the process we go through in creating those texts. Creating an assembled text, as Kathleen Blake Yancey demonstrates, is not a simple linear process; for digital composers, it is better thought of as a coalition of *engagements* (technological engagements, architectural engagements, interface engagements, media engagements, textual engagements, code engagements, template engagements, etc.), as well as *negotiations* of the *embedded expertise* in those engagements. Learning to create assembled texts involves learning more about each of these engagements, but it also involves, on a more abstract level, a process of managing these coalitions of engagements and negotiating among the various areas of expertise embedded within them.

ENGAGEMENTS: THE GATHERING OF MATERIALS

An "assemblage," whether in art or in rhetoric, is an object made out of other objects. In applying this concept of assemblage to the process of creating texts, I use the term *engagement* to refer to the pieces assembled during composition. These pieces will vary from project to project, person to person, and refer not simply to content, but also to tools as well as to the composer's background knowledge, interests, and values.

For digital projects, there is always a set of technological engagements: the collection of software tools that a maker uses to build the object. A digital project will also include design engagements (issues of color, typography, images, etc.), interface engagements, information architecture engagements, and content engagements, as well as social engagements and personal engagements. Different students bring their own unique sets of engagements to an assemblage project.

NEGOTIATION

During the process of assemblage composing, engagements are assembled into a coalition. A major part of the intellectual labor of creating assemblage compositions involves negotiating between these engagements. One of the recurring misconceptions of assemblage composition is confusing the process of learning more about individual engagements with the negotiations between those engagements out of which an assemblage emerges.

Students can profitably learn more about their various engagements: read books, ask their classmates for help, look up issues on Google. They can workshop their texts and improve them through feedback, dialogue, and revision. The same is not true of a negotiation, which involves a much more abstract balancing act and which cannot be workshopped. You can study what others have done and learn from their choices; you can reflect, after the fact, on what you did well and what you want to do better next time.

While I have always valued the process of having small groups of students workshop their projects, students don't always share this value. Too often small groups fail to rise above the level of pointing out typos, critiquing color choices, or sharing tips on using software—that is, focusing on their engagements, as these engagements are visible and easy to critique. Getting students to talk through their ongoing negotiations *between* engagements is a much bigger challenge. It is not that the students don't want to talk about these bigger issues so much as that they don't know how; moreover, each student's coalition of engagements is unique to that student and to his or her project. Finding ways to get students to reflect on and talk about the *ways they are negotiating engagements* is an enduring challenge in teaching assemblage composition. On the other hand, when everything clicks, and a group of students reflectively talk through their negotiations, the result can be magical.

EMBEDDED EXPERTISE: TEMPLATES, DEFAULT SETTINGS, AND WEB 2.0 TOOLS

In today's Web 2.0 world, virtually every website starts as a template of some sort (Kalmbach, "Mechanization"). A content management system such as WordPress creates pages on the fly, pulling text and images out of a database and flowing them into a template. These templates are a form of embedded expertise: someone has decided what fonts and colors the template will use, how many columns it will have, where the menus will appear, etc. When this paper was drafted in July of 2015, the open-source version of WordPress offered an archive of 1,962 themes, while Drupal, another open-source content management system, offered 2,146. As Stephen J. McElroy points out, there is a legacy effect to assemblage: many of these themes have been adapted from other themes to solve a specific problem for a particular organization and then shared with the larger community. When students choose a WordPress theme for a project, they are working with a gathering of strategies, engagements, and compromises that has been designed to solve a specific problem at a specific time, in a specific place, and in a specific social context—none of which is likely to be relevant to their specific projects. To use such a template effectively, students must visualize how these compromises will play out as they are attempting to solve their own problems at a different time and in a different place.

Templates, however, are not limited to database-driven sites; all Web-authoring software and Web 2.0 platforms make use of templates. Dreamweaver, for example, offers a variety of templates, file types, and starter pages (see Figure 4.1). These starter pages, designed to serve as the basic framework of a website, contain both embedded and explicit expertise. If you view the code, you'll find that the author of the page has included extensive commentary about the decisions that were made in creating the layout as well as advice on how best to use the starter layout (see Figure 4.2).

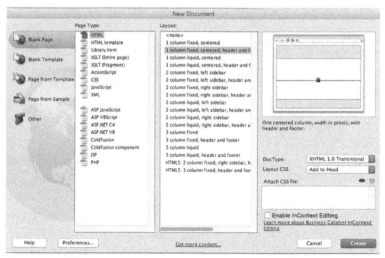

Figure 4.1. The starter page layouts available in Dreamweaver.

```
/* ~~ Element/tag selectors ~~ */
ul, ol, dl { /* Due to variations between browsers, it's best practices to zero padding and
margin on lists. For consistency, you can either specify the amounts you want here, or on the
list items (LI, DT, DD) they contain. Remember that what you do here will cascade to the .nav
list unless you write a more specific selector. */
    padding: 0;
    margin: 0;
}
h1, h2, h3, h4, h5, h6, p {
    margin-top: 0;    /* removing the top margin gets around an issue where margins can escape
from their containing div. The remaining bottom margin will hold it away from any elements that
follow. */
    padding-right: 15px;
    padding-left: 15px; /* adding the padding to the sides of the elements within the divs,
instead of the divs themselves, gets rid of any box model math. A nested div with side padding
can also be used as an alternate method. */
}
```

Figure 4.2. Advice embedded in the code of a Dreamweaver 5.5 starter layout.

Each new software tool a student adds to his or her project adds a new voice to a cacophonous conversation. Increasingly this embedded expertise is found in Web 2.0 tools: students may use paletton .com to create a color palette, css3generator.com to create a code snippet, photo-collage.net to create an image collage, 3dtextmaker .com to make a graphic header, screencast-o-matic.com to make a screen-capture video. The urge to assemble is an urge to distribute expertise instead of focusing that expertise in a limited set of tools.

What is this give and take between complex engagements and embedded expertise like? I find it helpful to compare assemblage composition and its negotiations to parenting. There are many actors in a parent's activity network, centered on your child or children—grandparents, spouses, siblings, and friends, as well as the child's toys, electronic devices, schools or daycare centers, favorite play sites, etc. You try a variety of strategies to manage this network: you talk to your spouse, your friends, your parents. You may read books about parenting, visit online forums, even watch reality television. You think about your children constantly, reflecting on what is working and what isn't while picking apart your decisions with your friends. And while these activities all help, you still feel as if you are hanging on by your fingertips, that you are a fraud and everyone else is doing it better. What is worse: your kids keep growing; they keep changing. You may find something that works, but a month later your child will have moved on, and you must figure out something else. Parenting is an act of continual creativity. That is what it feels like to create a digitally multimodal assemblage.

Helping students handle these engagements and the negotiations between engagements has been the core activity of my thirty-five years of teaching. In the next section, I offer a very brief history of this teaching so that I can then tell the story of three students: Hannah, Jared, and Kelly, each of whom took a very different path to negotiating his or her engagements while creating assemblage projects in recent classes.

HOW I CAME TO ASSEMBLAGE

I began teaching print-based multimodal composition at Michigan Technological University (where I taught from 1980 to 1987 and where a young, brash Johndan Eilola was one of my students) in a course called Publications Management. For this class, I developed what I now recognize as an activity-theory focus (though, alas, not an activity-theory vocabulary). I emphasized the analysis of ephemeral organizational documents—such as flyers, brochures, newsletters, and pamphlets—and the ways that those documents functioned in organizational activity networks. Students used type gauges (fancy rulers that could identify the size and spacing of type) to unpack the decisions designers had made in producing these documents, and they interviewed publishers about the work they hoped the documents would do, in order to write ethnographic studies and critical analyses of these goals and design choices.

In those pre–personal computer times, there were not many opportunities to create media-rich assemblages. We worked with pen and paper, scissors, and adhesive tape. I taught my first computer-based versions of the course in the mid-1980s on Macintosh Plus computers running PageMaker 1.2, on 400K floppy diskettes that had to be swapped in and out of a single disk drive whenever you changed a font. I taught my first Web-focused version of that course (after I had moved to Illinois State University) a decade later, in the spring of 1995. In the course, I had students create a project on three different platforms: HyperCard, Storyspace, and HTML. Comparing platforms got students to think about the hidden trade-offs in each and about design as an abstract activity rather than as a software-specific activity. It was an assemblage activity: students were learning to negotiate the expertise embedded in a range of tools.

While the students found this multiplatform approach to be quite engaging, the World Wide Web quickly came to dominate multimodal composing; I responded by pivoting the course to focus entirely on composing for and on the Web. Inspired by Jerome Bruner's notion of a spiral curriculum, I developed a series of assignments to engage students while returning them again and again to the same activities with an increasingly sophisticated understanding each time of what they were doing. First, they would repurpose a print paper they had written into a website; then they would create a site that explored some aspect of their identity. Finally, in the last half of the course, they would create a website on any topic.

This model worked for about ten years. Students were engaged, produced strong work, and got good jobs once they graduated. Unfortunately, as the Web grew more complex and more nearly ubiquitous, my focus on creating unique websites became more problematic. The experience of creating a website from "scratch" was becoming largely irrelevant and increasingly overwhelming for many of the students. Employers were no longer looking for employees who would create websites for them; they wanted people who would maintain the content on websites that were already in production. The world had changed: the most advanced Web-design skills I had learned how to teach from one point of view had become the entry-level skills for writers, editors, and designers from another.

My response to this problem was to return to the more overtly assemblage-based model I had used in my early, digitally focused, multimodal classes. I split the new course into two parts: in the first half of the semester, I asked students to create and then re-create a single project using different Web-authoring tools. The exact platforms changed each time I taught this new course. Most recently, students first created a website on Wix.com whose interface grammar mimics the floating, draggable objects of InDesign. Next they re-created this site in a custom WordPress.org install, in which students could install themes and plug-ins that would help them solve problems in their projects. Finally, they re-created the site, yet again, in Dreamweaver and HTML. At this point, students wrote reflections on their projects, comparing the strengths and weaknesses of each platform.

In the second half of the semester, students picked topics that engaged them as well as which Web-authoring platform they would use to turn that topic into a website. They were not limited to the platforms we had originally studied; they could pick different platforms or software packages as long as they could justify their choices. Past students have used iWeb, Notepad, Weebly, WikiSpaces, Blogger, and Drupal Gardens, among others. The goal was to provide students with enough experiences using different processes of creating websites so that they could make informed decisions about which platforms fit their projects, their personal work styles, and the problems they were trying to solve. Put another way, I was asking them to negotiate between their content engagements and the technological engagements embedded in their tools.

THREE STUDENTS NEGOTIATE ASSEMBLAGE PROJECTS

To illustrate how students negotiate the embedded expertise of their engagements, I offer the stories of three students: Hannah, Jared, and Kelly. Hannah struggled to make use of her past experiences working on the campus newspaper when creating an interactive PDF project, while Jared and Kelly created websites using Dreamweaver. Jared's engagement with code ultimately led him to neglect the content of his sites, while Kelly's engagement with her content ultimately led her to make peace with HTML.

Hannah: A Liminality of Expertise

Hannah was a communications major, a senior editor of our campus newspaper, and a student in a course focused on social media. For her final project, she decided to create an 11×17-inch interactive PDF newspaper to present her research on how newspapers are making use of social media. We did some initial investigation of tools, which suggested that Adobe InDesign was the best tool for creating an interactive, media-rich PDF. Since Hannah had used InDesign in the process of producing issues of the campus newspaper, we both assumed she would not have any problems. Toward the end of class, however, she asked for help. When we met in a computer classroom, I found that though she had spent many hours using InDesign to produce print editions of our campus newspaper, her knowledge of InDesign was fairly shallow. She had primarily used the program to complete a limited set of tasks again and again: flowing text and images into prebuilt newspaper templates. While she was quite comfortable working in the program's interface, she had not had much experience using InDesign to solve her own communication problems. On the other hand, the hours she had spent flowing text into newspaper templates were not without value. InDesign has a complex interface that can challenge beginners. When I showed Hannah the advanced features she would need for her project, she understood them almost at once. She had been trapped in a liminal space: she was neither a beginner nor a problem solver, but her experiences with the program helped her to move through that space. The colorful, interactive PDF she created included embedded videos (set to autostart, giving the newspaper a very Harry-Potterish feel), weather forecasts, interviews, advertisements, and a variety of social-media screen captures.

Jared: The Long Shadow of jQuery

Jared was an English major with a technical communication emphasis. He was taking my Web-design course his last semester at Illinois State while simultaneously taking a code-focused HTML course in our College for Applied Sciences and Technology. Jared wanted to use jQuery, an open-source JavaScript library he had studied in that class, in his final project for my class. He had proposed creating a website celebrating Derrick Rose (a point guard for the Chicago Bulls who had, at that time, captured the city's imagination), and he hoped to use jQuery to include image sliders as well as a responsive design that would reflow the content of the website from multiple columns to a single column when the user viewed the site on a smaller screen.

Jared's project included a number of technological engagements: He created his site ID in Photoshop and his headlines in CSS, but he struggled mightily to understand the logic of the responsive template he was using as well as the process for integrating a jQuery slideshow into his site. While he eventually solved these problems, the result was a fairly ordinary website without much original insight into or celebration of Derrick Rose: he spent so much of his time engaged with jQuery that his content suffered. The pages felt more like placeholders for a prototype website, waiting to be pitched to an editor before further development. Of course, Jared might have chosen to build his website using one of the many WordPress, Wix, or Weebly templates that had built-in jQuery support for slideshows and responsive designs, but his engagements were centered on understanding code. He wanted to solve his own problems.

The engagements that Jared pursued and the compromises he made are typical of those I had seen when my course was focused exclusively on Dreamweaver. During those semesters, many students were so exhausted by the problems of getting their code to work that, by the final project, they were out of ideas, and the quality of their content suffered, even while their technical expertise may have improved. The increasing difficulties I had observed as my students sought balance between their technological and their content engagements was one of the primary reasons I moved away from teaching specific software to an assemblage model that provided students with a range of software options and an emphasis on understanding the strengths and weaknesses of those different platforms. While Jared's struggle demonstrates this problem, his struggle was also complicated by the fact that he was taking two very different Web courses at the same time: one focused on code, the other on design. He was hearing two very different voices in his head talking over one another; I am not sure he ever reconciled them.

Kelly: A Commitment to Content

Kelly was a publishing studies major who had just completed an elite publishing internship that involved working on a variety of print journals and books and included extensive experience using print-production software. In our first project, she fell in love with Wix and its InDesign-like interface, producing a strong how-to website that celebrated advanced nail polish techniques with complex step-by-step instructions using photographs taken with her phone. When I talked to her about how she might make that site more visually dynamic by creating fewer, but stronger, visual lines and framing her content with white space, she got the idea instantly, and the results were striking. After I did a unit on color and introduced various online color wheels, I saw her creating and referring to color palettes throughout the rest of the semester. Her publishing background really helped her to deepen these engagements.

Kelly suffered through my units on WordPress and Dreamweaver with fairly good humor, creating nice variations of her nail-polish site on each platform. For her final project, she decided to create a genealogy site using research she had already gathered about her family. She wanted desperately to use Wix for this project, as it had deeply resonated with her print-publishing experiences. Unfortunately, as a result of the genre research I required for this project, she had decided that she also wanted to create a graphic of a family tree. When users rolled over a name on that tree, a small box of information about the person would appear. Wix did not offer this level of interactivity, nor did any other content-management system that I was aware of, but Dreamweaver had a fairly straightforward interface to a process of making content appear and disappear on mouseover and mouseout using embedded JavaScript functions.

Kelly stewed for a week about what platform to use until finally deciding that her content engagements and her commitment to her topic, to her vision of the site, and to her family were more important than her apprehension about working with HTML again. The result was a pretty striking project, but that product did not come easily. Kelly spent quite a long time developing the family-tree image that would be the base of her image map. I had encouraged her to create that graphic in InDesign (rather than Illustrator) because she was comfortable with the program, but I had underestimated her perfectionist drive, and I was beginning to despair about whether she would be able to finish on time. Would this engagement end up sidetracking her project?

When the image was finally finished, Kelly chained together an assemblage of tools, using features of several software packages for the final text: Photoshop to create a site ID, paletton.com for help in developing a color palette, and Dreamweaver for a custom Google font (Vollkorn). Toward the end of class, I talked her through the process of using Dreamweaver's behaviors interface to make her content divs appear and disappear, but that interface was pretty clunky. Numerous steps were required to create the mouseover and mouseout events needed for each of the ancestors in her sixteen-node tree. At one point, I was showing her the underlying code trying to help her understand what all these seemingly endless steps were doing, and she asked, "Can't I just copy and paste that bit of code and tweak the function?" A big smile split my face: Kelly had negotiated a balance between her content engagements and her apprehensions about technology. I knew she would finish.

We see in Hannah, Jared, and Kelly three students, each of whom was trapped in a different sort of liminal space and as a result had to work through very different negotiations. Hannah had extensive experience with the interface of InDesign but had not used the software to solve problems. Jared was caught between my emphasis on design and his other Web teacher's emphasis on code. Kelly was caught in a liminal space between print and Web publishing, but her commitment to her content and to her family led her to successfully tackle some very sophisticated technological problems.

WHY ASSEMBLAGE MATTERS

As any teacher of assemblage composition knows, the stories of Hannah, Jared, and Kelly are not unique or even particularly unusual. I have seen negotiations like these play out repeatedly with different levels of success as students struggled to create successful projects. Assemblage may offer a new and more useful way of talking about this process, but what does it add to the conversation? My answer to this question returns to Johnson-Eilola and Selber's essay and their argument about plagiarism and the enduring trope of the lone genius writer slaving in his or her garret to create original texts.

Johnson-Eilola and Selber note that despite the reality of our everyday experience creating digital texts using processes of assemblage, bricolage, collage, and remix in order to solve real-world problems, we continue, as a field, to embrace the trope of the lone writer creating a new, unique, and individual text. While our field has long attacked the idea of the lone genius in the attic slaving away on a piece of written work (Porter; Selzer), we still hew pretty close to this ideal when dealing with issues of plagiarism. We may value assemblage in the abstract, but in our lived-through, daily experience working with students, we tend to fall back on the idea of writers as loners composing original texts in their garrets. There is a similar trope speaking to the subtle relationship of engagements and negotiations in assemblage composition: the trope that writing is a muscle, the idea that we get better as writers through hard work, by grueling individual and solitary exercise:

Writing is a muscle. Smaller than a hamstring and slightly bigger than a bicep, and it needs to be exercised to get stronger. Think of your words as reps, your paragraphs as sets, your pages as daily workouts. Think of your laptop as a machine like the one at the gym where you open and close your inner thighs in front of everyone, exposing both your insecurities and your genitals. Because that is what writing is all about. (Nissan)

It is a trope with many amusing visual memes (see Figure 4.3). You can almost read the click-bait headline: "You won't believe what these writers did to become famous."

Why do these tropes matter? Johnson-Eilola and Selber argue that they are evidence of a gap between our theories and our everyday, lived-through experiences. We know rationally that writing is a complex social process and that creating a multimodal composition or website involves more than exercising individual engagements, but we still fall back on an old familiar trope that focuses on a single engagement. Part of the argument for viewing texts as assemblages is that if we better understand the components and purposes of

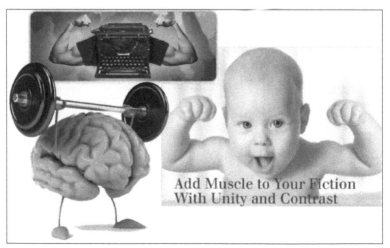

Figure 4.3. The trope of writing as a muscle.

everyday documents that solve problems, we will ideally be able to better resist these totalizing tropes.

This gap between our theories and our everyday perceptions is reminiscent of Sherry Turkle's 1995 observations about the gap between postmodern theories of fragmented identity and the reality of the unitary self in everyday life:

> While in recent years, many psychologists, social theorists, psychoanalysts, and philosophers have argued that the self should be thought of as essentially decentered, the normal requirements of everyday life exert strong pressure on people to take responsibility for their actions and to see themselves as intentional and unitary actors. This disjuncture between theory (the unitary self is an illusion) and lived experience (the unitary self is the most basic reality) is one of the main reasons why multiple and decentered theories have been slow to catch on—or when they do, why we tend to settle back quickly into older, centralized ways of looking at things. (15)

The disjuncture Turkle writes about "between theory (the unitary self is an illusion) and lived experience (the unitary self is the most basic reality)" haunts us to this day. In the concept of assemblage, we see the same tensions between theories of the assemblage text and an assemblage process versus our lived experience of a unitary text and a unitary process. When I talk to teachers, I see them again and again reducing assemblage projects and processes to the individual engagements that make up the project and to the work involved in getting better at those engagements, rather than focusing on the harder and much more complex work of negotiating our assemblages of engagements and their embedded expertise. We need to continually work at making this complexity visible.

EMBRACING NEGOTIATION IN THE CLASSROOM

Because managing the tension between engagement and negotiation is so difficult, I end with three small steps that teachers at all levels can take.

Choosing Their Own Topics

As we saw in Kelly's story, a strong commitment to a topic can go a long way in helping students to negotiate technological engagements. Unless students have a problem that they really want to solve with an assemblage composition, they are unlikely to invest in the negotiations among engagements from which strong projects emerge. Such a problem could be aesthetic, personal, political, critical, or organizational; good projects come in all forms and in all disciplines, but the problem has to be more than "What can I do that will get an A in this course?" Helping students to find good topics is another of the enduring challenges of teaching assemblage composition; giving students too little guidance (write about anything that interests you) is just as bad as giving them too much direction.

Choosing Their Own Tools

Letting students choose their software tools for a project is an argument that has been made for years, most recently by Nick Carbone, Richard Holeton, and others. If students chose their own tools, where, I wondered, were the opportunities to problematize those choices, pushing them to learn more deeply and to solve more complex and more interesting problems? Nonetheless, I eventually came to understand that Carbone and Holeton were right. While assigning a specific software package like Dreamweaver to use for a specific project did provide me with opportunities for just-in-time interventions, I was turning the project into a banking activity, an exercise in giving the teacher what he or she wanted. The problem too many students, like Hannah, were trying to solve was how little of Dreamweaver they could get away with learning and still get a good grade. When we ask students to pick the software they will use and to defend those choices, we are highlighting the importance of problem solving from the beginning of the project.

Letting students choose their own tools does not, however, mean the teacher has no role in managing technological engagements. There are still opportunities for just-in-time teaching. Teachers can help students engage with software in a variety of ways, for example, pushing students to explore new options or use new features when it is obvious that the students' current engagements cannot solve their problems. Teachers can also create sandbox opportunities, during which students are encouraged to play with software without the pressure of creating a deliverable. Open-ended exploration prior to using a new platform to solve a problem is almost always more productive than watching step-by-step videos. Sandboxing can be as simple as scheduling time during which students are asked to explore a new platform without trying to solve a problem or as complicated as creating a stripped-down environment within a platform where students can experiment with a new technology without getting lost in its more advanced features (Carroll). When I taught the publications management classes mentioned earlier, I always started students learning page layout software (first Page-Maker, later InDesign) by having them work on one-page documents, because much of the troublesome complexity of the software involved managing the flow of text and images across multiple pages. Likewise, students can use an online CSS editor to modify the appearance of a short poem so as to reflect their experience of reading that poem; students use CSS rules to make meaning without the burden of also learning all the messy details of creating and publishing a complete webpage.

Using Critique to Make Negotiations Visible

I have long believed in the importance of critical, reflective writing (see Kalmbach, "Agonies"). It pulls students away from the urge to make something work by asking them to reflect on why they are trying to use this feature in the first place. Critical reflection is an essential balance to the pleasures of technological engagement. Having experimented with a variety of critical, reflective assignments, I have concluded that students benefit from two different sorts of critical writing. The first is a careful, critical analysis of an individual website or multimodal artifact involving a close examination of the different engagements in that website or artifact, a consideration of how well those engagements were implemented, and an overall assessment of the effectiveness of the site or artifact.

This sort of reflective writing encourages students to study the individual design decisions in the embedded expertise within a single artifact. However, students also benefit from comparing several different multimodal artifacts or websites that are similar to a project they plan to complete. Particularly important in such an assignment is asking the students to start their genre analysis by articulating problems they were trying to solve in their own projects. These two forms of critique complement each other. Studying an individual multimodal artifact encourages students to look closely at its engagements, while comparing how a variety of artifacts try to solve a problem provides insight into more abstract negotiations. Good reflective writing should encourage students to move their critical lenses back and forth between engagement and negotiation.

Ultimately, the core competency we develop in learning to create assemblage projects may well be neither the specific content of technological engagements nor the negotiations between the embedded expertise of these engagements, but rather this cycling back and forth between engagements and negotiations, keeping our minds perpetually open to new possibilities, hanging on by our fingertips, clinging to acts of continual creativity.

WORKS CITED

Bruner, Jerome S. *The Process of Education.* Cambridge: Harvard UP, 1960. Print.

Carbone, Nick. "Re: FW: June/July issue of Innovate." Listserv posting to techrhet@interversity.org, 4 June 2005.

Carroll, John M. *The Nurnberg Funnel: Designing Minimalist Instruction for Practical Computer Skill.* Cambridge: MIT P, 1990. Print.

Holeton, Richard. "How Much Is Too Much New Media for the NetGen?" *RAW (Reading and Writing) New Media.* Ed. Cheryl E. Ball and James Kalmbach. Cresskill: Hampton, 2010. 209–30. Print.

Johnson-Eilola, Johndan, and Stuart A. Selber. "Plagiarism, Originality, Assemblage." *Computers and Composition* 24.4 (2007): 375–403. http://dx.doi.org/10.1016/j.compcom.2007.08.003.

Kalmbach, James. "The Agonies of Virtuality: What If Anything Should English Majors Know about Web Design These Days?" Computers and Writing Conference: Virtual Worlds, Purdue U, 22 May 2010. Talk.

———. "The Mechanization of the Web and the Tragedy That Is Template Rot." Computers and Writing Conference: Mechanization and Writing, Frostburg State U, 8 June 2013. Presentation.

Nissan, Colin. "The Ultimate Guide to Writing Better Than You Normally Do." *Timothy McSweeney's Internet Tendency.* 10 Apr. 2012. Web. 13 Sep. 2016.

Porter, James E. "Intertextuality and the Discourse Community." *Rhetoric Review* 5.1 (1986): 34–47. *EBSCOHost.* Web. 22 Oct. 2016.

Selzer, Jack. "Interextuality and the Writing Process: An Overview." *Writing in the Workplace: New Research Perspectives.* Ed. Rachel Spilka. Carbondale: Southern Illinois UP, 1993. 171–80. Print.

Turkle, Sherry. *Life on the Screen: Identity in the Age of the Internet.* New York. Simon, 1995. Print.

II   IN THE CLASSROOM/ON CAMPUS

5

Assemblage Composing, Reconsidered

Michael J. Michaud

WHILE I'VE PROBABLY PRACTICED THE ARTS OF ASSEMBLAGE (i.e., mix-tapes, scrapbooks, photo albums, and poster-collages) for many, many years, I first thought in a systematic way about assemblage as related to the teaching of writing while collecting data for my dissertation, which focused on the literacy practices of adult learners returning to college. I was sitting with one of my research participants, a paramedic-turned-EMS-administrator named Tony Vaccaro, and he was sharing samples of his workplace writing, when we came to a booklet-like document that Tony called the "competency manual," essentially a collection of competencies that all new hires at his ambulance company had to demonstrate during their first ninety days on the job. I asked Tony how he had composed the competency manual, and he explained the process in this way:

> I actually got the template for the manual from the hospital and then made a few modifications. They've got a whole website full of competencies. So, let's say you're looking for one on rhythm interpretation—you can go on and if there is a competency posted you can just right-click-steal it and then modify it to suit your purposes. I kept their grid, but I took their logo off and put ours on. I changed around the headers and I changed the actual wording for each of the competencies—which took the most amount of time. The hospital did not have any of the competencies that I needed, so in the end we had to create the actual wording for each of the competencies from scratch, or in some cases, we found the language we

needed for a competency on the Internet and right-click-stole it. (Michaud 252)

Right-click-steal. From where I sat as a teacher of college writing, it was a phrase that made me nervous. From where Tony sat as a long-time member of the EMS community and a busy administrator at his ambulance company, right-click-steal was an assemblage-like composing strategy that allowed him to "solve a writing or communication problem in a new context" (Johnson-Eilola and Selber 381). In a fast-paced professional environment in which *how* you produced documents seemed to matter less than *what* you could do with them, right-click-stealing was an expedient means of getting work done on the job. Furthermore, right-click-stealing seemed to embody the ethos of shared knowledge or distributed cognition that informed Tony's workplace. "I share stuff with the hospital all the time," he went on to explain, "I tell them, right-click-steal. It's really more like right-click-borrow. I share anything I have with anybody. I do not try to capitalize on anything" (Michaud 252).

As our discussion continued and as Tony shared several more documents he had assembled on the job—sometimes on his own, sometimes collaboratively—I came to see how pervasive this composing practice was in his day-to-day work. As interesting, perhaps, I came to understand how naturalized assemblage composing had become for him. And by assemblage, I mean, simply, a document that mixes "original and found content from numerous sources" (Johnson-Eilola and Selber 381). Looking back now on my conversations with Tony, I can see in those moments we spent discussing his assemblages a kind of contact zone opening up between us. He brought with him the culture of the workplace, where, as Anne Beaufort and many others have shown, "the purpose for writing is to take action," and where writing differs from that which is produced in the academy in terms of "content, form, tone" and standards of authorship (4–5). I brought with me the culture of the school, where the purpose for writing is instrumental in a different way, focused on facilitating student learning and the assessment of that learning. As a result of my education, training, and institutional positioning within higher education, I failed to appreciate or understand the "culture clash" that occurred when Tony presented me with his workplace assemblages. I couldn't help imposing my ways of knowing and seeing on artifacts that embodied a different set of discursive values. Rather than see right-click-stealing or assemblage as a viable composing strategy suited for myriad composing situations, I worried that what Tony was doing was, essentially, stealing, and I struggled even to acknowledge the competency manual as a legitimate form of writing.

I no longer see it that way. From the vantage point I now occupy, as a teacher of mostly traditional-age undergraduate students steeped in conventional academic genres of writing and in a composing culture usually insisting on "original work only," I have come full circle on assemblage: now I seek out opportunities to incorporate instruction in assemblage into my teaching. Through working with people like Tony Vaccaro and, more recently, with writing interns, I have seen how pervasive assemblages are outside of school. From promotional posters to blog posts, from news articles to newsletters, the interns that I supervise assemble myriad texts for the public and professional audiences their organizations serve. To take just one example, consider Figure 5.1, a screenshot of a blog post that a student intern with whom I worked recently created while working at the Rhode Island Historical Society (RIHS). In this post, the student works within a template provided by the website Tumblr to combine original text of her own creation, borrowed text (old-time seafaring recipes), and rich visual imagery from the RIHS archive of old postcards to assemble a blog post that brings to life the food and feel of an earlier era.

The more I have seen of assemblages like this one, the more convinced I have become of the importance of providing students with instruction in assemblage composing. In the remainder of this chapter, I situate my discussion about assemblage composing within two larger conversations about writing and pedagogy in the field of composition, then move on to explore how engaging students in composing in two genres, blogs and white papers, can help them both understand writing in new ways and practice the arts of assemblage that are ubiquitous in public and professional writing.

Figure 5.1. Assemblage from the Rhode Island Historical Society website.

SITUATING ASSEMBLAGE
WITHIN COMPOSITION STUDIES

An argument for teaching the arts of assemblage can be situated within two broad contemporary conversations in the field of composition, the first about the value of teaching nonacademic forms of writing and the second about the value of teaching students to compose multimodally in new media or in digital and/or multimedia environments. In recent years, as we have sought to define a vision of our field's pedagogical work, an increasing emphasis has been placed on teaching academic forms of writing. First-year composition, basic writing, Writing Across the Curriculum (WAC), and Writing in the Disciplines (WID)—all of these areas have received considerable scholarly and pedagogical attention, and all take as their mission, in large part, a focus on teaching students the means of effective participation in the discourse of the academy. At the same time, courses in professional writing, public or civic writing, and creative nonfiction further a long-standing tradition in the field of teaching students to write for nonacademic audiences and purposes.

Doug Hesse has outlined a number of persuasive arguments for furthering a curriculum that looks beyond higher education and its various forms of academic writing, pointing out that most undergraduates will not go on to produce writing aimed at academic audiences after they graduate and reminding us that academic discourse is dwarfed by "a much larger and more complex realm of public and political discourse" that circulates outside of the academy (10). While Hesse does not dispute the value of learning to analyze and produce academic writing, traditionally conceived, he argues that for their own success in that larger realm of worldly discourse and for the success and health of a democratic society, "college graduates must be able to write for public audiences, not only to transmit information but also to argue positions" (8). In sum, teaching the arts of assemblage, a kind of writing that is decidedly different from the conventional forms of traditional literacy that are most valued in the academy, aligns nicely with calls made by those like Hesse, who argue for attention to nonacademic forms of writing.

The argument for teaching the arts of assemblage can also be situated within the conversation in composition about the role of multimodal composing instruction in new media and in digital and multimedia writing. While assemblages come in all shapes and sizes and are by no means exclusively creations of the screen—as demonstrated by Stephen McElroy, Kathleen Blake Yancey, Jody Shipka, and even James Kalmbach in this volume—many composition instructors today are asking their students to produce new kinds of compositions, like assemblages, in digitally mediated environments. The ease with which one can locate images, text, and/or video and remix these into new compositions using templates and online composing tools is staggering. But what role should new media and multimodal composing play in a postsecondary composition curriculum, and what principles should guide our teaching practice?

The chorus of voices arguing for an increased role for these kinds of instruction has grown in recent years. Some, like the National Council of Teachers of English and the Writing in Digital Environments (WIDE) Research Center Collective, note the prominence of digital composing *outside* of school and the opportunity this presents for engaging literacy learners in relevant and meaningful writing instruction. Others, such as Elizabeth Daley, point to the ubiquity of the screen in our society and warn of our inevitable irrelevance should we choose to ignore the changes in communication practices taking place all around us. Scholars like Cynthia Selfe, Kathleen Blake Yancey, Ann Frances Wysocki, and many others argue for the excitement and possibility of teaching students to interact rhetorically in new composing environments. Meanwhile, Gunther Kress, building on previous scholarship in conjunction with the New London Group (Cazden et al.), has worked to theorize the multimodality of communication across print and digital media. And Collin Gifford Brooke, in his "New Media Pedagogy" chapter of *A Guide to Composition Pedagogies,* offers those who are interested in or already engaged in teaching in new-media environments a list of four "principles and attitudes," drawn from his own work in the classroom. Because of its usefulness to my discussion of assemblage composing, I'd like to linger over Brooke's list for just a moment before moving on to discuss the arts of assemblage.

Brooke's first principle is that "[n]ew media pedagogy is more than 'teaching the text'" (180): when writing teachers work to adopt new technologies in the classroom, we must think not just about the *products* our students will compose, but also about the *practices* in which we are asking them to engage. Brooke points to Prezi as an example, arguing that although it's traditionally used in place of PowerPoint to present information, its real function (and usefulness) stems from the way it allows users to arrange information spatially that would otherwise be delivered sequentially.

Second, Brooke argues that multimodal tools should function as a "writer's laboratory, a site of experimentation" (180). While it's good practice to try to link new composing tools with existing course outcomes, it's sometimes productive to experiment with new and unknown platforms, testing their affordances and limitations.

Third, Brooke urges instructors to consider the ways in which new media operate on a different timescale from traditional media: the platforms hosting our students' multimodal compositions (and assemblages) operate on "Internet time," which is, of course, different from the classroom time that most of us are accustomed to. He encourages teachers to consider our responsibility to help students reflect on the role of *kairos,* the moment, in online interactive environments (181).

Finally, Brooke cautions us to consider the ways in which our own expertise with new media and multimodal composing tools may influence our practices: when experimenting with the platforms that contemporary composers use to create assemblages, expertise can flow in many directions—teacher-to-student, student-to-student, and student-to-teacher. Brooke urges us to be open to this multidirectionality.

In sum, Brooke's guidelines for composing in new-media environments serve as a useful heuristic for those working to bring the arts of assemblage into the composition classroom. If we situate instruction in assemblage composing within the broader conversation about multimodal, new-media, digital, and multimedia composing in which Brooke and many others are engaging, we find much support for assemblage in the community of composition.

What practices are entailed in assemblage composing? Johndan Johnson-Eilola and Stuart Selber offer a tentative articulation when they suggest that creativity, within an assemblage paradigm, consists of "extensive research, filtering, recombining, [and] remixing" (400). They situate their argument for assemblage within a rhetorical framework, arguing that "creating assemblages requires the same rhetorical sophistication as any text" (391). And herein lies the problem for many students of composition: raised on the five-paragraph theme and the literary-analysis essay, many students lack the kind of rhetorical sophistication that good writers, of assemblages or anything else, possess.

Further, because assemblages in digital environments usually remix visual and textual elements, students must attend not just to the words they are producing, but also to the texts and images they are borrowing and the interaction between the textual and visual elements of their assemblages. As they learn and practice the arts of assemblage, students begin to develop a new sense of rhetorical *and* visual sophistication, but this process takes time.

HELPING STUDENTS LEARN TO
THINK LIKE ASSEMBLERS

Overall, usage of font size and image placement makes the design of the page *easy to follow and interesting.* Your eye is drawn immediately to that first headline, and then is drawn to the picture below. To see the entire picture you must scroll down, leading to the next headlines. *The purpose of the site is made clear* in the upper left-hand corner, and the tabs directing you to the different areas of the site are *easy to follow and straightforward.* Even opening up the page on different devices, such as an iPhone or mobile device, the page opens to a much similar, if not the same, format, and the main headline *is easily readable.* (Sarah, italics added)

How does one help students begin to compose rhetorically sophisti-cated assemblages? In my experience, the process can usefully begin with analysis of existing assemblages. The passage above is drawn from a short analytical essay written by a student, Sarah, who was enrolled in a Digital and Multimedia Writing course I taught re-cently. The assignment asked students to find an assemblage from their day-to-day lives and analyze it, drawing on the language of vi-sual rhetoric and design they were learning in class. It asks students, in short, to *disassemble* an existing assemblage in order to discover its compositional logic.

Sarah's words in the preceding passage reveal the challenges in-structors sometimes face in the early stages of working with stu-dents on assemblage composing. As the italicized passages illus-trate, Sarah's initial reading of her assemblage is mostly positive. While she is learning to think with concepts and terms she is learn-ing about in class, she is not yet able to deploy these in a critical way. Sarah is not alone. As in the case of analyzing more traditional print-based texts, when students are first asked to analyze digital assemblages the texts sometimes cast a kind of spell of inevitabil-ity over them. Students assume that what the creators of the as-semblages have put together "works"—is rhetorically effective and visually successful—merely by virtue of the fact that it has been published online. There is, perhaps, an analogy here with the way a typed and printed page has a "finished" quality to it that can make opaque the very much *un*finished nature of a text at an early stage of production. Documents that have been "published," including assemblages, must, some students seem to conclude, be rhetorically effective simply because they have been published. Consequently, they go on, sometimes exclusively, to praise the assemblages they have found, commenting on how the texts are "easy to follow," "clear," and "readable." Although some students exercise more criti-cal acumen when analyzing assemblages, it generally takes time to help students think critically about a "published" text, assemblage or otherwise, in order to articulate what works, what doesn't work, and why.

Finding resources to talk with students about such issues and to get them thinking, seeing, and speaking/writing in new ways is an important first step when teaching students the arts of assemblage. Although many academic and professional writing textbooks introduce students to visual and document design, assigning students simply to examine existing assemblages and read about multimodality, visual rhetoric, or document design will likely not be enough. It takes time to help students learn how to apply new concepts and to use them to think critically about assemblages—those they are encountering in the world and those they themselves are composing. With regard to Sarah's analysis, I pulled up the assemblage she was analyzing in class, the homepage of her college's athletic department website, and used it as an opportunity to talk with the entire class about visual rhetoric and design. Upon closer, collective analysis, our evaluation revealed that the page was, contrary to Sarah's initial appraisal, not as "easy to follow and straight-forward" as it may have seemed. In fact, our analysis found that, from a document-design perspective, the page was, as one student put it, "a hot mess"—cluttered with information that could have been sequenced in different ways and busy with clashing colors and incompatible fonts. In sum, instruction in assemblage can usefully begin by helping students to develop a critical vocabulary for talking about assemblages and deploying that vocabulary to investigate the compositional logic of assemblages that already exist.

GENRE AND ASSEMBLAGE

Johnson-Eilola and Selber identify several genres of writing that function as assemblages: while assemblage (the noun) is a term that one can use to describe a specific type or kind of text, it's also help-ful to identify the specific genres that one will help students learn to assemble (the verb). A great deal of research in composition about teaching genres has been published over the past twenty years, as writing teachers, theorizing genres of writing as constituted by fea-tures and as instantiations of social action (Miller; Russell; Devitt), have tried to teach students not just what a genre looks like but also how it functions rhetorically. As Irene Clark and Andrea Hernan-dez have pointed out, "Through explicit teaching of a particular genre, students may be able to create a text that imitates its form and style—sometimes quite successfully. But without genre aware-ness, they will not understand how the text 'works' to fulfill its purpose" (67).

In my own work with assemblage instruction, I try to employ a "both/and" approach, not only attempting to help students learn about the formal features of, say, a blog or white paper, but also working to help them understand the rhetorical functions that such genres accomplish in the world. For many students, just learning the form and style of a new genre can take a good deal of time and, of course, this process is sometimes hindered if a student fails to un-derstand the larger rhetorical concerns of genre production—(i.e., who composes a given genre, for whom, for what purposes). In short, pedagogies that, borrowing the language of Douglas Downs and Elizabeth Wardle, teach students both *how to* produce a genre and *about* that genre itself are probably best suited to achieving lasting results.

Two genres of writing that I have used to help students learn about and explore assemblage composing are blogs and white pa-pers. In what follows, I share and reflect on assignments I have devised to teach these genres, in order to convey a sense of what instruction in assemblage composing might look like from a genre perspective.

BLOGS

Weblogs, or blogs, may be among the most common types of as-semblage genre (Johnson-Eilola and Selber 388). Blogs combine "a wide range of materials: quotations from (words, texts, images both still and moving), links to, and summaries of other texts on the Web; updates on books, movies, and music the weblog author is currently reading, viewing, or listening to; commentaries on the weblog author's experiences; short or even long original essays; and more" (388). They provide a terrific means of helping students learn to produce rhetorically and visually interesting and effective assemblages.

In a Digital and Multimedia Writing course that I teach regu-larly, I ask students to experiment with blogging for six weeks as they investigate self-selected topics related to the course theme, sustainability. Students spend several weeks researching potential areas of inquiry—reading about rhetoric, visual design, and blogging; investigating blog platforms; and enlisting external readers for their blogs before they get down to the nitty-gritty of actually publishing their first blog posts. Once they've gathered some understanding of their topics, developed beginners' knowledge of the genre of the blog, and chosen platforms and templates for their blogs, students blog weekly, using multiple opportunities to experiment with blogging and the skills in assemblage composing that are required to produce engaging blog posts. Each week they receive feedback from their peers, their external readers, and me, a pattern that assembles their experiences:

- Step One: Students draft a new blog post for the first class meeting of each week and save this draft in their blogging platform;
- Step Two: On the first day of class each week, students print out and share their draft posts with peers in small groups, giving and receiving feedback on their works in progress;
- Step Three: Once the peer-review session has ended, students have the opportunity to work, in class, to edit/revise their posts and conference with me;
- Step Four: On the second day of class each week, the "graded" versions of students' newest blog posts are due. During the first thirty to forty-five minutes of class on the second day, students read and post comments on a set number (usually three) of their classmates' newest blog posts.

There are two principal affordances of this approach or one like it. First, while writers outside of academic settings frequently produce the same kinds of texts repeatedly over the course of many years, in the process developing a deep understanding of the textual and rhetorical characteristics of a given set of genres, in school we often assign students one type or kind of writing and then move on to something else. The assignment sequence I outline above attempts to approximate the way writing is learned and produced outside of school by nudging students back toward the same genre each week and encouraging them to work to incorporate and apply feedback they are receiving from different readers. Second, the sequence allows students the opportunity to experiment with a range of different assemblage skills—the use and placement of visual images; the intersection of textual and nontextual elements; the incorporation of video footage; the multimodal use of color, design, and layout; the "how to" of writing for nonacademic audiences; and the development of a nonacademic style or voice appropriate to a wider audience of readers/viewers.

There are also challenges to using weblogs to teach students about assemblage composing. As James Kalmbach suggests in this volume, templates provided by blogging platforms can present difficulties as students seek to do things with their posts that are not possible given the constraints of the template. Likewise, some students resist the admittedly more complex task of incorporating nontextual elements (and links) into their blogs, preferring to create posts that are primarily verbal and which sometimes reproduce or transfer the conventions of academic writing, traditionally conceived (see Figure 5.2). Finally, students' initial attempts to produce visually and rhetorically effective blog posts are, as one might expect, not always elegant. Photos get stretched, font colors don't always coordinate, images/videos are dropped into posts without contextualization, linking is either nonexistent or performed inexpertly, and titles and headers don't always accurately convey a sense of the content to follow—in other words, the students' initial forays into composing with multiple modes may be extensive or even robust without being successfully coherent. Over time, with feedback and the opportunity to continue to read/view their peers' work, students will iron out many of these problems. Some students even find ways to be inventive with their blogs that go beyond my expectations. Figure 5.3, for example, illustrates the way one student, annoyed that he couldn't find a background template within his chosen blog platform that could adequately convey a sense of his topic, manufactured his own background by researching images that made more sense and investigating the tools within the blog platform that allow customization.

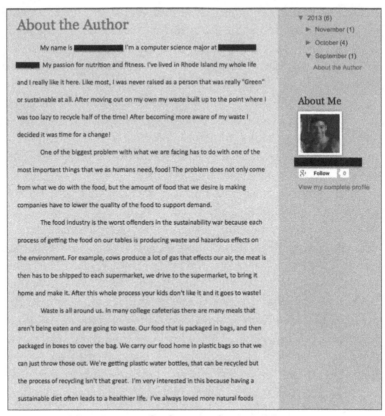

Figure 5.2. Negative transfer from academic writing.

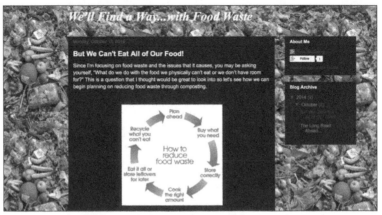

Figure 5.3. A customized blog background.

In sum, in this blogging assignment, as students experiment with various skills of assemblage, they go through the same iterative process that writers outside of school frequently go through when learning new genres, producing, at first, approximations of the genre based on their somewhat limited understanding of the forms and conventions, but, over time, more successful instantiations reflecting their growing awareness of the "deep structures" of the genre and its rhetorical function through the careful coordination of modes. Importantly, they get repeated opportunities to experiment with assemblage composing, remixing all sorts of borrowed content from the Web and original content that they themselves have created.

Blogging templates also play a role in this assignment as in others, as Kalmbach eloquently explains, and there is more to writing, of course, then merely filling in a template. "One must do much more as a designer [of assemblages]," write Johnson-Eilola and Selber, "than download templates and replace their placeholder items with real content" (391). This is undoubtedly true, and yet templates seem deceptively simple to use, sending an implicit message that writing with them is basically an exercise in filling in the blanks. Even selecting a template, as Anders Fagerjord argues, involves a complex decision-making process in which one considers interface, design, and genre precepts that will shape one's composing experience. When assembling compositions, students thus will need opportunities to experiment with different templates in order to discover the affordances and constraints each makes available. This process of experimentation, when combined with discussion and reflection, can further develop students' rhetorical skill.

WHITE PAPERS

A second genre especially conducive to assemblage is the white paper: as with the blog, instruction in this genre usually begins with an overview of the genre itself. Model white papers on just about every topic imaginable are easily available online for students to examine and use to familiarize themselves with this genre.

One of the great affordances of white papers, as instructional genres, is the way in which they encourage students to think more expansively about how one shares and presents research. As students browse model white papers, noting the incorporation of visual media and the use of engaging colors, fonts, and layouts, I draw their attention to the ways in which well-designed white papers can make a type of writing that students often perceive to be dry and boring (researched writing) lively and engaging. I point out that white papers offer one model of the way writers outside of academic settings incorporate research into their work, thus helping students see how practices they are learning in school can have implications for life beyond the classroom.

I have asked students to assemble white papers in several different courses. Each time, students are provided with new opportunities to think about the skills of assemblage: remixing, filtering, researching, and designing. One assignment uses the white paper to build on students' prior work with blogging: students take what they learned about their sustainability topic over the course of their six weeks of blogging and repurpose this information into a white paper that describes a sustainability problem, explains its causes, and argues for a range of possible solutions. In this assignment, one resembling McElroy's observation in this volume about assemblage effecting new contexts and compositions, students are not "starting from scratch" as far as researching their topics goes, but are encouraged, instead, to filter their own writing to discover content that is suitable and usable for this new genre and new task. As they compose their white papers, students are able to draw on or borrow images, text, and ideas from their earlier blogging production, and these images, texts, and ideas are, themselves, often borrowed from the various sources that they investigated while blogging. I often use the word *repurposing* to help students think about this assignment—they are repurposing content from their blogs and remixing this into something new and coherent that works to address a new and different rhetorical problem.

A second assignment I have used in a first-year seminar on the theme of food asks students to collaboratively compose a white paper sharing findings from peer-reviewed research on food consumption. Here students draw on the Cornell University Food

and Brand Lab website to learn about different areas of food research. With their groups, they work to identify a unique food-
related problem, summarize the research on this problem, and suggest solutions. In this way, students are challenged to learn about a
particular domain of knowledge by reading peer-reviewed research
that has already been organized and cataloged for them, experiment with a new genre of writing allowing them to engage in assemblage composing practices, and practice the rhetoric involved in
transforming academic research aimed at specialized audiences into
prose that is accessible to more general audiences.

In sum, white papers as a genre are especially valuable for introducing students to the arts of assemblage. Students can work
alone or in groups to assemble white papers on topics that they
have already begun to research or on entirely new topics. The genre
helps students think about how to share and present research in
ways that are different from and perhaps more engaging than some
might have found traditional academic papers or essays to be, and
it allows them the opportunity to further develop skills that assist
in assembling rhetorically sophisticated and engaging documents.

THE PLEASURES OF ASSEMBLAGE

I began this chapter on assemblage composing by recalling my experiences working with and learning from Tony Vaccaro. In my interviews with Tony, he narrated his struggles with writing in school,
including failing English classes multiple times in high school. He
carried this sense of struggle with him into his professional life and
work, avoiding positions that required substantial writing, traditionally conceived. For Tony, assemblage provided a successful
composing strategy as he began to move out of EMS work and
into EMS education, a move that meant new and different kinds
of writing.

At the time of our interviews, Tony had taken on the role of education and training coordinator at his ambulance company, a position causing him to spend more time, as he put it, "driving the desk."
While he struggled to get through the occasional memo or docu-
mentation, he reveled in the opportunity to assemble documents

that allowed him to do the important new work of training and supporting his ambulance company's EMS technicians and para- medics. Toward these ends, he had assembled a multichapter orien- tation manual and PowerPoint presentation to facilitate the three- day orientation sessions he frequently ran.

As I listened to him talk about the way he had built a feedback process into the orientations to assess the effectiveness of his docu- ments, I sensed both the pride and the pleasure he took in com- posing and recomposing these texts. Here was a writer enmeshed in a real-world rhetorical situation, producing documents—as- semblages—that helped solve problems and get work done in the world. Here was a man who had struggled with writing his entire life, finding pleasure in the iterative and recursive process of draft- ing, publishing, soliciting feedback, and revising. Little in Tony's earlier academic experience with writing had shown him that this was what writing is actually about. Assemblage composing was a kind of back door through which Tony was now, finally, beginning to learn about the process(es) of writing—and to find pleasure in them. With this in mind, I'd like to close this chapter with a final rationale for teaching the arts of assemblage: it offers a new op- portunity to make *pleasure* a part of teaching and learning to write. There is pleasure in repurposing, in remixing, in borrowing and mashing up and assembling new texts to solve new problems. And pleasure, as we know but sometimes forget, is a very important part of the process of learning to write, no matter the kind of writing you are trying to teach or learn.

WORKS CITED

Beaufort, Anne. *Writing in the Real World: Making the Transition from School to Work*. New York: Teachers College P, 1999. Print.

Brooke, Collin Gifford. "New Media." *A Guide to Composition Pedagogies*. 2d ed. Ed. Gary Tate, Amy Rupiper Taggart, Kurt Schick, and H. Brooke Hessler. New York: Oxford UP, 2014. 177–93. Print.

Cazden, Courtney, et al. "A Pedagogy of Multiliteracies: Design- ing Social Futures." *Harvard Educational Review* 66.1 (1996): 60–92. *ProQuest*. Web. 23 Oct. 2016.

Clark, Irene L., and Andrea Hernandez. "Genre Awareness, Academic Argument, and Transferability." *WAC Journal* 22 (2011): 65–78. Web. 23 Oct. 2016.

Daley, Elizabeth. "Expanding the Concept of Literacy." *Educause Review* 38.2 (2003): 33–40. Web. 15 June 2014.

Devitt, Amy. "Transferability and Genres." *The Locations of Composition.* Ed. Christopher J. Keller and Christian R. Weisser. Albany: State U of New York P, 2007. 215–28. Print.

Downs, Douglas, and Elizabeth Wardle. "Teaching about Writing, Righting Misconceptions: (Re)Envisioning 'First-Year Composition' as 'Introduction to Writing Studies.'" *College Composition and Communication* 58.4 (2007): 552–84. *ProQuest.* Web. 23 Oct. 2016.

Fagerjord, Anders. "Prescripts: Authoring with Templates." *Kairos* 10.1 (2005). Web. 23 Oct. 2016.

Hesse, Doug. *Writing beyond Writing Classes: Resources for University of Denver Faculty.* 2d ed. U of Denver Writing Program, 2010. Web. 13 Sep. 2016.

Johnson-Eilola, Johndan, and Stuart A. Selber. "Plagiarism, Originality, Assemblage." *Computers and Composition* 24.4 (2007): 375–403. http://dx.doi.org/10.1016/j.compcom.2007.08.003.

Kress, Gunther. *Multimodality: A Social Semiotic Approach to Contemporary Communication.* New York: Routledge, 2010. Print.

Michaud, Michael J. "The 'Reverse Commute': Adult Students and the Transition from Professional to Academic Literacy." *Teaching English in the Two-Year College* 38.3 (2011): 244–57. *ProQuest.* Web. 23 Oct. 2016.

Miller, Carolyn R. "Genre as Social Action." *Quarterly Journal of Speech* 70.2 (1984): 151–67. *Taylor and Francis Online.* Web. 9 Sep. 2016. http://dx.doi.org/10.1080/00335638409383686.

National Council of Teachers of English. "Voices on Reading and Writing in the Digital Age." *Reading and Writing Differently.* Nov. 2008: 15–16. Web. 13 Sep. 2016.

Russell, David R. "Rethinking Genre in School and Society: An Activity Theory Analysis." *Written Communication* 14.4 (1997): 504–54. doi: 10.1177/0741088397014004004.

Selfe, Cynthia L. "Technology and Literacy: A Story about the Perils of Not Paying Attention." *College Composition and Communication* 50.3 (1999): 411–36. *ProQuest.* Web. 23 Oct. 2016.

Writing in Digital Environments (WIDE) Research Center Collective. "Why Teach Digital Writing?" *Kairos* 10.1 (2005). Web. 9 Sep. 2016.

Wysocki, Anne Frances. "The Multiple Media of Texts: How Onscreen and Paper Texts Incorporate Words, Images, and Other Media." *What Writing Does and How It Does It: An Introduction to Analyzing Texts and Textual Practices.* Ed. Charles Bazerman and Paul Prior. Mahwah: Erlbaum, 2004. 123–64. Print.

Yancey, Kathleen Blake. "Made Not Only in Words: Composition in a New Key." *College Composition and Communication* 56.2 (2004): 297–328. *ProQuest.* Web. 23 Oct. 2016.

6

Copy, Combine, Transform: Assemblage in First-Year Composition

Stephen J. McElroy and Travis Maynard

AS OTHER CHAPTERS OF THIS COLLECTION DEMONSTRATE, assemblage as a compositional concept and practice is of growing import in the field. And, like the authors of those other chapters, we can point to Johndan Johnson-Eilola and Stuart Selber's 2007 article "Plagiarism, Originality, Assemblage" for insights about effective composing practices and ways of teaching composition. In this regard, Johnson-Eilola and Selber pose a set of provocative questions. What might happen, they ask, "if we tell students that their goal is not to create new, unique texts but to filter and remix other texts in ways that solve concrete problems or enact real social action? What if we expect and encourage them to copy other texts?" (380). Guided by these questions, we designed and delivered two nearly identical sections of a course in first-year composition (FYC) whose central organizing principle was considering all "texts as assemblages" (Johnson-Eilola and Selber 376).

In this chapter, we provide an account of this course. We have four goals here: (1) to describe the conception and development of this first-semester course; (2) to present an overview of the major assignments, activities, readings, and discussion topics; (3) to offer our own observations—and those of our students—about how the design of the course helped students learn about becoming better writers; and (4) in light of those observations, to articulate some of the ways in which an assemblage approach to FYC may be advantageous for the field. We are motivated to share these experiences and reflections by a sense that assemblage provides first-year college writers with a unique entry into and framework for understanding the rhetorical role that writing and composing play in the world around them; we hope that our explanation and analysis will provide a springboard for those who might want to take a similar curricular approach.

WHY ASSEMBLAGE?

This course in FYC was conceived among a constellation of several factors and events, chief among which is the growing literature on assemblage, which we see connecting with our field's ongoing attention to multimodal composing. In addition to Johnson-Eilola and Selber, other scholars in composition studies have pointed to assemblage as a way to rethink composing. Byron Hawk, for instance, suggests that a "Deleuzian ontology of assemblage could ground the notion that writing is situated" (75). Like Johnson-Eilola and Selber, Hawk is interested in how composers act in and on the world. For Hawk, "writing with/in assemblages would entail processes of engaging with situations . . . that contribute to the production and evolution of those situations" (81). In each case, the goal—as it is for Michael Michaud in his work with upper-level students described in this volume—is for composers to see earlier texts as resources for composition and their own compositions as having consequences. This sense of engaging and contributing was one aspect of assemblage we saw as potentially—and especially—valuable for first-year writers.

Similarly, scholarship on assemblage outside of composition studies suggests its potential for understanding and engaging in social action, a point that Jacqueline Preston also makes. Working in geography, for example, Ben Anderson, Matthew Kearnes, Colin McFarlane, and Dan Swanton describe the "remarkable proliferation" of the term 'assemblage' across their discipline as they assess "what *assemblage thinking* offers social-spatial theory" (171–72, emphasis ours). Part of their answer is remarkably similar to what compositionists say assemblage offers our field: "assemblage enables an *ethos of engagement* with the world" (176, emphasis ours). Like Hawk, Anderson et al. call on Gilles Deleuze, stating that "for Deleuze . . . assemblage describes the 'co-functioning' of heterogeneous parts into some form of provisional, open, whole" (177). Thinking of texts as assemblages, then, is to consider texts as made of parts of other texts while also considering the ways in which those texts act in and on the world.

It was against this backdrop of scholarship that our own interest in assemblage began to grow. McElroy's research was located in assemblage theory and its applications, especially as the concept related to multimodal composing in print. Maynard became interested in assemblage by revisiting poststructuralist theories of "text" as it intersects with assemblage theory. As we shared our ideas with each other, we began to see assemblage as something more central to the work of composing than previously understood, as a concept and practice that, in combination with multimodality, should be made more explicit for our students. Thus, in putting assemblage at the center of the course and in helping students to 'see, think, and do' assemblage, we hoped that students would become more experienced with the work of composing writ large, a goal shared with Michael Michaud and Jody Shipka.

WHAT ASSEMBLAGE OFFERS AS AN APPROACH TO FYC

We began our planning for the course with the hypothesis implied, if not forwarded, by Johnson-Eilola and Selber, that all texts are assemblages. We took this broad premise on its face and considered what it meant for composing as a practice and as a subject of study. If texts are assemblages, we concluded, then composing becomes less about creation and more about making new meaning through the selection and arrangement of components and elements of preexisting texts. If, as we supposed, composing in any case—and in any medium or genre—is a matter of the arrangement of semiotic material, then it made sense for us to imagine what it might be like to *start* a course with that supposition and build out from there. Put another way, starting with assemblage allowed us to synthesize, in a relatively seamless way, discussions of key composing topics, including invention, genre, media, multimodality, rhetorical situations, reflective composing practices, and strategies for revision—

concepts that we see as indispensable to composition pedagogy. In addition, in developing this curriculum, we also learned that using assemblage as a starting point is valuable because it incorporates the act of reading/experiencing as a necessary component of the work of writing/composing.

AN ASSEMBLED CURRICULUM

The syllabus we designed for this FYC course—ENC1101, the outcomes of which include introducing students to college-level composing—prompts students to compose in a number of different ways for a number of different purposes. Students wrote alphabetic essays, but they also created videos, posters, podcasts, webpages, and so on, and they were prompted to understand essays, videos, and posters all as falling under the same umbrella of the work of composing.

Moreover, working under the assumption that all texts are interconnected, an assemblage approach to composition establishes a common ground for students no matter their personal interests: given the necessity of reading/experiencing in composing, the musicians in the class, the film buffs, the creative writers, the graphic designers, and the rest all thus already had something to contribute when they came to the class on the first day. Drawing on their experiences, they could offer their own examples of assemblage and remix right away—e.g., a parody film mimicking an iconic scene, or the use and reuse of a specific sample in songs. And, as the semester went on, students were prompted to see the connections between their own composing interests and those of their classmates, both inside and outside the classroom. Retrospectively, we see the common ground established by assemblage as one potential model for the "new curriculum for the 21st century" (295) called for by Kathleen Blake Yancey.

In "Made Not Only in Words: Composition in a New Key," Yancey envisions the possibilities of this new curriculum, outlining some examples of "what students aren't asked to do in the current model" but would be in the new model (311). Yancey's examples include considering the "issue of intertextual circulation," considering "what the best medium and the best delivery" might be for a given instance of communication and for a given audience, thinking "explicitly about what they might 'transfer' from one medium to the next," and considering "how to transfer what they have learned in one site and how that could or could not transfer to another" (311). As we will show, our course assignments, readings, and activities asked students to do each of these—not just once or twice, but repeatedly and routinely, prompting students to develop a habit of thinking and doing that attends to the assembling of modes, media, genres, and rhetorical situations in ways that reflect what we see as the vital work of composing.

THE COURSE: UNITS, READINGS, ACTIVITIES, AND ASSIGNMENTS

In the following sections, we present our rationale for the three units of the course, including the accompanying major assignments, readings from the field of rhetoric and composition, and activities we employed to support our learning outcomes. Broadly speaking, we structured the course across four major concepts, each one concerning a different principle in the field: assemblage, our foundational principle; multimodality; genre; and rhetoric. The four concepts were divided across three major units and accompanying assignments: units on assemblage, accompanied by an analytical essay; on multimodality and genre, including a remediated text; and on rhetoric, concluding with a rhetorical assemblage. To alleviate students' initial shock at terms that were new and perhaps opaque, we framed each of the four concepts in the form of a question (with an answer) that points to our goals for the course:

- What are the processes by which we compose? (Through assemblage.)
- What material and semiotic resources do we employ in textual production? (Material: modes; semiotic: preexisting texts.)
- How are the texts we produce categorized and recognized by composers and audiences? (With genre.)
- How do the texts we produce function in the world outside the classroom? (With effect, i.e., by employing rhetoric.)

In showing our students that composition is a product of assemblage, we first had to show how assemblage works—through copying and transforming existing materials into new combinations. It is this idea of *how* that serves as our foundation; as composition teachers, we are at the very least tasked with providing a skill set—our students expect us to teach them how to write—and that is our ultimate goal. But since the process of assemblage is so different from what many students have been taught in high school about composing, we also showed them a way of seeing what composition *is,* of defining it more capaciously than as an inspired author creating an original text in isolation—as is often the case in high school (Yancey, Robertson, and Taczak). Instead, we wanted students to see that—whether through quotation, sampling, working within a template, relying on genre conventions, or conforming to or deviating from the discursive practices of a culture—composers rely on other texts to facilitate both composition and the co-creation of meaning with an audience.

Our first series of readings is intended to introduce students to assemblage via what we see as the three principal activities of composition—copying, (re)combining, and transforming—a framework we ourselves reappropriated from Kirby Ferguson's 2010 video series *Everything Is a Remix*. In the first week of class, we screened two episodes of the series—"The Elements of Creativity" and "The Song Remains the Same"—to show students how two well-known innovators—Steve Jobs and the musical group Led Zeppelin—either copied ideas from other companies or lifted whole texts from other artists.[1] In addition, we screened a short interview clip with Alfred Hitchcock, in which he describes the process of filmmaking as one of "assembly" to show how film is also a product of assemblage.[2] Moving from popular texts to academic discourse, we assigned Joseph Harris's introduction to *Rewriting: How to Do Things with Texts*, which illustrates scholars' reliance on the preexisting literature to build arguments. By demonstrating the ways in which both public and academic cultures are intertextual, these viewings and readings built toward students reading Johnson-Eilola and Selber's "Plagiarism, Originality, Assemblage," which articulates the central focus of the course. To assist students in their first academic writing assignment for this unit, described below, we also included selections from our program textbook that support academic style, planning, and drafting.

To hone this way of seeing intertextuality, the first assignment of the course asked students to conduct an intertextual analysis in a 1,600-to-2,000-word essay. Dubbed a "genealogy," this assignment prompted students to engage in one of two possible analyses. First they could delineate a "semantic unit"—e.g., a quotation, a character, a chord progression—and show how it has been transformed across three different textual manifestations. For instance, students could write about the ways that forbidden lovers are depicted in Shakespeare's *Romeo and Juliet*, Leonard Bernstein and Stephen Sondheim's *West Side Story*, and Baz Luhrmann's film adaption *Romeo + Juliet*. Second, and alternatively, students could construct the "ancestry" of a primary text, seeking out its references and influences and then tracing the influences of those secondary sources to find tertiary influences—for example, tracing allusions in T. S. Eliot's *The Waste Land* to Arthurian legend, religious scriptures, and other literary texts. Conceptually, we framed this analysis to prompt students to see the use and reuse of semantic units—phrases, gestures, symbols, melodies, and so on—so that they begin to see textual production as an ongoing cultural endeavor and consider themselves as potential active participants in that endeavor, able to draw on preexisting texts, quote source materials, and make textual allusions. Recognizing that the composition of texts necessarily relies on those that came before, students begin to understand that to create new compositions, they must arrange elements of preexisting texts. On perhaps a more practical level, the students are also conducting a textual analysis, working on developing an academic prose style, and becoming accustomed to the peer-review format of FYC. In the assessment of this assignment, we look for attention to detail in students' prose that shows a critical reading of the intertext of their semantic unit as a tentative understanding of how popular and literary texts are products of assemblage.

UNIT TWO: MODES, CONVENTIONS, GENRES, AND MEDIA

Our question opening the second unit of the course addresses multimodality: "What material and semiotic resources do we employ in textual production?" With an understanding of preexisting texts as semiotic resources, our second unit anatomizes texts into the "raw materials" of composition in the form of the Kressian modes (visuals, sound, layout, temporal arrangement, font, motion, and so on) that composers use to make meaning. As composers enmeshed in a multimedia ecology, students may face any number of exigences that would be best addressed by a textual form other than print; further, as they attempt to reach audiences whose reading habits are not tethered to print media, it is important they become aware of the wide array of material resources available to them. By making explicit the variety of available modes, we hope to prepare students to navigate rhetorical situations that work within and across the constraints of different media and the affordances of different modes. By illustrating that forms of media are assemblages of different modes working in concert with one another, much as James Kalmbach suggests in this volume, this unit helps students realize that all of composition—print and digital—is multimodal, a realization that prepares them for the explicitly multimodal assignments to come in the course. In learning about these concepts, students gain (1) a broad-based understanding of the material resources of composition and a more acute ability to analyze media in terms of their constituent modes, understanding how they are combined to make a particular meaning, and (2) a sense of how texts circulating across media through the process of remediation necessarily are changed by the affordances and constraints of each medium.

Together, our discussions about assemblage and multimodality provide students with an understanding of both the processes and the materials used to create texts and a way of analyzing them for their component parts. We then turn toward applying these concepts to existing texts to see how they function. Our readings on genre pose the question, also during the second unit, "How are the texts we produce categorized and recognized by composers and audiences?" As a segue into this topic, we end our discussions of multimodality by emphasizing the recursive relationship between cultures, media, and modes, showing the ways that different modes are given preference in different cultures: academics in the humanities preferring discursive—written and verbal—modes, mass culture being more based in the visual, and so on. With the thread of culture tying our discussions of assemblage and multimodality together, we introduce the social nature of genre conventions as a heuristic for students to understand the types of texts they encounter and for their use as starting "templates" in their own compositions. Explaining genre conventions as a set of flexible "expectations" rooted in cultural traditions, we hope that students grow comfortable working within and departing from them for their own rhetorical purposes. Three additional conceptual outcomes include understanding how intertextuality allows genres to span different media, how discursive genres function to shape reading and composing, and how modes are manipulated within media to create and reify conventions of genres for audiences. The readings, activities, and discussions in this unit lead into the second major assignment, which prompts students to remediate their essay from the first unit into a new textual form and demonstrating their understanding of mode and genre.

The first reading of the unit is the first chapter of Jay David Bolter and Richard Grusin's *Remediation,* which provides an introduction to the concepts of immediacy, hypermediacy, and remediation. Using as an example one of the most commonly recognizable forms of remediation—film adaptations of popular novels and comic books——Bolter and Grusin enable students to see that characters and plotlines are copied from the discursive medium and transformed to suit the film. With this baseline knowledge of media, we analyze media for their component modes, introducing multimodality through the work of Gunther Kress, specifically a clip from an interview titled "What Is Multimodality?" and Anne Wysocki's response to Kress in her article "awaywithwords." Wysocki's piece, both short and accessible, helps students to contextualize the work of Kress, whose concepts can be difficult for first-year students. Wysocki also gives us an avenue to discuss the temporal and spatial dynamics of multimodality, a tension addressed in "awaywithwords." Finally, Wysocki's examples in the text—water as a weapon and crayons as unacceptable for academic writing—illustrate the socially constructed preferences for certain modes. In order to introduce genre, we return to the second episode of *Everything Is a Remix,* which gives a brief overview of the concept, and have students read Daniel Chandler's "Introduction to Genre Theory" as an overview of the vocabulary and perspectives of genre. Finally, we select short essays from the textbook as a way to introduce conventions of discursive genres.

In the classroom, students engage in two different mapping activities. First, they map out genres with the conventions that might be common across genres; second, they create a concept map of the course using the vocabulary of the course—remix, assemblage, media, modes, and genre. Although difficult, this second task helps students synthesize ideas based on the interrelationships among these features of composition.

The readings on multimodality and genre during the second unit of the course prepare students to remediate their genealogy essay from an alphabetic text into some other form. Pragmatically, the assignment allows students to put the axiom of "copy, combine, transform" into action by carrying over the message of their essay into a new medium. In doing so, they also gain experience in new composing spaces. For example, one student transformed his genealogy essay, which analyzed Spotify's interface as an assemblage of features from preexisting music library applications like iTunes and social media platforms like Twitter, into the more visual platform of Prezi, allowing viewers to see screen shots from the various applications assembled to create the Spotify interface. Accompanying the remediated text is a 700-to-1,000-word reflective essay in which students articulate their rhetorical choices, consider what is gained and lost in their remediation, and navigate the relationships among media, genres, conventions, and modes toward the goal of making meaning. In the remediation, we look for student projects that effectively copy relevant material from the essay to the new medium and work well within the chosen genre, showing some adherence to conventions—or conscious deviations, as the case may be. The reflection allows students the space to articulate choices such as these deviations from conventions, and ideally show a metacognitive awareness of the selection of relevant material and of the ways the medium, modes, and genre work together to communicate the genealogy of their topic.

UNIT THREE: RHETORICAL ASSEMBLAGES

In the culminating activity of our course, students consider the rhetoric of composing by investigating a question familiar to both Michaud and Kalmbach: "How do the texts we produce function in the world outside the classroom?" This unit's placement within the chronology of the course was of concern because in our program rhetoric is usually the guiding frame for FYC. In this assemblage-oriented course, rhetoric is as important as all the other concepts, but were it placed first, persuasion would serve as the central concept of the course. Instead, students encounter assemblage as the guiding principle, and they work with this more capacious conception of all writing rather than one prioritizing persuasion. Thus, with a broad understanding of assemblage, modes, and genre as the "composition of composition," students turn their focus to persuasive composition outside of the classroom as one mechanism for thinking about the transfer of writing knowledge and practice. Using the material they learn early in the course as a lens, students analyze rhetors' uses of modes, media, and genre—the available means of persuasion—to respond to exigences targeted at particular audiences. Students consider the salient rhetorical, modal, and generic aspects of a variety of situations, including for example a State of the Union address, a magazine advertisement, a scholarly article, and a text message inviting a friend out for dinner. After conducting these analyses in class, students craft and work within their own rhetorical situations to understand how material and semiotic resources assist in persuasion in an assignment dubbed a "rhetorical assemblage."

Providing a thorough definition of the nature of composition, students consider composition outside the classroom through the rhetorical situation and a preliminary vocabulary in classical rhetoric. Opening with Lloyd Bitzer's 1968 essay "The Rhetorical Situation" to introduce the concepts of exigence and audience, we include Aristotle's rhetorical proofs and the Ciceronian model of arrangement. With this rudimentary understanding of rhetoric as context, students review multiple example-texts in class, identifying exigences and audiences. Because the concept of constraints can be challenging for composition students, we visualize on the whiteboard how an exigence and audience "constrain" the type of arguments available to a composer, narrowing down the available means of persuasion. And given that different audiences respond positively to different types of texts, we attempt to show that the fittingness, in the Bitzerian sense, of media, modes, and genres is also constrained by the exigence and audience of a given situation.

To engage all the concepts covered in the course, our final assignment is a "rhetorical assemblage" requiring students to select an exigence and audience and compose an argument addressing that exigence. In doing so, they must assemble elements from at least five different texts to support their rhetorical argument. As with most multimodal projects, student work can take any form as long as there is a justifiable fit between exigence, audience, and artifact. Accompanying this assemblage is a 2,000-to-2,500-word reflection essay that attends to rhetorical situation, the use of media, mode, and genre, and the ways students copy and transform their source texts. This assignment asks students to apply what they have learned throughout the semester—about textual creation in relationship to assemblage, multimodality, genres, media, and conventions—in response to a specific and explicit rhetorical situation. One student, for example, developed a seminar targeted to her first-year classmates concerning the prevalence of sexual assault in American universities and administrations' inaction concerning the matter. More generally, the reflective essay demands a similar response to that of the remediation reflection, but adds the layer of Bitzerian exigence and audience for students to consider, allowing them to see media and modes as constraints of the rhetorical situation. A successful rhetorical assemblage will copy, combine, and transform texts appropriate for the rhetorical situation and present them in a genre that is accessible to the target audience. A successful reflection will show both awareness of exigence and an appropriate selection of audience(s) and an awareness of the fittingness of the assembled texts, medium, and genre for the selected audience. It will also speak to the process of assemblage: which texts were copied, how they were transformed, and how those texts serve their rhetorical purpose.

In the last few class meetings, we encourage students to reflect on the course as a whole, asking them to identify five key terms for the course and map them any way they see fit. In tandem with this activity, we ask students to write a 700-to-1,000-word final reflection in which they talk about whether and/or how their view of composition has changed and whether/how they will transfer course concepts to future writing situations, both academic and beyond. It is through this final reflection that we gain a sense of students' overall progression as composers and the ways they saw the course as beneficial to their academic careers.

OBSERVATIONS: THE STUDENTS' VIEWS

One of our biggest reservations as we put the course together was the possibility that the concept of assemblage would be too broad and too complex for first-year writers to adopt for their writing practices. However, students were overwhelmingly positive about the course content in both their anonymous course evaluations and their final written reflections. One student, Will, placed emphasis on assemblage in his final reflection while referring to one of the "Everything Is a Remix" videos that we watched on the first day of class:

> The whole idea of assemblage is that the composer is putting the necessary components of something together to make something whole. True originality is hard to find no matter what kind of text it may be in. Henry Ford didn't make the first assembly line or the first car even, but he combined the

two to mass-produce the car industry and made millions of dollars in doing so. Assemblage is one of the major components of writing and is the word I will remember as most influential after having taken this course.

Another student, Nick, wrote that he initially had the kind of trouble with "assemblage" that we had feared, but that he eventually saw its value as a generalizable framework for understanding creativity:

When we first started talking about assemblage I was very confused. The first reading we were given was not easily understood. . . . Once I understood what assemblage was I was able to see creativity and writing very differently. I was aware that people had inspirations for the different texts they had created but I was unaware that everything is a combination of separate ideas.

And another student, Katie, made an explicit connection between assemblage and writing:

An important theory that I learned in this class is that all pieces of writing are assemblages of previous compositions. Even though when you write something as your own, you are transforming and remixing other people's work and making it your own.

These perspectives represent a general consensus among the students in both sections—that despite a steep early learning curve, assemblage eventually made sense to them and helped them understand composing in new ways.

Despite our reservations about students' ability to grasp—as well as our ability to teach—the concept of assemblage, we hoped that, once the initial hurdle was passed, students would be able to use assemblage as a bridge toward invention. We imagined that the concept would help to demystify aspects of the creative process, that examining instances of assemblage in popular culture would teach students about the value of contextualized heuristic practices, and that our discussions about assemblage would help establish for them an ethos of rhetorical engagement. As the classes played out and as we received feedback from the students in their final reflections, it became evident that students saw assemblage as a helpful concept for composing and writing. For example, Payton, writing about her experience researching for and writing her genealogy project, said in her reflection:

> The collecting of these works . . . showed me the ways that over the years people have used the idea of copy, combine, and transform and how in the future people will continue to use this idea. It has also helped me by showing me a way to create ideas and projects for papers that I will have to complete in the future when it comes to school as well as throughout my lifetime.

Another student, Andrew, described how assemblage thinking gave him the license and freedom to support claims and arguments that he made in his writing with the words of experts who came before him:

> This gives me a new confidence when I take a stance on a subject because I realize that I am not the first person to have a certain opinion about a particular subject. Any argument route I decide to take with a particular topic can be reinforced by publications of someone who feels the same way prior to you.

These comments point to the ways in which assemblage is a useful concept for thinking about heuristics of invention: that to begin to write requires thoughtful consideration and engagement with preexisting texts, and that composing is a way of contributing to an ongoing conversation.

We also learned through reading these reflections that intentional and deliberate discussions of the use and reuse of existing textual material provided students with a helpful framework for understanding the meaning and nature of plagiarism. Being explicit about assemblage helps to remove the taboo associated with the reuse of others' work and sheds light on the gray area between proper and improper reuse. Brandy, for example, was explicit about the "fear" that she formerly felt about plagiarism and how the readings about assemblage helped her overcome that fear:

> [Johnson-Eilola and Selber's] article allowed me to see all writing differently because many great pieces of writing are just different versions of others. In the future, I will keep an open mind while looking at other works, while still abiding by the [FSU] plagiarism guidelines.
>
> Johnson-Eilola and Selber's article, along with our first assignment, has allowed me to be less fearful when using others' works as a reference.

Another student, Bailey, connected her newfound understanding to her future academic work, noting the importance of citation as a component of scholarly assemblage:

> The last project was on creating our own assemblage. We had to use preexisting texts and use them to help build our own argument. I believe that we had to do this because to show we really understand the concept of assemblage we had to be able to copy, transform, and combine our own work with others' work. I think that creating my own assemblage will help me throughout college because when writing papers I will be sure to do research to back up my argument and always give credit to these sources.

These students' reflections point to the ways in which discussions of assemblage help bring the salience of plagiarism—so often a nebulous term that gets recited uncritically in honor codes—to life, defining its parameters so that students know not only how to avoid it, but also why it matters.

CONCLUSION

Building on the growing body of literature on assemblage in composition studies, our FYC course makes assemblage the central theme that ties together other important concepts like multimodality, genre conventions, remediation, and rhetorical situation. To recap, the course features three units and major assignments: the first assignment, which prompts students to see assemblage in practice in the world around them, is an essay on the genealogy of three specific interrelated texts; the second assignment tasks students with remediating their first essay and explaining in an accompanying reflective essay the modes, genre, and conventions of their new creation; the third assignment prompts students to create a rhetorical assemblage, explicitly combining existing texts in such a way as to respond to a given rhetorical situation. The course, we believe, satisfies the WPA Outcomes 3.0 and enacts one potential manifestation of Yancey's vision for a "new curriculum for the 21st century" (295). Moreover, as we reflect on the experience of teaching the course and review our students' own reflections, we recognize three areas where the course seemed to be particularly effective: providing students with an adaptable heuristic for rhetorical invention, helping students understand the nebulous and often intimidating boundary between borrowing and plagiarizing, and prompting the transfer of rhetorical thinking across composing contexts and audiences. Our hope in sharing our experiences here is that others will see the potential for using assemblage theory and practice in FYC as an effective means of engaging students in the work of composing.

NOTES

1. Apple's innovation of the graphical user interface relied heavily on Xerox's previous operating systems, and Led Zeppelin's catalog is peppered with unattributed copies of blues songs.

2. We came across this video by way of a Johnson-Eilola tweet.

WORKS CITED

Anderson, Ben, Matthew Kearnes, Colin McFarlane, and Dan Swanton. "On Assemblages and Geography." *Dialogues in Human Geography* 2.2 (2012): 171–89. doi:10.1177/2043820612449261.

Bitzer, Lloyd F. "The Rhetorical Situation." *Philosophy and Rhetoric* 1.1 (1968): 1–14. Print.

Bolter, Jay David, and Richard Grusin. *Remediation: Understanding New Media.* Cambridge: MIT P, 1999. Print.

Chandler, Daniel. "An Introduction to Genre Theory." *Visual-Memory.co.uk/daniel,* 1997. Web. 13 Sep. 2016.

Council of Writing Program Administrators. "WPA Outcomes Statement for First-Year Composition (3.0), Approved July 17, 2014." *WPACouncil.org.* 17 July 2014. Web. 17 Oct. 2016.

Ferguson, Kirby. "Everything Is a Remix Part 1: The Song Remains the Same." *Vimeo,* 12 Sep. 2010. Web. 13 Sep. 2016.

————. "Everything Is a Remix Part 2: Remix, Inc." *Vimeo,* 1 Feb. 2011. Web. 13 Sep. 2016.

————. "Everything Is a Remix Part 3: The Elements of Creativity." *Vimeo,* 20 June 2011. Web. 13 Sep. 2016.

Harris, Joseph. *Rewriting: How to Do Things with Texts.* Logan: Utah State UP, 2006. Print.

Hawk, Byron. "Reassembling Postprocess: Toward a Posthuman Theory of Public Rhetoric." *Beyond Postprocess.* Ed. Sidney I. Dobrin, J. A. Rice, and Michael Vastola. Logan: Utah State UP, 2011. 75–93. Print.

Hitchcock, Alfred. Interview by Fletcher Markle. "Hitchcock Explains about Cutting." From "Telescope: A Talk with Hitchcock, Part 1." Canadian Broadcasting Corporation, 1964. *YouTube,* 29 Jan. 2009. Web. 16 Sep. 2016.

Johnson-Eilola, Johndan, and Stuart A. Selber. "Plagiarism, Originality, Assemblage." *Computers and Composition* 24.4 (2007): 375–403. http://dx.doi.org/10.1016/j.compcom.2010.09.007.

Kress, Gunther, with Berit Henriksen. "What Is Multimodality?" MODE, Institute of Education, U of London, 2012. *YouTube,* 15 Mar. 2012. Web. 13 Sep. 2016.

Preston, Jacqueline. "Project(ing) Literacy: Writing to Assemble in a Postcomposition FYW Classroom." *College Composition and Communication* 67.1 (2015): 35–63. *ProQuest.* Web. 23 Oct. 2016.

Wysocki, Anne Frances. "awaywithwords: On the Possibilities in Unavailable Designs." *Computers and Composition* 22.1 (2005): 55–62. http://dx.doi.org/10.1016/j.compcom.2004.12.011.

Yancey, Kathleen Blake. "Made Not Only in Words: Composition in a New Key." *College Composition and Communication* 56.2 (2004): 297–328. *ProQuest.* Web. 23 Oct. 2016.

Yancey, Kathleen Blake, Liane Robertson, and Kara Taczak. *Writing across Contexts: Transfer, Composition, and Sites of Writing*. Logan: Utah State UP, 2014. Print.

7

ePortfolio Artifacts as Graduate Student Multimodal Identity Assemblages

Kristine L. Blair

REMEDIATION. REMIX. CONVERGENCE. ALL ARE CONCEPTS our field has adopted from the likes of Jay David Bolter, Lawrence Lessig, and Henry Jenkins to describe the participatory composing processes of the late twentieth- and early twenty-first-century digital age. Bolter and Richard Grusin's *remediation* has traditionally described the ways electronic writing remediates, repurposes, and alters the conventions of the print book while maintaining some conventions of alphabetic literacy, while *remixing* is Lessig's depiction of the creative borrowing and meshing of multiple, preexisting media artifacts to create a read-write culture in which citizens use media to produce as much of that culture as they consume. Jenkins's emphasis on *convergence* has chronicled the relationship between such media to disseminate culture and ideology in a participatory system of citizen users relying upon citizen vernaculars. Regardless of which concept we rely on, as several authors here have explained, each helps us describe the cultural shift from our roles as consumers of alphabetic texts to producers of multimodal representations of work, play, and self.

These representations have themselves shifted from a Web 1.0 era of the static website presence to the Web 2.0 era of the blogosphere and other forms of social media and are as much a part of our academic identities as they are our social ones. For example, in my recently completed seminar on scholarly publishing, a pair of doctoral students guided conversations about the evening's topic of publishing the dissertation by having students create memes of key points from the readings (see Figure 7.1). In this instance, the genre of the meme represents the concepts that begin this chapter, yet it also represents a form of assemblage, or what Johndan Johnson-Eilola and Stuart Selber define as "texts built primarily and explicitly from existing texts in order to solve a writing or communication problem in a new context . . . constructed from the conceptual, linguistic, and sociopolitical forces active in several different locations" (381). Genres and artifacts like the meme in Figure 7.1 deploy an existing image, text, or media mode for composers, in this case graduate students, to layer with their own textual commentary to express simultaneously humor and anxiety about the print-based "culminating requirement for the degree" that doesn't

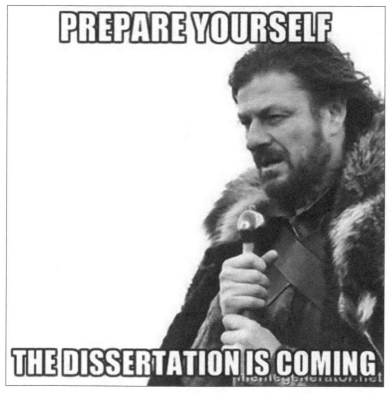

Figure 7.1. Amy Wrobel Jamieson dissertation meme.

afford them—in most cases—the same opportunity to "assemble" via multiple modes and genres. For Kendall Leon and Stacey Pigg, such "digital writing becomes the connective thread through which individuals do professional work" while often representing genres that are "not traditionally the focus of studies of academic professionalization" (4).

While the meme is a useful example of an emerging genre of assembled preexisting media artifacts circulating within a specific rhetorical context, genres such as the dissertation have traditionally trumped these social media representations in establishing academic ethos and identity. Yet academic genres require equally substantive analysis of the rhetorical contexts that reinscribe their status as coin of the realm across disciplines. Similarly, portfolios, both print and electronic, garner capital as professional genres, typically in the job-market process. In focusing on academic ePortfolio artifacts within this chapter, however, I do not intend to reinscribe Leon and Pigg's concern that we don't focus enough on the role of digital nonacademic genres. Instead, I stress that because of the role various Web 2.0 genres play in our representation of "professionalism," our collective understanding of the genre of the ePortfolio and the typical artifacts contained within that genre should better account for the concept of assemblage as a framework for development and delivery. Put simply, the ePortfolio genre is a personal and professional assemblage in which multiple artifacts are repurposed in varied modes and within varied networked spaces hosting students' equally multiple identities.

To showcase this process, this chapter overviews the role that ePortfolio artifacts play in developing multimodal identity assemblages for graduate students as future faculty charged with fostering similar new-media assemblage processes with their undergraduate students. Through a case study of a graduate-level studio course in computer-mediated writing, this chapter documents how two representative ePortfolio artifacts, the literacy narrative and the teaching philosophy, enable experimentation with the affordances of assemblage. These affordances include the time and space for students to experiment with remixing not only academic writing genres in digital form, but also their identities as professionals in the field, an exercise especially important given Caroline Dadas's recent contention that it is vital for job seekers to "consider how they present themselves online" (86). With that call in mind, this chapter promotes a broadened definition of ePortfolios as assemblages that subvert—in productive and challenging ways—the assumption that representing academic professionalism is a unified, stable, and inherently alphabetic process. Ultimately, this broadened scope allows ePortfolios to play a vital role in professional identity assemblage over time and across multiple spaces.

WHY EPORTFOLIO ARTIFACTS?

Although ePortfolios are not new to our discipline, what makes them such a complex genre is their multiple purposes, audiences, and platforms. Indeed, in introducing their 2013 collection *ePortfolio Performance Support Systems*, Katherine V. Wills and Rich Rice ask "readers to consider ways in which ePortfolios . . . facilitate sustainable and measurable writing-related student development, assessment and accountability, learning and knowledge transfer, principles related to universal design for learning, just in time support, interaction design and usability testing" (3). Based on this list, ePortfolios can assume any role in the writing process, in any context, and in multiple genres. I too have used metaphors of remix and remediation to overview the role of ePortfolios as genres and spaces for graduate student exploration of professional identity, specifically within Computer-Mediated Writing Theory and Practice, a course designed for students enrolled in Bowling Green State University's doctoral program in rhetoric and writing. Assemblage, as I shall thus stress throughout this chapter, is not only about the process of combining digital artifacts for a professional portfolio, but also—and perhaps even more significantly—about the process of representing stages of identity formation. For graduate students, this is a liminal process—from being to becoming and back again—as they experiment with multiple tools and genres, even when the larger disciplinary culture encourages a more stable sense of self and academic ethos through genres such as the alphabetic cover letter and curriculum vitae intended to meet the expectations of hiring committees.

Because the concept of assemblage has its origins in artistic contexts and genres of collage between older and newer media, it becomes apt as a framework for ePortfolios. Moreover, the emphasis on artistic processes, as emphasized by Michael Michaud in this volume as the arts of assemblage, applies to courses like Computer-Mediated Writing that rely on a studio review and assessment process in which feedback itself is an assemblage of both face-to-face and online interactions with artifacts, as students work at computer stations to offer formative feedback on works in progress and explain online commentary orally to their peers. Based on this feedback, students then develop revision plans that allow them to prioritize feedback for short-term, end-of-semester deadlines, as well as for long-term professional portfolio development for the academic job market. In this way, peer review is a complex process in which multiple texts and multiple voices within multiple feedback locales affect the development of artifacts over time and space.

Over the two decades I taught the course, the portfolio development process has relied on proprietary Web-authoring, digital imaging, and video and audio editing applications emphasizing what I until very recently considered to be an important consistency of design and identity in the form of a static website, a genre that Kristin Arola contends has become as obsolete as the typewriter or the rotary telephone. With the advent of Web 2.0, however, design and identity are anything but consistent, as the menu of public composing spaces privileges ease of use and immediacy of digital presences through a post, a tweet, a share, a tag, a pin, and—let's not forget—a meme, in what is a frequently template-driven interface. As Arola notes, "If we are to critically engage with the rhetoric of the interface and critically engage with Web 2.0, we must pay attention to how Web 2.0 interfaces are shaping our interactions and ourselves" (7).

Paying attention is as important for teachers as it is for students; increasingly, students' use of tools like Academia.edu, Facebook, LinkedIn, and Twitter outside the class, in both professional and social contexts, has influenced the reconceptualization of both online identity and the ePortfolio as a singular container, be it within a learning management system like Blackboard or the increasingly obsolete Web 1.0 website. By the time they begin pursuing an academic job search, my students have often moved to a more interactive blog-based interface. As they have discovered, the ability or desire to maintain a consistent presence across platforms can lead to a form of identity overload where we are only peripherally active within these spaces. Although writers as diverse as Nicholas Carr, Cathy Davidson, James Gee, and William Powers either celebrate or lament what is now a life of constant connection, we must address how these layers of connectedness affect our understanding of what it means to assemble a professional online identity across and within spaces over time, and how both our alphabetic genres and our digital genres endemic to the academy, including ePortfolio artifacts, are changing as a result.

Both undergraduate and graduate students have more access to and in many cases more comfort with the composing practices within digital spaces than previously. Graduate students in BGSU's program, for example, may have a WordPress blog, a LinkedIn account, a Twitter account, and an Academia.edu account, as well as others. In these contexts, ePortfolio artifacts have the potential to move beyond our more academic conception of and even desire for stable, finished, academic reflections of the identities they simultaneously contain and constrain. Moreover, as members of a field, we don't always prioritize these issues, as Kathleen Blake Yancey suggests. In her discussion of the concept of remix as "concept, material, and method," Yancey ("Re-designing") acknowledges that our field's attention to the invention of digital space is not as prominent in graduate education as it could or should be, and that we must "attend to the concerns of the current moment" (11), in this instance the moment that is Web 2.0.

To document how an ePortfolio represents a multigenre assemblage of Web 2.0 artifacts and identity, I focus on two specific academic genres that doctoral students in my Computer-Mediated Writing course typically complete as part of their portfolios: the literacy narrative and the teaching philosophy statement. I have chosen these genres in part because of their ubiquity as reflective documents in our discipline, but also because of the shift in expectations we may have about what those genres might look like and how as increasingly multigenred artifacts they contribute to equally multigenred assemblages of identity formation in dialogue, as Johnson-Eilola and Selber suggest, not just with existing texts and genres but also with different versions of texts developed and repurposed across time and space.

DIGITAL LITERACY NARRATIVES

Through the work of Gail Hawisher and Cynthia Selfe, the field of computers and writing is grounded in narratives of technological literacy acquisition across media, genres, cultures, and identities as a mechanism for students' understanding the politics of access and theorizing technological attitudes and aptitudes over time. Thus, in Computer-Mediated Writing, I have stressed such narratives as the opening reflective components of an ePortfolio. Like Hawisher and Selfe, I have adapted the genre to allow students to theorize their own experiences of technology as mediated by issues of gender, class, age, and ethnicity to stress that lack of access to or comfort with technology is not innate, but is instead culturally bound. As the following assignment context suggests, the literacy narrative also represents an opportunity to develop, over time and for low stakes, Selber's 2004 continuum of "multiliteracies" as functional, critical, and rhetorical:

Technological Literacy Narrative

What is a literacy narrative? In Computer-Mediated Writing Theory and Practice, it is a reflective statement of about 750 words, or the equivalent, about your histories of technological literacy. When did you first learn to use a computer? In grade school? At a first job? What was that like? Exciting? Scary? How has your access to and comfort with various writing and communication technologies changed over time, from childhood to the present? What are your current digital literacy practices? How have these practices impacted you as a student or as a teacher? If these questions don't resonate with you, consult the questions from page 223 of Kitalong, Moore, Bridgeford, and Selfe's (2002) "Variations on a Theme," or perhaps you might find inspiration by also consulting the Digital Archive of Literacy Narratives: http://daln.osu.edu

The purpose behind this assignment is threefold: (1) to allow you the opportunity to engage in **critical** reflection about your technological histories; (2) to begin to develop **functional** literacies in multimodal composing; and (3) to see those literacies develop throughout the semester into **rhetorically** effective digital writing that successfully balances form and content.

Here's the good news: There's no right way or wrong way to complete this first assignment. Admittedly, for some that may be bad news because the choices are infinite as a result. The thing to remember is that this is a technological literacy narrative.

Format: This must be a digital, multimodal text of some kind: a website, an audio essay, a video, a Prezi. A word-processed document is not an option. But another piece of good news is that you will continue to work on this document throughout the semester, so that in the end the document will be very different from what you started with.

The final version will be part of your portfolio submitted at the end of the term, which gives you about three months to experiment and play. So have fun!

The language of assemblage is not part of this written assignment, and the extent to which individual students' responses constitute experiential collages of media, genres, cultures, and identities can vary based on their rhetorical choices. In my earliest assignment of the literacy narrative, I relied, as the assignment suggests, on a textual frame of reference, assuming in an admittedly static, Web 1.0 fashion that responses would be minimally multimodal, an HTML document with images added. As Jonathan Alexander and Jacqueline Rhodes argue, this language represents a rhetoric of "techno-inclusion" (45–56) that may promote the integration of multimodality, but in the service of alphabetic conventions and genres (e.g., in an "essay") that maintain instructors' subject positions as authority figures on genres with which they are most familiar and comfortable. For Alexander and Rhodes, this limits student experimentation and identity representation through varied genres and modalities. Despite these limitations and biases within my assignment prompt, more recent student responses have been as diverse as the Web 2.0 tools that enable them, from audio narratives recorded in Audacity and stored on SoundCloud, to presentations created in VoiceThread, to comic genres that present literacy acquisition as a complex graphical story arc.

A strong model of the latter is Adam Sprague's "Awesome Adam versus the Technologies," a literacy narrative developed within a comic generator, and certainly a model that moves beyond the traditional expectations of my assignment in its linear multimodal identity assemblage of strip panels (as well as a chiptune electronic music soundtrack) documenting his academic and personal computing life. Adam evolves into superhero Awesome Adam (Figure 7.2), an identity shift to an empowered technological alter ego, to combat Lord Technology, a personified representation of both educational and larger social media practices throughout Adam's life that have made technology less relevant and admittedly more distracting. Awesome Adam defeats this nemesis, and after a story arc that visually depicts a child, adolescent, adult, and superhero self, he reverts to his real-time identity as a college-level writing instructor (Figure 7.3).

Prior to his enrollment in Computer-Mediated Writing, Adam already had an ePortfolio created with Wix. Rather than start from scratch, Adam assembles his portfolio with both Wix and Adobe Dreamweaver interfaces, creating links from the newer Dreamweaver interface hosted on a webserver at BGSU to the older Wix-based platform (see Figures 7.4 and 7.5).

Figure 7.2. From Adam Sprague's literacy narrative, with Adam as a superhero.

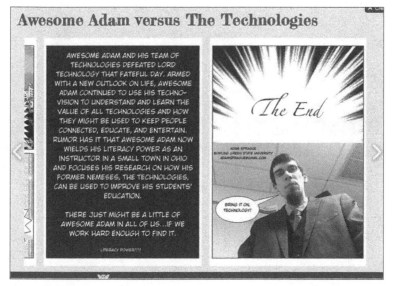

Figure 7.3. From Adam Sprague's literacy narrative, with Adam as himself.

Figure 7.4. Adam Sprague's ENG7280 portfolio interface.

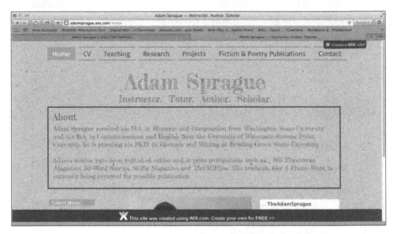

Figure 7.5. From Adam Sprague's original Wix portfolio.

As the two ePortfolio interfaces suggest, design plays a powerful role in the representation of professional identity, as one interface reflects the conventions of a comic genre, including thought bubbles and vivid color schemes, and the other represents a more retro style. While it is very common for students to repurpose artifacts from an earlier ePortfolio to a newer one, it is less common for students to maintain the two interfaces simultaneously. Initially, I suggested to Adam that he develop a "consistency" of design between interfaces that could have enhanced his visual theme but would have significantly diminished his ability to honor the digital work he had done before the course. Inevitably, identity is not consistent in such spaces, nor should it be, and regardless of the version viewers might prefer, both ePortfolio interfaces represent Adam's multifaceted identities, with Figure 7.5 celebrating his multiple roles as instructor, tutor, author, and scholar, and Figure 7.4 linking to a Twitter identity through the use of the microblogging icon. Not unlike his multiple comic selves within the literacy narrative, Adam uses the comic genre as a platform for combining past and present identities. Such examples represent the potential of ePortfolio artifacts and interfaces to function, as suggested earlier, as liminal spaces between being and becoming in both form and content. This includes the potential of digital literacy narratives to chronicle the shift from student to teacher and of the ePortfolio to chronicle the growth from novice to experienced multimodal composer.

TEACHING PHILOSOPHY STATEMENTS

In their article "Teaching with Technology: Remediating the Teaching Philosophy Statement," Phill Alexander and his coauthors argue that despite the ubiquity of this stock academic genre it is "undertheorized, underscrutinized, and underutilized" (23). Nevertheless, even in its print form, a teaching philosophy statement represents a complex triangulation of theoretical alignment, e.g., from Dewey to Freire to Selfe, to abstract curricular values such as "active learning" or "participatory democracy," to more concrete pedagogical practices that manifest those theories and values. Within an ePortfolio, the teaching philosophy, typically in print, is itself a form of assemblage as it integrates other curricular-pedagogical genres such as sample course syllabi and assignment descriptions to establish a relationship between theory and practice, not unlike the rhetorical assemblages designed by Stephen McElroy and Travis Maynard in this volume. For Alexander et al. and many others, the philosophy has multiple purposes: documenting teaching effectiveness, getting a job, and so forth. Yet the philosophy has the potential to reinscribe teacher identity as stable and summative rather than fragmented or, again, liminal. Alexander and his coauthors highlight the process of "remediating" their teaching philosophies in multimodal form in Dànielle DeVoss's graduate seminar Teaching with Technology, noting that DeVoss provided guiding questions that broke down the binary between literacy narrative and teaching philosophy. Equally significant, key threads that evolved during the remediation process included "recognizing the multiple and layered transformations that occurred as we moved our teaching with technology philosophy statements across media and across time; and addressing how the complexities relate to representations of professional identity across digital media and remediations" (29). These threads support an operational definition of assemblage that recognizes the role of multiple tools, genres, and spaces, and not necessarily within a singular timeframe such as a single course, but over a series of career or life experiences.

Similarly, in Computer-Mediated Writing, the literacy narrative, because of its chronological pattern in many cases, is often aligned with, or when possible linked to, what I call the techno-educational philosophy. The two genres represent opportunities for students to reflect on their teacherly identities and their experiences, positive and negative, in teaching with technology, experiences that are influenced by past histories and yet ever-evolving. To help students establish such relationships, I provided them with access to past samples, along with the following prompt:

Techno-Educational Philosophy
What: An artifact that reflects your current attitudes about teaching with technology and technology's role in fostering your particular pedagogical goals. For instance, if you value collaboration, or student-centered learning, what role does technology play in fostering that goal?

How:
- **Form:** You decide. You may do an HTML document, a video or audio essay, a presentation, and so forth. Think about how you can integrate modalities; for instance, you could do a Prezi

that is both visual and textual with the ability to embed media as well.

- **Content:** You are more than welcome to use an existing philosophy statement, but you must revise it to emphasize technology's role.

Some Pointers:

- **Be specific:** Philosophy statements are all too often loaded with buzzwords that don't say much: "I value active learning"; "I encourage critical thinking." How do you do that, and what role does technology play (or not)?
- **Get to the point:** If you were applying for a job, trust me, the search committee wouldn't necessarily want a ten-page philosophy or even a five-page philosophy. Keep it shorter.

As I review my own assignment, I concede that despite my encouragement of a more multimodal approach, the language of my directives privileges print. The rationale for this approach, in part, is that for new multimodal composers, there are fewer points of comparison as to "How long should it be?" Regardless of this limitation, I have been increasingly surprised by the diversity of composing tools students have selected, including tools such as Prezi that are designed to assemble and present information in a dynamic way. For example, a Prezi by former doctoral student Tina Arduini, organized around the theme of active learning (see Figure 7.6), met the assignment directives to be more concrete in her discussion of active-learning practices she has developed over time and within fully online and hybrid classroom spaces. For Tina, this is a purposeful assemblage of artifacts documenting her ability to align theory with practice and maintain the expectations readers would have of the teaching philosophy as a genre. As a result, Tina's philosophy includes links to and embedded Microsoft Word screen captures of assignments, such as small-group activities and peer editing, to document the specific way she fosters more collaborative, interactive relationships among students in both face-to-face and digital form. While Prezi seems to represent a singular composing space, it allows for the collage of multiple genres that represent multiple aspects of her identity. Tina's selection and arrangement of artifacts, including visuals that mesh with the overall theme of her portfolio (Figure 7.7), allowed her to represent a teacherly identity that, while possible to document within a solely alphabetic space, is less representative of the assembled nodes of activities and spaces that constitute Tina's course, including her use of face-to-face peer review groups, the Microsoft Word commenting feature in student essays, and the discussion forum in the course management system. The use of Prezi, as the Web 2.0 alternative to Microsoft PowerPoint, provides a unique opportunity for fostering the basic understanding of assemblage as multigenred, multi-artifacted, and multi-interfaced. Such assemblages also extend to Tina's overall portfolio interface, a powerful and carefully designed comic-based theme with links to other sections of her portfolio, including a website for her technology autobiography and a video for her classroom observation. As Jeff Rice contends in his discussion of YouTube, "The writer . . . is not writing as an individual; she composes in a space where a variety of identities are shaped (or disassembled) as connections form and break apart" (33). Tina's work suggests that this composing process inevitably applies to ePortfolio artifacts as well, as students negotiate how and where to position their multiple identities as student and teacher, novice and expert, within both professional and social contexts. Such a positioning of identity is multimodal and multigenred, given Tina's use of an image of herself as a gamer on the opening interface for her portfolio (Figure 7.7). She also discusses her gamer identity in her literacy narrative by including images and commentary about early computer games on systems such as Atari and Nintendo and the access she inherited or "borrowed" through siblings.

By representing her identities in these ways, Tina's portfolio artifacts represent not only an assemblage of modalities and genres, but also an assemblage of time and space as she reflects on the impact of earlier literacy practices on current practices. Although Johnson-Eilola and Selber's conception of assemblage focuses in part on the redeployment of existing texts, Tina's work strongly suggests that assemblage can encompass the process of literacy acquisition itself,

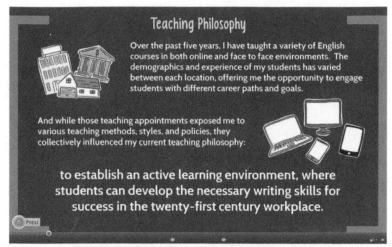

Figure 7.6. From Tina Arduini's Prezi teaching philosophy.

Figure 7.7. From Tina Arduini's ePortfolio.

in that her earlier and ongoing practices as a gamer are situated within the socioeconomic contexts of family and school. These earlier practices have influenced her current practices as a teacher, as represented in both Tina's narrative and her philosophy.

CONCLUSION: AN *ASSEMBLAGE* OF TERMS?

I began this chapter with the comment that computers and writing scholars have applied a range of interrelated terms to describe the process of migrating print genres and alphabetically literate representations of identity into digital space, much as we see in Christine Tulley's "Migration Patterns: A Status Report on the Transition from Paper to Eportfolios and the Effect on Multimodal Composition Initiatives." Tulley's reliance on migration as a concept is useful in documenting the "common methods for creating, exchanging, and evaluating eportfolios" (103), including commercial ePortfolio tools with software suites, standalone commercial ePortfolio software, homegrown ePortfolios, and open-source software. Yet migration is not necessarily transformation, particularly if our understanding of the ePortfolio remains rooted in print-text-based assumptions. However, my own experience as someone who has used ePortfolios across the curriculum shows that this need not be the case, and, given our current digital Web 2.0 culture, current and future generations of both undergraduate and graduate students, and their teachers, can benefit from opportunities to establish connections between identity and multimodality. Assemblage plays a role in making those connections. Throughout this chapter, I have emphasized the literacy narrative and teaching philosophy to suggest that our understanding of the form that ePortfolio artifacts can take is ever-evolving as the tools themselves move us from more alphabetic to visual, interactive modes and to forms of identity collection and representation that are assembled across multiple spaces and multiple genres. Such spaces and genres are ones that graduate students and faculty in writing studies have typically been trained neither to teach in functional, critical, and rhetorical ways nor to assess, though many of our students frequently use such tools in nonacademic contexts. Although assessment is beyond the scope of this chapter, I would encourage, as Yancey has long done ("Looking"), a similarly broadened understanding of portfolio and ePortfolio assessment that encourages the affordances of genre, medium, and modality, considering as criteria questions such as "What arrangements are possible? Who arranges? What is the intent? What is the fit between the intent and the effect?" (96).

Clearly, the language we use to describe these arrangements in our theoretical discussions as well as our assignment prompts represents the Burkean adage that "a way of seeing is a way of not seeing" (49). And as Yancey, Stephen J. McElroy, and Elizabeth Powers conclude, "we needed to develop a new vocabulary and a new set of practices: viewing/reading; the mapping of representations; [and] spatial, embodied and collective pin-up reading." (24). What makes *assemblage* an important term to add to the mix of nomenclatures is its presumption of pluralities and multiplicities of representation, identity, and making and circulating knowledge; ePortfolios themselves are genres aligned with these concepts. They are designed to be assemblages in the literal sense, rhetorically purposeful selections and deselections across genres and modalities and over time. Both Adam's and Tina's artifacts represent this diversity, of genre, of modality, and of identity, in ways that extend our understanding of ePortfolios as a singular container to a series of textual spaces that students assemble to deploy identities of student, teacher, comic fan, gamer, and professional in the field. Their reliance on assemblage as a governing principle, whether or not they define it as such, mandates that digital writing teachers reconsider the language of their assignments, as I am learning to do myself, to encourage a more diverse conceptual model of multimodal composing that reflects the current skills and processes of assembling that are active across many Web 2.0 writing spaces. In doing so, we foster broadened forms of digital identity exploration among graduate students as teacher-scholars as they come to explore in similar ways the identity assemblages of their current and future students.

WORKS CITED

Alexander, Jonathan, and Jacqueline Rhodes. *On Multimodality: New Media in Composition Studies.* Urbana: NCTE, 2014. Print.

Alexander, Phill, Karissa Chabot, Matt Cox, Dànielle Nicole DeVoss, Barb Gerber, Staci Perryman-Clark, Julie Platt, Donnie Johnson Sackie, and Mary Wendt. "Teaching with Technology: Remediating the Teaching Philosophy Statement." *Computers and Composition* 29.1 (2012): 23–38. http://dx.doi.org/10.1016/j.compcom.2011.12.002.

Arola, Kristin L. "The Design of Web 2.0: The Rise of the Template, the Fall of Design." *Computers and Composition* 27.1 (2010): 4–14. http://dx.doi.org/10.1016/j.compcom.2009.11.004.

Bolter, Jay David. *Writing Space: Computers, Hypertext, and the Remediation of Print.* 2d ed. Mahwah: Erlbaum, 2001. Print.

Bolter, Jay David, and Richard Grusin. *Remediation: Understanding New Media.* Cambridge: MIT P, 1999. Print.

Burke, Kenneth. *Permanence and Change: An Anatomy of Purpose.* 3d ed. Berkeley: U of California P, 1984. Print.

Carr, Nicholas. *The Shallows: What the Internet Is Doing to Our Brains.* New York: Norton, 2011. Print.

Dadas, Caroline. "Reaching the Profession: The Locations of the Rhetoric and Composition Job Market." *College Composition and Communication* 65.1 (2013): 67–89. *ProQuest.* Web. 23 Oct. 2016.

Davidson, Cathy N. *Now You See It: How the Brain Science of Attention Will Transform the Way We Live, Work, and Learn.* New York: Viking, 2011. Print.

Gee, James Paul. *What Video Games Have to Teach Us about Learning and Literacy.* New York: Palgrave, 2003. Print.

Hawisher, Gail, and Cynthia Selfe. *Literate Lives in the Information Age: Narratives of Literacy from the United States.* Mahwah: Erlbaum, 2004. Print.

Jenkins, Henry. *Convergence Culture: Where Old and New Media Collide.* New York: New York UP, 2006. Print.

Johnson-Eilola, Johndan, and Stuart A. Selber. "Plagiarism, Originality, Assemblage." *Computers and Composition* 24.4 (2007): 375–403. http://dx.doi.org/10.1016/j.compcom.2007.08.003.

Kitalong, Karla, Michael Moore, Tracy Bridgeford, and Dickie Selfe. "Variations on a Theme: The Technology Autobiography as a Versatile Writing Assignment." *Teaching Writing with Computers: An Introduction.* Ed. Pamela Takayoshi and Brian A. Huot. Boston: Houghton, 2002. 219–33. Print.

Leon, Kendall, and Stacey Pigg. "Graduate Students Professionalizing in Digital Time/Space: A View from 'Down Below.'" *Computers and Composition* 28.1 (2011): 3–13. http://dx.doi.org/10.1016/j.compcom.2010.12.002.

Lessig, Lawrence. *Remix: Making Art and Commerce Thrive in the Hybrid Economy*. New York: Penguin, 2008. Print.

Powers, Williams. *Hamlet's Blackberry: A Practical Philosophy for Building a Good Life in the Digital Age*. New York: Harper, 2010. Print.

Rice, Jeff. "Networked Assessment." *Computers and Composition* 28.1 (2011): 28–39. http://dx.doi.org/10.1016/j.compcom.2010.09.007.

Selber, Stuart. *Multiliteracies for a Digital Age*. Carbondale: Southern Illinois UP, 2004. Print.

Tulley, Christine. "Migration Patterns: A Status Report on the Transition from Paper to Eportfolios and the Effect on Multimodal Composition Initiatives." *Computers and Composition* 30.2 (2013): 101–14. http://dx.doi.org/10.1016/j.compcom.2013.03.002.

Wills, Katherine V., and Rich Rice, eds. Introduction. *Eportfolio Performance Support Systems: Constructing, Presenting, and Assessing Portfolios*. Anderson: Parlor, 2013. 5–15. Print.

Yancey, Kathleen Blake. "Looking for Sources of Coherence in a Fragmented World: Notes toward a New Assessment Design." *Computers and Composition* 21.1 (2004): 89–102. http://dx.doi.org/10.1016/j.compcom.2003.08.024.

———. "Re-designing Graduate Education in Composition and Rhetoric: The Use of Remix as Concept, Material, and Method." *Computers and Composition* 26.1 (2009): 4–12. http://dx.doi.org/10.1016/j.compcom.2008.11.004.

Yancey, Kathleen Blake, Stephen J. McElroy, and Elizabeth Powers. "Composing, Networks, and Electronic Portfolios: Notes toward a Theory of Assessing ePortfolios." *Digital Writing Assessment and Evaluation*. Ed. Heidi A. McKee and Dànielle Nicole DeVoss. Computers and Composition Digital Press/Utah State UP, 2013. Web. 23 Oct. 2016.

III   IN THE WORLD

8

To Gather, Assemble, and Display: Composition as [Re]Collection

Jody Shipka

> To renew the old world—that is the collector's deepest desire when he is driven to acquire new things.
> —Walter Benjamin

> Collecting is an act of very personal commitment. It's about erecting a bond between yourself and an object; it's all about what you choose to be responsible for.
> —Marilynn Gelfman Karp

IN "PLAGIARISM, ORIGINALITY, ASSEMBLAGE," Johndan Johnson-Eilola and Stuart Selber argue for "a view of writing that shifts the emphasis from *performance* to *action* or *effect in context* . . . and that [values] the remix practices that can now be found in many forms of discourse, including student writing and communication" (375), an argument illustrated as well by Stephen J. McElroy and Travis Maynard in this volume. Suggesting that teachers often expect students to produce "thoroughly 'original' texts—texts that make a clear distinction between invented and borrowed work, between that which is unique and that which is derivative or supportive" (375–76)—a concern echoed by several authors here, including Michael Michaud—Johnson-Eilola and Selber advocate treating assemblages as a "valid and valued form of student writing—and of writing in general" (380). Like Johnson-Eilola and Selber and these colleagues, I am interested in teasing out the potentials for a framework for writing, or, stated more broadly, *for composing*, that takes seriously, and that recognizes the rhetorical and material sophistication, rigor, and flexibility associated with, the production of texts as assemblages.

Of course, one could argue, as I will here, that we *cannot help* but create assemblages, that we are always creating and subsequently trading on them—that making meaning from existing/available stuff is all we ever do, *all we really can do*. If, following Jay Lemke, we accept that "each new item to be read or written is some small variation on many familiar ones read or written before" (291), then it is possible to see both that and how the text I am composing now—one in which I've taken up and remixed (or reassembled) alphabetic and numeric characters, marks of punctuation, individual words, figures of speech, syntactical moves, discourse conventions, conceptual metaphors, ideas and quotations from other scholars, etc.—is, in fact, an assemblage—a linear, print-based argumentative text "built primarily and explicitly" (Johnson-Eilola and Selber 381) from existing stuff. Put otherwise, following Marilynn Gelfman Karp, I attempt here to take responsibility for and erect a bond between me (i.e., the points I want to make, the work I mean to do) and but a few of the sociohistorical meaning-making resources I have to hand.

In this chapter, I draw on theories of collecting as a way of pointing to new possibilities for both theorizing and tracing the various agents and agencies associated with rhetorical and material (re)production—of composing, if you will. The collection-based framework offered here works to illustrate and explore the potentials of treating composers as collectors, and of conceptualizing research and composing processes as heterogeneous, complexly layered rearrangements of humans and nonhumans.

RENEWING OLD WORLDS: ON THE POTENTIALS OF A COLLECTION-BASED FRAMEWORK FOR COMPOSING

In "Collecting as an Art," Kevin Melchionne takes issue with theories of collecting that equate it with conspicuous consumption or obsessive-compulsive disorder, suggesting instead that collecting be viewed more broadly and robustly, as a practice involving "the complex world of wandering, hunting, rummaging, examining, selecting, bargaining, swapping, buying, preserving, restoring, ordering, cataloguing, completing, upgrading, researching, and displaying" (151). Melchionne draws on the work of Norbert Hinske, particularly Hinske's concept of *Weltaneignung*, translated roughly as "world acquisition" or "world appropriation," which conveys an attitude of allowing oneself to "be enchanted by the world" (151). As Melchionne notes, for Hinske collecting is "less a world-denying regulation of neurotic life" than an "attitude of adoration, amazement, and insouciant curiosity about the world": "it becomes a means of learning about and appreciating the world" (151).

As an increasingly committed collector of strangers' memory objects, I appreciate Melchionne's and Hinske's highlighting many of the physical, material, intellectual, and affective aspects associated with this work. In particular, Melchionne's detailing of the constellation of practices associated with collecting (or with being a collector) describes accurately the activities I routinely engage in while combing flea markets, antique stores, and estate sales in hopes of finding other people's scrapbooks, photo albums, travel diaries, letters, slides, and home movies. Importantly, in addition to naming many of the activities I engage in while trying to secure these material traces of other people's lives, he also names many of the processes I engage in, and activities I undertake, while preparing these artifacts for publication (see, for example, "Other People's Lives" and "To Preserve, Digitize, and Project"). Then, too, I am concerned with *selecting, examining, preserving, ordering, researching, transforming, and displaying* these artifacts so that I may share them with others.

Insofar as collectors can be defined as engaging in the "selective, active, longitudinal acquisition, possession, and disposition of an inter-related set of differentiated objects," including, but certainly not limited to, "material things, ideas, beings, or experiences" (Belk et al., qtd. in Pearce, *Museums* 49), I'm cognizant of still other ways in which I am positioned as a collector (and, if you will, as a collection), and that I've long been positioned as such, albeit certainly without thinking of it in those terms or identifying myself in this way. I refer now to what I take to be my scholarly or pedagogical "collections," which include, but are certainly not limited to:

experiences with students and of being a student; collections of student work; various assignments and activities (my own and those adapted from others); theories of multimodal discourse; histories of rhetoric and composition; theories about mediation, play, and creativity; knowledge about classroom and discourse conventions and expectations, as well as a vast assortment of pedagogical and scholarly techniques or "moves" that range from more-or-less successful to those I try to avoid. In keeping with one of the central themes or principles of collecting scholarship, I have attempted, with both my scholarly and my pedagogical work, to "renew the old world" (Benjamin 61). Put otherwise, one of the aims informing my uptake, arrangement, and display of items in my scholarly and/or pedagogical collections has been "to construct something new out of the old, to connect what may appear dissimilar in order to achieve new insights and understanding" (Shanks 189). In what follows, I detail how a collection-based framework provides us with ways of developing more robust notions of meaning-making practices—notions that foreground complex, rhetorically and materially savvy processes of choosing, curating, making, arranging, and displaying—while highlighting the role that *both* humans and nonhumans play in these processes. Following this, I offer a description of an activity that positions composers as collectors and that requires them to create complex texts fashioned from existing materials. In offering this example, I provide readers with a better sense of how this framework might be enacted. Finally, I conclude the chapter by suggesting ways that a collection-based framework—in addition to providing us with an alternative to narrowly defined, human-centered notions of invention, negotiation, production, and creativity—creates opportunities for students and scholars alike to engage in rigorous-productive play.

ON CHOOSING, MAKING, ARRANGING, TRANSFORMING, AND DISPLAYING

Like the New London Group's "Available Designs/Designing" framework, a collection-based framework emphasizes the active, dynamic aspects of meaning-making processes. It too is based on the understanding that the "process of shaping emergent meaning involves re-presentation and recontextualization," transformation, and "making new use of old materials" (22). Like the term *design,* *collect* also affords a certain "felicitous ambiguity" (20) as it points to the "organizational structure of products" (i.e., the collection), and to the processes involved with *both* amassing the objects in the collection and putting the collection together (i.e., to collect, collecting). What a collection-based framework adds to the mix, however, is a much greater emphasis on the role nonhumans play in our composing processes, drawing our attention to the participation of what Ben Highmore calls "the thingly world" (58). As Highmore reminds us:

> Things act on us (affect us, entice us, accompany us, extend us, assist us) and we act on things (make them, break them, adjust them, accredit them with meaning, join them together, discard them). There seems to be a symbiotic relationship between them and us; a mutually constituting interaction between people and things. (58)

Like Highmore, Jane Bennett, Bruno Latour, Laura Micciche, and others whose work is invested in expanding discussions of agency to include "humans, non-humans, and the environmental surround" (Micciche 489), I'd underscore here the value of extending and so redefining notions of collaboration as highly distributed and complex human-nonhuman coordinations, or, following Micciche, as a kind of "coexistence": "To think of writing as a practice of coexistence is to imagine a merging of various forms of matter—objects, pets, sounds, tools, books, bodies, spaces, feelings and so on—in an activity not solely dependent on one's control but made possible by elements that codetermine writing's possibility" (498). An expanded sense of agency, collaboration, and materiality allows us to move beyond a consideration of the assemblages or remixes that Johnson-Eilola and Selber have in mind— those designed for and intended to be experienced on the page or screen—allowing us to consider as well the processes involved with the composition of three-dimensional, material artifacts, multipart rhetorical objects and events, and live performances.

By inviting us to think about authors or composers as "collectors," the framework has at least two additional benefits. First, as mentioned earlier, the idea of author-as-collector allows for a much broader idea of the range of materials or resources that might be collected, remixed, and displayed in one's work (objects, experiences, ideas, words, images, sound files, etc.). Second, and related to this, since a term like *author* tends to be equated with the production of words/alphabetic text—and often, with the (human/individual) point of origin of a text—adopting a term like *collector* positions us in ways that makes it difficult to ignore the immensely social, material, highly distributed, and emergent aspects of composing (or collecting) processes. As Susan Pearce maintains:

> Collections, then, come about because individuals select objects and specimens out of all the available material of the world, and put them together in a way which renders the meaning of the group more than the sum of its individual parts. . . . Collections spring from existing individual and social constructions, but they also underwrite and perpetuate these constructs. Collections are endowed with a life of their own, which bears the most intimate relationship to that of the collector, so that the collector sees them, in the most literal sense, as parts of himself. (*Museums* 66)

MANAGING ORDER/DISORDER: WORKING WITH (AND AGAINST) THE AGENCY OF THINGS

In the seminal 1931 essay on collecting titled "Unpacking my Library," Walter Benjamin underscores the tension between order and disorder in the life of the collector, maintaining that "to a true collector the acquisition of an old book is its rebirth" (61). As Benjamin goes on to describe this process of death and rebirth, remediation, or de- and recontextualization, he underscores a childlike aspect of collecting, suggesting that for children "collecting is only one process of renewal; other processes are the painting of objects, the cutting out of figures, the application of decals—the whole range of childlike modes of acquisition, from touching things to giving them names" (61). Like Melchionne, Kevin Moist takes issue with conceptions of collecting that too narrowly equate the practice with passive or mindless consumption, and, following Benjamin, suggests that collecting involves "the cultural production of meaning as collectors find creative ways to renew their particular old worlds" (100). Underscoring something of the "dynamism of the collecting process" (153), Melchionne notes that often a new find or acquisition will reveal "an ignorance or blindness that went untended" (152). In this way, the "decision to acquire can have a transformative effect upon the object as well as the rest of the collection. Through the new acquisition, the meaning of the collection as a whole is called into question" (152).

In yet another example, one that foregrounds both the dynamism Melchionne alludes to and how meaning develops as the result of the complex interaction between the human and the nonhuman, or between the viewer and the objects being viewed, Pearce focuses on a red jacket worn by an infantry officer at the battle of Waterloo, an object housed at the National Army Museum in London. As Pearce explains, when the viewer stands in front of the showcase, "he makes use of the various perspectives that the object offers him, some of which have already been suggested: his creative urges are set in motion . . . and the dynamic process of interpretation and reinterpretation begins, which extends far beyond the mere perception of what the object is" ("Objects as Meaning" 26). It is as a result of this complex human-nonhuman transaction, Pearce maintains, that the "dynamics of viewing are revealed":

> The object is inexhaustible, but it is this inexhaustibility which forces the viewer to his decisions. The viewing process is selective, and the potential object is richer than any of its realizations. . . . In one sense, it is reflecting the developing personality of the viewer and so acting as a kind of mirror; but at the same time the effect of the object is to modify or change the viewer, so that he is a slightly different person from the one he was before. (26)

As Pearce suggests here, "at the heart of this relationship is an ambiguity of control; sometimes the collector shapes the collection and sometimes it shapes him—another way of saying that objects are always active and passive" (*Museums* 66).

The idea of redefining, redirecting, reorganizing, or renewing the old world—of providing new life, context, and potential for old, familiar things—constitutes a common refrain in collecting scholarship and aligns with rhetoric-composition and new-media scholarship. In particular, it resonates with Johnson-Eilola and Selber's notion of assemblages and with Jay David Bolter and Richard Grusin's theory of remediation, with its emphasis on the way newer media forms "honor, rival, and revise" (or "refashion") older media forms and vice versa (15), as well as with the vision of composition that Geoffrey Sirc articulates in *English Composition as a Happening*—one based "on choosing rather than fabricating" (44), with material "chosen from a vaster field than the disciplined one" (47). Beyond resonating with theories of assemblage, remix, and remediation, the idea of renewing the old world, or discovering new possibilities and futures for old or familiar things, aligns with theories of invention that highlight its social, historical, and interpersonal dimensions. The task of invention, as Daniel Royer argues, might best "be understood as a response to both the world as it is given and to the lure of possibility" (171). Like Royer, the archaeologist Michael Shanks sees invention as simultaneously *about finding and creating*, with a logic "of conjunction, making connections. It is both/and, between self and other, not either/or. The thing I have found, the site I visit is both this and that, it is there and here, past and of the present" (135).

ON CULTIVATION, CARE, AND HUMAN–NONHUMAN CONNECTIONS

To conceive of authors or composers as collectors provides us with alternatives to narrow, human-centric notions of invention and collaboration while simultaneously allowing us to attend to the complex relationship between people and the "thingly world" (Highmore 58). This conceiving also provides a point of entry for thinking about issues of care, cultivation, curation, and responsiveness/responsibility, highlighting the affective dimensions of texts, objects, performances, and composing practices. Like Karp, Melchionne notes the connection between collecting, care, and commitment, arguing that a "carefully assembled collection represents an exercise in cultivation" (154). "Cultivation," he explains, "is essentially a process: we do or make things in order to have experiences with them, internalized through habit and reorganized and redirected upon reflection. . . . The temporal dimension of cultivation is especially evident in collecting, where each acquisition redefines the direction for future ones" (154).

To think about composing in terms of collecting and curating practices allows us to attend as well to the affective dimension of the work that we, and that our students, accomplish. Again, with Karp's words in mind—collecting is "all about what you choose to be responsible for"—it proves helpful to think about academic, pedagogical, and/or scholarly collections (or collecting practices) in terms of care, choice, commitment, and responsibility. Whether I am creating a print-based linear text, a piece of video scholarship, an assignment, or an in-class activity, I can consider the ways in which, and the degree to which, I have committed to and assume responsibility for the experience or product I share with others. Thinking about composing in this way allows us to consider more carefully what it is that we connect with (or fail and/or refuse to connect with), and what we choose (or refuse) to take responsibility for. Finally, it allows us to attend more closely to why and how certain connections are forged (or resisted), and to consider how those connections (or collections) help to shape, alter, and transform us, our worlds, and the work we hope to do.

In their work, both Melchionne and Moist go to great lengths to suggest that collecting is not simply mindless consumption. In a similar fashion I would underscore here that thinking about composing as collecting (or to think of final texts/products as collections) does not suggest, nor equate with, mindless gathering and production. Nor is it "tantamount to stealing" (Johnson-Eilola and Selber 391). To view assemblages this way, Johnson-Eilola and Selber insist, "misses what is really going on, at least in many projects" (391). Far from being a matter of thoughtlessly cobbling together bits of existing design elements and texts, creating assemblages, they argue, is "decidedly rhetorical," requiring of their creators "the same rhetorical sophistication as any text," if not more. Following Johnson-Eilola and Selber, I would suggest that creating texts from already existing materials is decidedly rhetorical, decidedly sophisticated, and requires not only a different way of working, but a decidedly different mindset for working, for thinking about the kinds of texts and meanings one hopes to produce. More specifically, it requires a shift away from asking oneself, "What do *I want* to say, do, or mean here?" and becomes more a matter of contemplating potential—what it is that one can possibly do, say, or mean in light of, or in relationship with, the resources, conventions, materials, etc., one has to work with. In sum, it becomes a matter of shifting the focus away from issues of representation, and of attending instead to rhetorical/material action, potential, and the complex relationship between human and nonhuman agency.

While working with existing materials, then, one is acutely aware of what Pearce calls the "ambiguity of control" as one works with (and at times against) the agency exerted by the members of one's collection—of the various components he or she hopes to assemble successfully. Indeed, "sometimes the collector shapes the collection and sometimes it shapes him" (*Museums* 66). By way of illustration, I offer an example of a half-day workshop designed for scholars and teachers interested in working with (and against) the agency of objects—an experience that requires participants to juggle human/nonhuman agency and input in this way.

EXPLORING THE POTENTIALS OF EVOCATIVE OBJECTS

The Evocative Objects Workshop[1] invites teachers and scholars to consider the impact of doing something beyond, or in addition to, merely thinking about (or with) objects—or, as is often the case, when objects are even considered and given their due, *writing about objects.* Instead, participants explore more fully what it might mean—and, indeed, how it feels—*to actually compose with objects* (see Figure 8.1). This hands-on, three-hour-long workshop requires participants to compose multimodal texts while working with (and

Figure 8.1. An evocative object.

against) the affordances of a wide variety of material objects. By inviting participants to compose complex 3D object-texts, the workshop serves an additional purpose by challenging a tendency in the field to equate "multimodality" with digital media or visual-verbal 2D object-texts.

In preparation for the workshop session, participants collect at least five physical objects and spend time reflecting on those objects' meaning potentials. Participants are asked to consider *both what and how* each of these objects means individually (what it conveys, what it is made of, how it is typically used, how it might be used, etc.), and to consider as well how their collection of objects might be juxtaposed, combined, or even modified to do certain kinds of rhetorical work—for instance, to tell a story, to move someone to action, to make an argument, to warn, to amuse, etc. In addition to considering the objects' potentials for meaning, use, and/or modification, participants are encouraged to consider the affective dimensions of the objects they have selected. Does an object convey or suggest a kind of sadness—or is it playful, frightening, boring, provocative, etc.?

While these preparatory tasks ask participants to think about their collection's existing potentials for meanings, the first part of the workshop proper forces them to think about (and, indeed, to grapple with) emergent meaning potentials. At the start of the workshop, objects are placed in new networks of circulation as participants trade one of the objects they brought to the workshop with another participant. At this time, I also provide participants with an additional object or two, again forcing them to grapple with emergent meaning potentials and to anticipate ways of working with (or against) the affordances of this unexpected occurrence/object. After items have been traded and handed out, participants spend an hour composing their object-texts, understanding that their final products must include the traded object and the objects they received from me, along with any of the other items they brought to the workshop. Participants are provided with additional materials or supports (glue guns, tape, scissors, hammers, pliers, lighters, etc.) to help them build, affix, and/or transform the various objects in their collections. The workshop experience requires that participants find new potentials for old/existing things and to bring into alignment their goals or vision for the final piece (what they hope to do, make, or convey with this work) and the various materials they have to work with. In requiring participants to trade objects and use the objects I have given them, the workshop experience forces participants to re-see or reconsider the meaning potentials of this newly reformed or emergent collection. Put otherwise, by working with items that they had not selected or thought about prior to attending the workshop, the experience requires them to remain mindful of (while working with) the affordances and constraints associated with a particular artifact or material.

During the second portion of the workshop, participants engage in an hourlong "rapid response round." A variation on speed dating, participants are split into two groups and sit facing one another. Participants on the left side of the table sit with their finished object-texts in front of them, taking notes on what the person sitting opposite them says or asks about their final products. After two minutes, people sitting on the right side of the table move one chair to their right and this process is repeated until everyone sitting on the right side of the table has had a chance to respond to everyone on the left side of the table.

Following this, the people sitting on the right side of the table place their object-texts in front of them, and the process repeats again with the people on the left side moving one chair to their right after two minutes. During the final portion of the workshop, participants engage in a large-group discussion, reflecting on the overall experience. At this time we discuss, among other things, what it means, and how it feels, to compose in ways and with materials they might not be accustomed to; how they negotiated the complex dance of human/nonhuman agency while working with their newly reconfigured collections of objects; and how the experience of composing with objects relates to, or contrasts with, more traditional (alphabetic/print-linear) ways of composing. (For examples of objects made during the workshop, see www.flickr.com/photos/remediatethis/sets/72157633057086437.)

The Evocative Objects Workshop points to a notion of composing not only as collecting (or as collections), but as a practice that demands of composers a certain facility with processes of de- and recomposition. By this I mean dynamic, ongoing processes that involve (or result in) breaking things down (or things breaking down), of select elements being reworked and/or recombined, and of all this happening with the understanding that whatever results from these processes will again, at some other time, be broken down and remixed and so given new purpose, meaning, and potential. Such a practice positions composers as collectors who must sort through various kinds of collections, searching for ways of remixing or bringing these diverse elements into alignment. The workshop experience demands of participants an openness to material, environmental, and rhetorical potentials, and a willingness to see beyond what is ("This is merely a pipe cleaner," or "This is just a vase"), and to imagine what that thing can or might otherwise be if, for instance, it is broken down, broken apart, recombined with something else—or, indeed, *with many other things*. In short, it requires participants to consider *what else* might be possible when something is shifted out of one communicative context and adapted to/for another. Importantly, the workshop experience functions to underscore for participants the agency or, at times, the seemingly *recalcitrant aliveness of things*, as the materials, genres, and/ or rhetorical moves participants hope (or are forced) to employ in their work often refuse to cooperate or align with their human collaborators' intentions, pointing the way toward (or, at times, even insisting upon) the exploration and subsequent realization of still other purposes, designs, outcomes, meanings, and potentials.

ON COLLECTING, CREATIVITY, AND RIGOROUS-PRODUCTIVE PLAY

Toward the end of "Plagiarism, Originality, Assemblage" Johnson-Eilola and Selber call for a reconfigured notion of creativity, one that is more in keeping with postmodern work and one that is more supportive of remix and assemblage as it invites composers to take "what already exists and make it something else, something that works to solve problems in new, local contexts" (400). In this way, creativity becomes less a matter of originality or attempts to "reinvent the wheel" and involves instead "extensive research, filtering, recombining, remixing, the making of assemblages that solve problems" (400). I am struck, but not surprised, by the similarities between Johnson-Eilola and Selber's definition of creativity and the definition of collecting I featured at the chapter's beginning. Theorists of collecting have long stressed the playful, emergent, and creative aspects of collecting. In "No Two Alike: Play and Aesthetics in Collecting," Brenda Danet and Tamar Katriel articulate some of these similarities, underscoring how collecting, like play, is often regarded as a voluntary activity engaged in for its own sake; provides a kind of "flow" experience resulting in a merging of action and awareness; is often linked with contest/competition and chance; and, finally, involves an element of make-believe, fantasy, or "as-if-ness" that manifests in the ability to see, or imagine, new possibilities and/or futures, for what currently exists (222–23).

While much of this rings true for me as a collector of other people's memory artifacts, it is the aspect of collecting and play concerned with "as-if-ness" that seems most relevant for the collection-based framework I'm advocating here. We see this emphasis on renewal and potential/possible futures in Melchionne's, Moist's, and Benjamin's work; it is evidenced as well in Matthias Winzen's claim that collecting "is the imaginative process of association turned material" (12). It is there too in the work of Susan Stewart, who argues that the collection is "a form of play"—one that involves the "reframing of objects within a world of attention and manipulation of context" (151). For Stewart, the function of this play is not about "the restoration of context of origin, but rather the creation of new context" (152).

Though not directly concerned with collectors or theories of collecting, the work of cognitive scientist Douglas Hofstadter on invention, creativity, "slippage," and "counterfactual worlds" (237–38) provides ways of thinking about the complex kind of reframing, renewal, or de- and recontextualizing that collectors—or, more specifically, in light of my purposes here, *that composers-as-collectors*— often engage in. Maintaining that making "variations on a theme is really the crux of creativity" (233), Hofstadter, much like Lemke, suggests that little of what one sees or encounters is truly novel or original, but rather represents variations, albeit of different types and degrees, on existing concepts, ideas, and materials. To illustrate his point, Hofstadter refers to a Rubik's Cube, claiming that when he looks at it, he merely sees "what is there," namely "a 3×3×3 cube whose faces turn" (232). He goes on to contrast this view of the cube and its potentials with the views of those who have seen instead "what is visibly *not there*"—for instance, "cubes with shaved edges, spherical 'cubes,' differently colored cubes, Magic Dominos, 2×2×2 cubes, 4×4×4 and higher-order cubes, skew-twisting cubes, pyramids," to name only a few of these variations on this particular object/concept (232).

For Hofstadter, creativity is not about coming up with something original—a "totally new idea" (233)—but rather involves attending to how things might "glide into alternate versions of themselves" (245), seeing "further into the space of possibilities surrounding what *is*" (247), noting how a concept or thing "reaches out toward things it is not" (250)—in short, it is the ability to see "one thing as something else" (251). What Hofstadter calls creativity is what I would term "rigorous-productive play." Rigorous-productive play, like Hofstadter's notion of creativity, demands of composers the ability to see "one thing as something else" (252), to see "further into the space of possibilities surrounding what *is*" (247), and, importantly, to devote enough time, effort, flexibility, and patience to tease out the implications of that difference, of those possibilities. It requires of composers what Shanks calls "sensuous receptivity"—a greater awareness and appreciation of how "every new insight about an object literally changes what that object is, its identity, and thus our attitudes and actions toward it" (112). Indeed, rigorous-productive play simultaneously requires and allows us to move beyond something's "immediately given state . . . and follow the process in which it becomes something else" (Shanks 43).

And so I end much as I began, by suggesting that there is an inherently creative or playful aspect to scholarship and most pedagogical practice: not only do they involve remixing or reassembling one's thoughts, beliefs, and experiences with those of others, but both are often motivated by the desire to imagine possible, better, or merely alternative futures for a classroom, discipline, or field—to explore potentials surrounding what is, and to imagine alternatives to what has been, or is currently being, accomplished.

NOTE

1. The Evocative Objects Workshop was first offered as a half-day workshop for the 2013 Conference on College Composition and Communication. The first workshop was designed and facilitated by Erin Anderson, Kerry Banazek, Amber Buck, and me.

WORKS CITED

Belk, Russell W., Melanie Wallendorf, John F. Sherry Jr., and Morris B. Holbrook. "Collecting in a Consumer Culture." *Highways and Buyways: Naturalistic Research from the Consumer Behavior Odyssey*. Ed. Belk. Provo: Association for Consumer Research, 1991. 178–215. Print.

Benjamin, Walter. *Illuminations: Essays and Reflections*. Ed. Hannah Arendt. Trans. Harry Zohn. New York: Schocken, 1968. Print.

Bennett, Jane. *Vibrant Matter: A Political Ecology of Things*. Durham: Duke UP, 2010. Print.

Bolter, Jay David, and Richard Grusin. *Remediation: Understanding New Media*. Cambridge: MIT P, 1999. Print.

Danet, Brenda, and Tamar Katriel. "No Two Alike: Play and Aesthetics in Collecting." *Interpreting Objects and Collections*. Ed. Susan M. Pearce. New York: Routledge, 1994. 220–39. Print.

Highmore, Ben. *Ordinary Lives: Studies in the Everyday*. London: Routledge, 2011. Print.

Hofstadter, Douglas R. *Metamagical Themas: Questing for the Essence of Mind and Pattern*. New York: Basic, 1985. Print.

Johnson-Eilola, Johndan, and Stuart A. Selber. "Plagiarism, Originality, Assemblage." *Computers and Composition* 24.4 (2007): 375–403. http://dx.doi.org/10.1016/j.compcom.2007.08.003.

Karp, Marilynn Gelfman. *In Flagrante Collecto (Caught in the Act of Collecting)*. New York: Abrams, 2006. Print.

Latour, Bruno. *Reassembling the Social: An Introduction to Actor-Network-Theory*. Oxford: Oxford UP, 2005. Print.

Lemke, Jay L. "Social Semiotics: A New Model for Literacy Education." *Classrooms and Literacy*. Ed. David Bloome. Norwood: Ablex, 1989. 289–309. Print.

Melchionne, Kevin. "Collecting as an Art." *Philosophy and Literature* 23.1 (1999): 148–56. doi: 10.1353/phl.1999.0021.

Micciche, Laura R. "Writing Material." *College English* 76.6 (2014): 488–505. *ProQuest*. Web. 9 Sep. 2016.

Moist, Kevin. "'To Renew the Old World': Record Collecting as Cultural Production." *Studies in Popular Culture* 31.1 (2008): 99–122. *EBSCOHost*. Web. 22 Oct. 2016.

New London Group. "A Pedagogy of Multiliteracies: Designing Social Futures." *Multiliteracies: Literacy Learning and the Design of Social Futures*. Ed. Bill Cope and Mary Kalantzis. New York: Routledge, 2000. 9–38. Print.

Pearce, Susan M. *Museums, Objects, and Collections: A Cultural Study*. Washington: Smithsonian Institution P, 1993. Print.

————. "Objects as Meaning; or Narrating the Past." *Interpreting Objects and Collections.* Ed. Pearce. New York: Routledge, 1994. 19–29. Print.

Royer, Daniel J. "Lived Experience and the Problem with Invention on Demand." *Reconceiving Writing, Rethinking Writing Instruction.* Ed. Joseph Petraglia. New York: Routledge, 1995. 161–78. Print.

Shanks, Michael. *Experiencing the Past: On the Character of Archaeology.* New York: Routledge, 1992. Print.

Shipka, Jody. "Other People's Lives: A Projection," in "*Master Hands,* a Video Mashup Round Table." Ed. James J. Brown Jr. and Richard Marback. *Enculturation: A Journal of Rhetoric, Writing, and Culture* 11 (2011): n. pag. Web. 13 Sep. 2016.

————. "To Preserve, Digitize, and Project: On the Process of Composing Other People's Lives." Video. *Enculturation: A Journal of Rhetoric, Writing, and Culture* 14 (2012): n. pag. Web. 13 Sep. 2016.

Sirc, Geoffrey. *English Composition as a Happening.* Logan: Utah State UP, 2002. Print.

Stewart, Susan. *On Longing: Narratives of the Miniature, the Gigantic, the Souvenir, the Collection.* 1984. Durham: Duke UP, 1993. Print.

Winzen, Matthias. "Collecting—So Normal, So Paradoxical." Trans. Astrid Böger. *Deep Storage: Collecting, Storing, and Archiving in Art.* Ed. Ingrid Schaffner and Winzen. New York: Prestel, 1998. 22–32. Print.

9

Assemblages of Asbury Park: The Persistent Legacy of the Large-Letter Postcard

Stephen J. McElroy

DURING THE JANUARY 14, 2014, BROADCAST OF NBC's *Late Night with Jimmy Fallon*, a denim-clad figure, wearing sunglasses and a red bandanna, emerges onscreen from a pall of shadows. He steps up to one of a pair of spotlighted microphones, strumming a guitar to the familiar tune of Bruce Springsteen's "Born to Run." Although the figure has been introduced as Springsteen himself, the performer is not the rock star from New Jersey but is actually the show's titular host in costume. As he begins to sing the first verse, his vocals and melody are recognizable to the audience, but the lyrics are new:

> In the day we sweat it out on the streets,
> stuck in traffic on the G-W-B.
> They shut down the tollbooths of glory
> 'cause we didn't endorse Christie.

As the song progresses, it becomes evident that this rendition, unlike the original, is not an everyman anthem about small-town fates, but instead a comedic take on the George Washington Bridge lane-closure scandal. This incident had recently embroiled the office of the New Jersey governor and self-professed Springsteen idolizer, Chris Christie. After Fallon sings the chorus of this version, with the lyrics, "We're stuck in Gov'nor Chris Christie's Fort Lee, New Jersey, traffic jam," a second figure, wearing a similar outfit and strumming his own guitar, emerges. This new figure, in fact the real Bruce Springsteen, sings a second verse, lampooning his high-profile fan as well as Christie's involvement with the scandal: "You've got Wall Street masters stuck cheek-to-cheek with blue collar truckers, and man, I really gotta take a leak." The song crescendos with both Fallon and Springsteen belting out the last lines of the updated lyrics:

> Someday governor I don't know when
> this will all end. But 'til then
> you're killing the working man
> who's stuck in Gov'nor Chris Christie's
> four-lane New Jersey traffic jam.

The performance—a multimodal assemblage of disparate elements, including a famous song, lyrics inspired by a headline-dominating news story, and an aging rocker's persona—was celebrated both by the audience in attendance and by millions of people who watched the segment on television and online afterwards. And with this assemblage, the "communication problem" (Johnson-Eilola and Selber) was perhaps more a set of problems: for Fallon, of course, it was to entertain and to garner attention for his show and his network, but it was also presumably for Springsteen to get some headlines and to execute what the *New York Times* two days later called a "very public snub" (Santora) of a governor who often invokes Springsteen's name and co-opts his public persona—despite the strong opposition of the two figures' political views.

I open with this anecdote because I am interested in the Fallon segment as a composition, a complex "expression of relationships" (Yancey 100)—creative, economic, political—but this chapter is neither about Fallon, nor about his show. And while I am also interested in the history of Chris Christie's fanatical and apparently politically motivated devotion to Bruce Springsteen—and return to it below in the context of a broader discussion on assemblage—this chapter is not about the governor of New Jersey, nor is it about the ideological leanings of "the Boss." Instead, this chapter is about mi-

Figure 9.1. Cover of Bruce Springsteen's debut album, Columbia Records.

crohistories of creativity; the formation and progression of textual instantiations over time; and the appearance, reappearance, and cultural resonance of generic forms across media (Figure 9.1). More specifically, this chapter is about the assemblages and divergent legacies of a textual genre—particularly the genre known as the large-letter postcard—and how examining those legacies allows us to see the ways in which assemblages not only have "effects in context" but also *effect contexts,* creating new circumstances in which, for instance, a rock star would appear on a talk show to lampoon a politician. On the basis of this discussion, I also contribute more general insights about composition that assemblage as a concept allows us to gain. I begin, however, with the large-letter postcard.

THE LARGE-LETTER GENRE, DEFINED

Roughly a century before Springsteen and Fallon got together to make fun of the governor of New Jersey, the picture postcard—a multimodal medium of communication that was newer to people in the United States then than the World Wide Web is to us now—was basking in the glow of its "Golden Age," an era often defined as the period between 1907 and 1915. The picture postcard (or "private mailing card," as it was called until 1901) had been legally introduced in the United States in 1898, for the first time allowing privately printed cards with a picture on the front to be mailed for a penny—conveniently priced at half the rate of a one-ounce letter. Before that, postal cards were strictly defined as prestamped cards, printed and sold directly by the postal service, of a certain size and thickness, and with only a mailing address on the stamped side and space for a written message on the other. The picture postcard added a new visual dimension to the postal medium, creating opportunities for the masses to exchange images of events, municipalities, landmarks, and loved ones as never before.

Curt Teich & Company, which would go on to become the largest postcard manufacturer in the world, was a Chicago-based company that specialized in picture postcards. One of Teich's most lasting products in terms of cultural legacy was arguably the assembled genre of the large-letter postcard. Few people outside the world of postcard collecting are familiar with the term *large letter*, but most will likely recognize large-letter postcards when they see them. In fact, the large-letter postcard is perhaps the most archetypal subgenre of "vintage" postcards. Large-letter postcards have a front design that consists of the name of a location, such as a city or state, in large block letters, and within each of those letters is an image of a scene or landmark from that location. The name of the location is often prefaced with a salutation, such that the whole message reads, for example, "Greetings from Gallatin, Tennessee" (Figure 9.2).

Although Teich popularized the large-letter postcard, he did not invent the genre in a vacuum. Since the early days of picture postcards, there had been various card designs, from a variety of manu-

Figure 9.2. Gallatin, Tennessee, postcard, author's collection.

facturers, that featured large words in block letters with images inside their borders. Often in these early days these multimodal print designs—featuring letters, lines, colors, shading, images, and carefully crafted layouts—contained images that were not scenes, but rather people's faces. For instance, the letters of a New York postcard postmarked in 1906 contain collages of a number of babies' faces (Figure 9.3). Other large-letter designs used similar assemblage practices for different commercial ends. The two cards shown in Figure 9.4, for instance, also feature faces in letters, but in these examples the letters spell out the names not of locations but rather of people—in this case, of Grace and Ethel. The similar designs of these two cards, coupled with the fact that they seem to have been published by the same company, suggest that this may have been a kind of template for a larger body of cards with names in similar styles. In this way, these cards bring to mind modern-day products that use similar design templates—such as key chains, coffee mugs, and shot glasses—with different individual names displayed on them, which points to the "personalization" that the large-letter genre/template forecast.

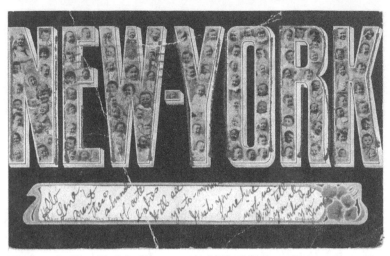

Figure 9.3. New York babies postcard, Florida State University card archive.

THE TEICH METHOD

As the above examples show, postcard designs of this type—with images inside the letters of words—had been around for a while before Teich began making his large-letter cards, sometime around 1920. Teich's defining innovation of the large-letter genre, first, was instituting the standard practice whereby the images inside the letters were a collection of scenes that represented the location being named. Teich's second innovation—both to the large-letter genre and to picture postcards more generally—was his invention of new methods of image colorization, bringing vivid shades and hues to the printed scenes in an era before color photography was practical. Here, I examine these innovations and their textual resonances over time and discuss what such examinations might mean for our understanding of assemblage composing.

ASSEMBLING TEICH LARGE LETTERS

Among the materials donated to the Curt Teich Postcard Archives[1] are more than a hundred thousand "job files"—manila envelopes each of which contains "original and edited photographs, inter-

Figure 9.4. "Ethel" and "Grace" postcards, Florida State University card archive.

office memos, and other documents" that, to varied extents, speak to the multimodal and often multimedia design and production history of a given postcard (McElroy). The job file for the Colorado large-letter postcard seen in Figure 9.5, for instance, contains a number of artifacts that allow us to see the ways in which processes of assemblage—specifically, portions of existing postcards being brought together to create a new postcard—played an explicit and integral role in the card's creation. The first artifact, the photo ticket, is actually not contained within the file but is affixed to it (see Figure 9.6). This artifact contains several pieces of critical

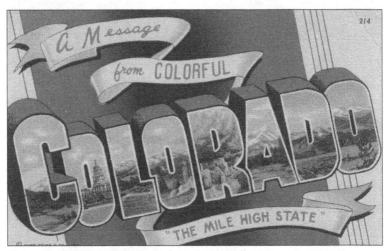

Figure 9.5. Colorado postcard, author's collection.

NO. 0B-H2699

SANBORN SOUVENIR CO., DENVER, COLO.

ORDER NO. 48138

DATE DEC 23, 1940

12½ M POST CARDS ART COLORTONE FULL FACE

(ALL OF THIS ON THE PICTURE SIDE)

PLACE OF TITLE: UPPER, LOWER, CENTER - BORDER.

TITLE (IN FULL) (IN PLATE)
A MESSAGE FROM COLORFUL COLORADO
THE MILE HIGH STATE
(C) CURT TEICH & CO., INC.
PRIV. NO. UPPER LEFT CORNER - 214

(ALL OF THIS ON THE ADDRESS SIDE)

FRONT NO. 3 R. M. YES

IMPRINT SAME AS ABOVE

PHOTO PROPERTY OF C.T.

COLOR DESCRIPTION
SUBMIT SKETCH
SEE SKETCH. IF POSSIBLE GET A BRIGHT SILVER & GOLD EFFECT ON THIS. IF NOT IT MUST BE SOME OTHER BRIGHT AND STRIKING COLOR COMBINATION. [illegible] USE LONG'S PEAK PRINT, SECTION OF CAPITOL PRINT, MT. EVANS, PIKE'S PEAK (4AH23), MESA VERDA PRINT, MT. ELBERT (7AH555), SIERRA BLANCA PRINT.

SUBMIT: RET. PHOTO REPHOTO B. L. & W. PROOF HANDCOL.PROOF YES RETURN PHOTO.

CURT TEICH & COMPANY, INC., CHICAGO
PHOTO TICKET

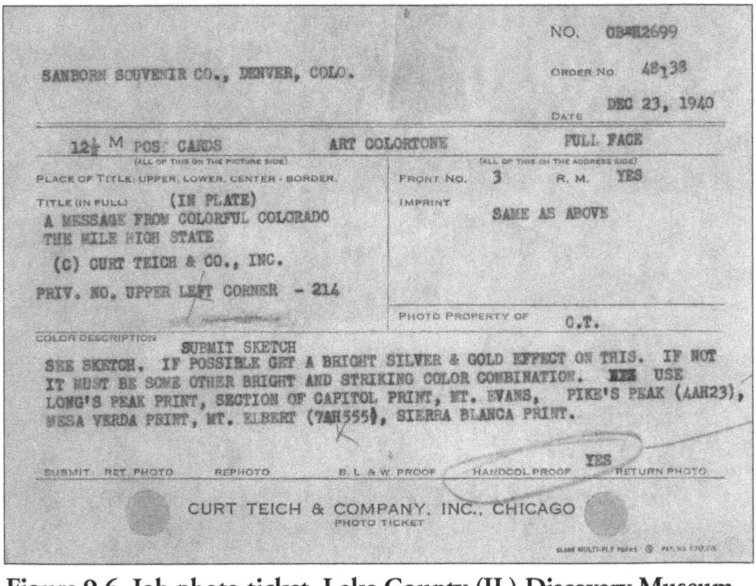

Figure 9.6. Job photo ticket, Lake County (IL) Discovery Museum, Curt Teich Postcard Archives.

information about the contents of the envelope and the production of the card it represents.[2]

At the top left of the ticket, the customer's name is printed. This line would often appear verbatim on the postcard back with publishing credits, as was the case with this Colorado card. In the upper right of the photo ticket are the serial number, the order number, and the date the order was submitted—in this case December 23, 1940.[3] Directly below the horizontal line that spans nearly the width of the ticket, from left to right, are the number of cards ordered, the process used to print the cards, and instructions to print the card "full face," i.e., without a border. Below that are two half-width sections. The left section has space for the title of the card and any other text that might go on the front, while the right section has space for any text that might go on the back. Below these sections is a full-width section for "color description." Specifications for the colorization of a postcard image would normally go here. In this case, where the card is a large-letter one, the instructions are for how these aspects of the card should be assembled—that is, what images should appear in the letters and what the background of the card should be.

The instructions on this photo ticket were apparently transcribed from a hand-drawn sketch accompanied by handwritten specifications contained in the job file and seen in Figure 9.7. Underneath a sketched layout that includes the words, "A Message from Colorful COLORADO The Mile High State," is a request for how the card should be assembled. The request reads:

> Is it possible to get a bright silver & gold effect on this. If not it must be some other bright and striking color combination. Use (1) Longs Peak print. Section of (2) Capitol print. (3) Mt. Evans. Pikes Peak 2114 (4A-H23)—Mesa Verde (4)— Mt. Elliot 2317 (7A-H555)—Sierra Blanca (5).

While it remains unclear who created this sketch and wrote these instructions, it is clear that the author is familiar with both the conventions of the genre and with the texts that are available to him or her to create this new design. The author refers to seven different texts (or "prints") that the Teich artists may use as they assemble the

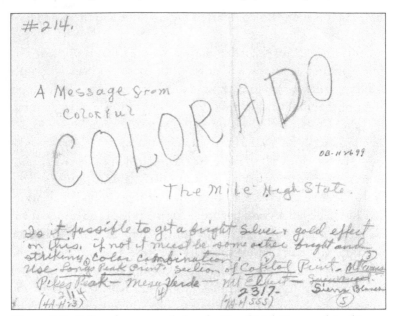

Figure 9.7. Colorado postcard sketch, Curt Teich Postcard Archives.

postcard, two of which—"Pikes Peak" and "Mt. Elliot"—are apparently preexisting Teich postcards, as the author provides Teich serial numbers for those. The other five are listed (1–5) in reference to a set of "real photo" postcards—i.e., prints made from photosensitive paper with a postcard back—that were correspondingly numbered and apparently sent, along with the order instructions, to Teich & Company. These cards can be seen in Figure 9.8. Provided with these instructions and existing texts, the artists went about designing the card, complete with its "striking" background.

By looking at the intermediate multimedia design, which remains in the job file and is shown in Figure 9.9, we can make some deductions about how the card was put together. The three major elements of the design are the background, the flowing ribbon with the "message" inside, and the large letters themselves. The background seems simply enough to consist of a half-dozen or so parallel, slightly off-vertical lines and a gradient shadow also running

Figure 9.8. Colorado postcard collage, Curt Teich Postcard Archives.

parallel through the center of the card. The ribbon appears to have been free-drawn, and the letters within it seem to have been inked by hand as well. Some physical evidence speaks to this inking process: the now seventy-year-old adhesive that was used to hold the elements of the design together is failing, and consequently we can see that the first attempt to ink the word *message* was considered unsatisfactory and was replaced with a second attempt that was affixed in its place. Similar adhesive-related evidence can be seen in the first letter in the word *Colorado*. From the portion of the letter that has come loose, we can see that photographic copies of each of the existing texts were made, portions of them were cut out in the

Figure 9.9. Colorado postcard design, Curt Teich Postcard Archives.

shapes of the letters' faces, and those portions were affixed to the design, which could then be sent on for colorization and printing. We can see from this example, then, the ways in which material assemblage was vital to the process of designing and producing large-letter postcards.

Assemblages, as Johndan Johnson-Eilola and Stuart Selber say, are built from existing texts, as in the case of the Colorado large-letter postcard. This definition has at least two important implications for research into the role(s) that assemblage plays in composing—of postcards or any other text. First, the combinatory nature of assemblages suggests that we can and should investigate the materials and activities involved with a given instance of assemblage. In other words, we should enumerate and examine the texts, including the modes and media, from which the composer/assembler draws; the segments, pieces, elements, and components of those texts that he or she selects and uses in the assemblage; and the means by which he or she puts them together to make a coherent whole. In short, we should work to understand instances of assemblage as instances of composing practices whether in print or digital. The preceding section on the physical assemblage of large-letter postcards is an example of an investigation in this category, demonstrating the ways in which the Curt Teich company used and reused photographs, postcards, paint, and other physical materials to create their postcard products.

Second, the nature of assemblages as not only *products of* but also *potential sources for* other assemblage practices prompts (if not requires) us to consider the textual or compositional lineage at play in assemblage over given spans of time. Built from existing texts, assemblages can also be assemblages of (other) assemblages. For instance, Existing Text A might be used in the creation of Assemblage B, which itself might be used some time later in the creation of Assemblage C. In this case, Assemblage C carries with it elements both of Assemblage B and of Existing Text A. Although this is a general statement, it articulates an important if very basic principle of assemblage lineages that I build on in the remainder of this chapter, where I present some specific lineages of large-letter assemblages. I argue that tracing these lineages allows us to see the ways in which assemblages not only have "effects in context" but also *effect contexts*—that is, assemblages both *draw from* the textual landscape and *contribute to* the textual landscape, thus creating new contexts within which composers may assemble, often in unforeseeable ways.

LINEAGES WITHIN TEICH & COMPANY

As we see in the example of the Colorado large-letter postcard in the preceding section, Curt Teich & Company relied on the methods of assemblage to create their large-letter cards, bringing together existing images and postcards of local scenes in a collage that would give viewers of the card a sense of what the titular locale had to offer. Here, I demonstrate that Teich & Company also had occasion to use the large-letter designs themselves as part of newer assemblages. Seen in Figure 9.10 (serial number 2BH1081), for instance, is a large-letter card representing the city of Tallahassee,

Florida, that was designed and initially printed in 1942 and, as will be shown below, reused in 1943 for the purposes of a new postcard text. Contained within the letters are images of a variety of key sights in and around Florida's capital city. In the background behind the large letters, in the lower right corner, is an image of the state capitol building. Unlike in the case of the Colorado card, the job file for this Tallahassee card cannot be found in the holdings of the Teich archives; thus, little is known about the specific parameters of its production. However, one year after it was produced, in 1943, the card's design was reused for the creation of a new postcard assemblage, this one a folder postcard.

The job file for the Tallahassee folder card, with serial number D7236, is in the holdings of the Teich archives. H. B. Dover is listed as the publisher/customer, the order date is listed as 4-26-43, and the color description for the front cover instructs the artists to "use photo no. 2BH1081," the Tallahassee large-letter postcard. For the back cover, the artists were to "use photo no. 0BH65"—i.e., the postcard of the state capitol building that also appears in the original large-letter assemblage. In addition to the photo ticket, the job file also contains the black-and-white arrangement that the art-

Figure 9.10. Tallahassee postcard, author's collection.

ists assembled. One other artifact in the job file also illustrates the methods of assemblage, but in this case the assemblage is not visual but rather verbal. The Tallahassee card contains a lengthy description of the city, and within the job file there is an artifact that sheds light on how this reading matter was produced. A typed missive on the letterhead of the New Hotel Mayflower (of Jacksonville, Florida) appears to be an early draft of the reading matter, and was stamped as being received at the Teich factory on April 27, 1943. On the back of the letterhead is a typed note that contains several points of interest about methods of assemblage used to produce the folder:

> This will now enable us to proceed with this folder edition of which I [secured] an increase from 6,500 to 25,000.
>
> George, [sic] evidently was so rushed at the end he forgot to secure this information and it has *taken [me] several hours to take out of various [pamphlets] I [secured] from the C of C* to get this together.
>
> Hope we can RUSH these out because Tallahassee has never had a folder before and we want to get ours on sale before Colourpicture's is out. (Emphasis mine)

We can see that in the second paragraph of this note its author claims to have assembled the reading matter for the folder together from "various pamphlets" that he gathered from the Chamber of Commerce, which suggests another kind of assemblage method in which Teich & Company engaged.

LARGE-LETTER LEGACIES IN CULTURE

As the number of large-letter titles available to consumers moved into the hundreds and even the thousands during the 1930s and 1940s, and as the familiar design template was used to represent cities from Miami to Seattle and states from California to Maine, the large-letter genre began to resonate outside the confines of the postcard industry. Through that resonance—through these new assemblage lineages—the meaning of the genre began to shift as well. Whereas individual large-letter postcards on a micro scale represented the inviting, coherent identities of, say, Sheboygan or St. Louis, the proliferation of large-letter postcards—and of their generic conventions across media on a macro scale—reified the conventions of the genre, transforming large-letter designs into widely recognized representations of identity-coherence and civic invitingness themselves. The cultural association with postcards—a medium that in the time of the large-letter design's invention was a popular means of everyday communication but that in the decades since has come to be largely associated with travel—also implies a sense both of the site being named as a destination and of a greeter calling out from that destination.

Large-letter postcards proliferated through countless assemblage lineages, each new assemblage contributing to the overall impact of the genre in our culture. In other words, each new large-letter assemblage effected new textual contexts in which future composers and designers would operate and from which they could pull. Three recent examples will illustrate that point here. The first example is a photograph that was taken inside a Logan's Roadhouse restaurant in Gallatin, Tennessee, in September 2014 (Figure 9.11). The photograph is of an arrangement of oversized reproductions of large-letter postcard designs that have been assembled together, framed, and hung on the wall of the restaurant. Here, these designs function not as the front of individual postcards to be purchased, handled, and mailed, but instead as a fixed, conglomerated symbol of Americana. Although a large-letter postcard for the city of Gallatin was produced by Teich (and can be seen in Figure 9.2), the managers for this particular Logan's elected to put on display an assortment of designs representing places as far away as Chicago and Los Angeles so that the emphasis is not on any one city or state but rather, through the assemblage of these decades-old designs, on a collectively nostalgic sense of these places all belonging under the same umbrella of America. Such nostalgia plays well into the aims of a company whose website has carried the tagline, in a bold font and in the middle of the screen, "Americana Atmosphere, Down-Home Service." In this case, the Teich card has been repurposed for these new commercial contexts, to leave a patriotic impression on the consumer.

Figure 9.11. Logan's Roadhouse postcard wall, photograph by author.

A similar commercial repurposing of Teich large-letter designs can be found in the Denver International Airport, where the Colorado postcard whose production is described in the earlier sections has been refashioned as the name and logo for a gift shop that sells Colorado-themed merchandise. The sign for the store, which can be seen in Figure 9.12, features the same color scheme, lettering, slogan, and images as the large-letter postcard produced by Teich & Company in 1940. However, the elements have been moved around such that the "Greetings from Colorful Colorado" slogan and its yellow-ribbon backing have been moved from its postcard position above the large-letter title to its new location to the left of the title. In this new instantiation, the design beckons shoppers to enter the store and to peruse and select from a wealth of hats, t-shirts, key chains, stationery, and (of course) postcards that can serve to remind them of their visit to the Centennial State. In this case, the Teich design has been repurposed so that it functions as a representation not of Colorado, as it once did, but instead of the opportunity and the invitation to shop for *other* representations of Colorado. The Teich-assembled postcard has effected new contexts,

Figure 9.12. Colorado store, photograph by author.

tying this large-letter design to a sense of coherent place that this airport gift shop taps into decades later.

Whereas the two examples illustrated in Figures 9.11 and 9.12 featured large-letter designs being used in new assemblages for commercial aims, the third and final example features a Teich design that has been reassembled for purposes having to do more with civic pride. The photograph in Figure 9.13 shows a mural that was commissioned in 2014 by the Tallahassee Downtown Improvement Authority and produced by students in Florida State University's Art Education department, with PhD student Sam Rosenstein as the lead artist. The mural, in the heart of the city's downtown, retains many elements of the postcard while updating others. As in the postcard, the mural's message still reads, "Greetings from Tallahassee, Fla., The Capital City." The lettering is very similar, although the words are rearranged—the biggest repositioning being that of "The Capital City" from above the city's name as in the postcard to its right. The state capitol building appears in the lower right corner of both the postcard and the mural. Some of the colors have also changed slightly, but the biggest change from the

Figure 9.13. Mural commissioned by the Tallahassee Downtown Improvement Authority, photograph by author.

postcard to the mural is to the images that appear within the letters in "Tallahassee." In the mural, the scenes have been updated to include images of local gardens, Florida A&M University, and the Tallahassee Museum.

As these examples demonstrate, Curt Teich & Company's large-letter postcards have left behind a significant cultural legacy embodied by assemblage lineages even decades after the company went out of business in the 1970s. Their designs also inspired numerous imitators within the postcard industry, imitators whose creations would spawn their own assemblage lineages. The Tichnor Company of Boston, for instance, not only assembled their own large-letter designs that borrowed the conventions of the trademark Teich & Company genre, but also hired many of Teich's executives and lead artists in order to better compete with the industry leader (Werther and Mott). One of the large-letter cards that Tichnor created was for the city of Asbury Park, New Jersey (see Figure 9.14). This card, a descendant of the Teich legacy, would itself be the source of a new lineage of assemblages that would emerge over

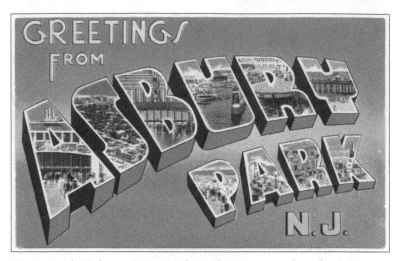

Figure 9.14. Tichnor Company large-letter postcard, author's collection.

several decades and that would play into both the history of rock music and the politics of the state of New Jersey.

LINEAGE CASE STUDY:
GREETINGS FROM ASBURY PARK

Unlike Teich & Company, the Tichnor Company did not use a serial-number convention that corresponded to the date of production. It is thus difficult to know when the "Greetings from Asbury Park" postcard in Figure 9.14 was produced, but we can reasonably guess that it was designed and printed, using assemblage practices similar to those employed by Teich & Company, sometime in the 1930s or 1940s. After "Greetings from Asbury Park" was produced, it existed in relative obscurity amid the abundant textual landscape of large-letter postcards. That remained the case for a few decades, until a young Bruce Springsteen, then on the verge of signing his first record deal with Columbia Records in 1973, plucked the postcard off a rack by the Asbury Park pier and resolved to appropriate the design for the cover of his first album. According to a report by Kirsty Fraser, Springsteen's plan was met with some resistance by his manager Mike Appel, because Appel knew that Columbia's policy at the time was that all "of Columbia's newly signed stars' debuts featured full-length snaps of the artist. This was to ensure that the music-buying public would latch on to the image of the artist when the singles started hitting the airwaves." What Appel did not know was that Columbia's chief art designer, John Berg, was himself a postcard enthusiast and thus would be receptive to Springsteen's vision, as Fraser explains:

When Appel saw [Springsteen's postcard] idea he thought it disastrous, but allowed Bruce to take it with him to a meeting they had with [Berg]. Appel—thinking that the idea would be shot down instantly—was in for a surprise. For when Bruce pulled the postcard from his pocket to show Berg, he un-knowingly tapped into Berg's love for postcard art. Pulling his very own wad of vintage postcards from a drawer for Bruce to croon over, Berg mulled over the idea of allowing this new artist . . . to deviate from Columbia policy. Bruce won out. The album cover became the colourful, simple design of the words, Greetings from Asbury Park, N.J., with pictures of the pier, beach and waters of the city enclosed within its let-ters. For Bruce, using the postcard was his way of inviting the audience into his world—of introducing his life and the characters within it to the masses.

Here, one assemblage of existing texts, the Tichnor Company's large-letter postcard for Asbury Park, effected new contexts, namely those in which Springsteen and Berg would decades later function as co-composers of the cover art for the album.

With its postcard cover, Springsteen's debut album (Figure 9.15) was released to critical acclaim that paved the way for his future musical and commercial success. As he gained that success, his work and public image were co-opted by various political machinations. Examining that co-opting reveals yet another stage in the lineage of the large-letter assemblage. Springsteen's music functions as a direct appeal to voters in New Jersey, and we can see such appreciation being expressed in a set of homage assemblages that emerged at the time of Chris Christie's reelection as governor in 2013, an homage

Figure 9.15. Cover of Bruce Springsteen's debut album, Columbia Records.

constituting an appropriation not only of Springsteen's fame, but also of the album art that had set the stage for that fame to emerge.

Upon Christie's reelection, his administration sent out email invitations for a celebration to be held in Asbury Park. These invitations contained an image of a large-letter design (Figure 9.16) whose features are both strikingly reminiscent of and divergent from Springsteen's debut, as Cathleen Decker, writing for the *Los Angeles Times*, observes:

> [T]he Republican governor offered a joking homage as he announced that his election night celebration next week would be—where else?—in Asbury Park. . . . The announcement of

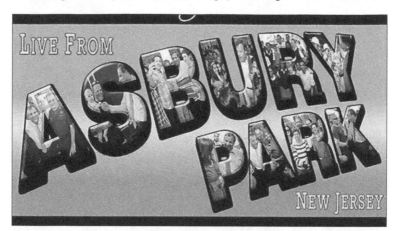

Figure 9.16. Chris Christie invitation design, courtesy of Mykwain Gainey.

Christie's event featured a mock-up, "Live from Asbury Park, New Jersey." Christie's signature is scrawled across the top of the faked postcard, as Springsteen's was on the album cover, and pictures of his face make up the letters, as pictures of Asbury Park did on the cover.

On the day of the celebration, the image was reproduced on a large banner that hung over the front of the venue (Figure 9.17).

CONCLUSION

As I have argued, assemblage thinking helps us see composing as a process that not only has effects in context but that also *effects new contexts*. The multimodal composition of large-letter postcards by Curt Teich & Company in the early 1900s effected new contexts in which new and unpredictable instantiations of the large-letter genre resonated within and across American culture—instantiations that themselves effected new contexts. A steakhouse chain hangs large reproductions of the cards in its dining room to invoke a connection between its food and Americana. The Downtown Improvement Authority for Florida's capital city adapts a seventy-year-old postcard design for a mural on the wall of a vacant downtown

Figure 9.17. Chris Christie banner in place, courtesy of Jake Tapper.

building, establishing a new civic attraction and a new backdrop for photographs and portraits that circulate through social media. A budding rock star incorporates an old postcard into the cover of his album, the design of which is itself adapted for political communications decades later. These instances of composers responding to contexts through assemblage demonstrate the ways in which those contexts were established by the work of previous composers. In this way, assemblage helps us better understand the practice of composing as borrowing from, building on, alluding to, and connecting with works that came before and are to come.

NOTES

1. The Curt Teich Postcard Archives have been housed by the Lake County Discovery Museum in Wauconda, Illinois, since 1982. In 2016, the transfer of the archive's holdings to the Newberry library in Chicago was announced.

2. Teich photo tickets remained consistent throughout the life of the company, so what's true of this example is true of most photo tickets.

3. Teich & Company was one of the only postcard firms to systematically link their serial numbers to dates of production. Beginning in 1930, one could tell what year a Teich postcard was printed simply by looking at the first two digits of the serial number. The letter stands for the decade, starting with A for the 1930s, and the number represents the year in that decade—so that 1A stands for 1931, 4B stands for 1944, and so on.

WORKS CITED

Decker, Cathleen. "Born to Run: Chris Christie Pays Homage to Springsteen." *Los Angeles Times* 29 Oct. 2013: n. pag. Web. 13 Sep. 2016.

Fraser, Kirsty. "Sleeve Stories: Bruce Springsteen's Greetings from Asbury Park." *Sabotage Times* 8 Feb. 2013. Web. 13 Sep. 2016.

Johnson-Eilola, Johndan, and Stuart A. Selber. "Plagiarism, Originality, Assemblage." *Computers and Composition* 24.4 (2007): 375–403. http://dx.doi.org/10.1016/j.compcom.2007.08.003.

Logan's Roadhouse. Home page, n.d. *Logansroadhouse.com*. Web. 15 May 2015.

McElroy, Stephen J. "Assemblage by Design: The Postcards of Curt Teich and Company." *Computers and Composition* 37 (2015): 147–65. http://dx.doi.org/10.1016/j.compcom.2015.07.002.

Santora, Marc. "Christie and Springsteen: A Tale of Devotion, and a Very Public Snub." *New York Times* 15 Jan. 2014: n. pag. Web. 13 Sep. 2016.

Werther, Mark, and Lorenzo Mott. *Linen Postcards: Images of the American Dream*. Wayne: Sentinel, 2002. Print.

Yancey, Kathleen Blake. "Looking for Sources of Coherence in a Fragmented World: Notes toward a New Assessment Design." *Computers and Composition* 21.1 (2004): 89–102. http://dx.doi.org/10.1016/j.compcom.2003.08.024.

10

Multimodal Assemblage, Compositions, and Composing: The Corresponding Cases of Emigrant Cemetery Tombstones and "A Line for Wendy"

Kathleen Blake Yancey

I BEGIN WITH TWO VERY DIFFERENT KINDS OF TEXTS relying on multimodal assemblage, both responding to death. The first is the tombstone, a multimodal material composition assembling verbal and visual fragments borrowing from high culture and low—poetry, biblical verses, religious sculpture, and vernacular visuals. The second is likewise an assembled text, the printed verbal memorial, a composition much like a eulogy, but performed or shared outside a funeral or memorial service. Because of their social nature in commemorating someone's loss, such memorial texts are hospitable to assemblage: they combine memories of many into a single composition unified through multiple modes, chief among them layout and juxtaposition. Here I focus on both dimensions of assemblage, text and process, first analyzing the contributions of assemblage to the tombstones themselves and their provision for the multiple identities of the person lost, and then describing, for one memorial text, its compositional process, especially the principal role that arrangement and layout play and the questions about authorship that are raised. Put succinctly, in

> **Grief is biologically determined.** Mourning is socially constructed. The elaborate artifacts of mourning, the dark reminders of loss, grew from common cultural experience with death, if not comfort with death. It is easy to confuse the two, but it's important not to.

considering how multimodal assemblage helps us understand both memorial compositions and the composing processes that go into them, we also learn more about everyday compositions and composing more generally.

LAYOUT AS COMMON MODE IN
LINEAR AND LYRIC TEXTS

There are many ways one can design a tombstone, one of the more recent using an online tombstone generator. The designer begins by choosing a style, then a kind of material, and then a color, and then drags in texts of various kinds, both verbal and visual: a name, a date, a bird sitting atop the online model. This process isn't difficult, in part because the online generator leads one through it, in part because of the ubiquity of tombstones and more particularly of their layout. Some genres—résumés, memos, and tombstones among them—seem to rely on overly conventionalized layouts that, perhaps unintentionally, lend themselves to borrowed texts that can help fill in the blanks. For such tasks, assemblage composing can provide a helpful, logical response, especially when we compose texts for the first time, or author texts that, like tombstones, we compose infrequently. With a genre's layout functioning as a frame or template, the composer can easily assemble blocks of verbal and visual texts into a new composition, a process through which a composer can simultaneously write within the conventions of a genre and personalize it.

Layout as a mode can also be critical in the verbal memorial in print, as it certainly was in "A Line for Wendy," a memorial text commemorating

A Line for Wendy

This is how I remember Wendy: writer, teacher, writer, mother—listening quietly at the back of a small Seattle Cs session only to gavel us a decade later; e-mailing about her family, her students, her next project and the six after that, and always about you, too; phoning from her beach, ocean waves and laptop keystrokes mingling with her voice over the line; torrenting language as if there would never be enough time for all those words—teacher, writer, mother, leader, writer, friend.
Doug Hesse

Who doesn't remember her first paper-giving experience?
My first: a last slot on Saturday. Three presenters, four audience members:
one friend for each speaker and my major professor.
Wendy Bishop,
"Against the Odds"

Wendy Bishop. In 2003, Jeanne Gunner, editor of *College English,* asked me to write a memorial text for rhetoric and composition scholar Wendy Bishop, who had died the previous month. To compose this text, I invited several of her colleagues and friends to send me "a line in remembrance of Wendy"; those lines became the material, the blocks of text, that I assembled into the print memorial "A Line for Wendy."

At the same time, both genres, the tombstone and the print memorial, also respond to death in different ways, a point made clear though lenses provided by Jennifer Sinor. In "Deserting the Narrative Line: Teaching the Braided Form," Sinor articulates the differences between two kinds of essays, what she calls linear design essays and lyric essays. The linear design essay, Sinor explains,

> assures more than just the inherent logic of the subject under study. Linearity suggests that the subject or the experience has been integrated and understood, and can be rendered as complete. The writer is implying in his choice of form that the parts add up to a whole and that the whole is best understood in relation to time. (189)

This logic governs tombstone compositions: the deceased as subject may not be completely integrated or understood, but tombstones display "parts add[ing] up to a whole," and that "whole is best understood in relation to time," in this case, typically, a birth and death that in bookending life provide one frame for it rendered in a tombstone composition. Put another way, a tombstone composition provides an opportunity to make available and public some kind of complete, if brief, story about the person remembered, and it does so by employing a temporal logic.

In contrast to linear essays, Sinor says, is the lyric essay.

> Often rendered in chunks of text on the page with white space in between, the lyric form behaves more like poetry, leaping from one image-laden paragraph to the next, asking readers to do the work of navigating the white space. The lyric form, like a mosaic, is only whole at a great distance. . . . More importantly, any sense of understanding or wholeness is temporary at best. The subject, the writer implies with the

lyric form, cannot be held; it slips and falls between our fingers, tiny bits of prose raining down like sand. (190)

It's often the case that when we try to make sense of the death of someone—especially someone who is young or whose death is unexpected, and someone about whom we care, especially when death itself isn't comprehensible in any existential way—that sense-making is necessarily contingent, which is what Sinor's lyric essay allows—and privileges. That kind of logic characterizes the memorial I assembled for Wendy.

Here, then, I consider assembled composition as text and assembling composition as process. More specifically, I consider, first, how the assemblage of tombstones provides for multiple identities and, second, how the process of assembling a memorial text relies on very specific modes, chiefly layout and white space, as it raises questions about authorship.

TOMBSTONES IN EMIGRANT CEMETERY, MONTANA

In 1881, Ellen Lee, the infant daughter of Bill Lee, a businessman and rancher in Emigrant, Montana, a small town lying next to the Yellowstone River thirty miles north of Yellowstone National Park, died. As was not uncommon in nineteenth-century rural America, she was buried on her family's property. Seven years later, Ellen's brother died, and he too was buried in the same plot, but what had been the family cemetery had by then become a resting place for other members of the small Emigrant community. That square cemetery, currently about half the size of a football field resting on the top of a hill under the protection of Emigrant Mountain, is, in the jargon of the trade, still active, with 250 graves, the last one created in the spring of 2013. Each burial plot is free, but only if the deceased is related to someone who has taken up residence there; otherwise, regardless of how long one has lived in the Yellowstone River Valley, there is no entry for what we might call posthumous residence.

The cemetery itself is a kind of assemblage, hosting a four-part set of multilayered compositions—first, the composition of the cemetery itself (in its layout, foliage, and so on); second, the tombstone compositions, which are richly multimodal assemblages; third, what I am calling tombstones extended, sites for improvisational compositions including flowers, flags, beer bottles, stickers, and children's toys; and fourth, the collective composition of the cemetery itself, the portrait it makes of the community which created it and which it represents. Inside this assemblage are the tombstones, the product of multiple modes, as suggested by the online site HeadstonesAndMemorials.com; the website lists multiple modes available for the making of meaning, although a single tombstone may employ one, some, or all of them:[1]

1. Color of the tombstone and font
2. Size and thickness of the stone
3. Inserts in the tombstone or figures added to it
4. Single or companion [or family]
5. Font size and style, including capitals and lower case
6. Verbal text, including name, date, epitaph/endearment
7. Borders
8. Graphics/images

Historically, early tombstones in North America, contextualized and assembled largely with religious verbal sentiments and visuals familiar to churches supporting cemeteries, were more uniform in their memorialization of the lost. Later tombstones, especially in community cemeteries like Emigrant Cemetery, often include a mix of the religious and the secular, especially visuals that are regionally oriented: images of mountains frequently occur in Emigrant Cemetery, those images visually echoing the mountains shadowing the cemetery itself and speaking to concerns both personal and collective.

One such tombstone commemorates Mildred J. Busby, a twelve-year-old who died in 1902. Her tombstone, a square block with upper corners rounded, sitting on another block, this one more nearly rectangular, includes a prominently placed visual commonplace, the lamb. Resting on top, the lamb, a Christian icon, sometimes refers to Christ, the Lamb of God, but in the case of children often refers to their innocence. At the top of and centered on the tombstone screen in capital letters are the child's name and the first letter of her middle name—Mildred J.; the next line identifies her in script—"Beloved Daughter of"—and "daughter" is spelled out with the important adjective "beloved" added, fronting the line and thus emphasizing it. Below that are the first initials and the name of the parents, J. & L. Busby, and the next line reporting, in script, "Died Oct. 20, 1902," with the following two lines—"Aged 12 Years 3 Mos"—completing what appears as a sentence functioning almost as a short obituary. Below the tombstone tablet, the space on a tombstone where names and other identifying information is provided, is the lower block, this one with an epitaph, "To live in hearts we leave behind is not to die," a nineteenth-century commonplace borrowed—without attribution—from *Hallowed Ground* (1825), a poem authored by the Scottish poet Thomas Campbell, celebrating both adult love and a life spent in battle. The poem's speaker links mature love, in "a kiss can consecrate the ground / Where mated hearts are mutual bound," to the noble purpose of war, as these two stanzas suggest:

> What hallows ground where heroes sleep?
> 'Tis not the sculptured piles you heap!
> In dews that heavens far distant weep
> Their turf may bloom;
> Or Genii twine beneath the deep
> Their coral tomb.
>
> But strew his ashes to the wind
> Whose sword or voice has served mankind,—
> And is he dead, whose glorious mind
> Lifts thine on high?—
> To live in hearts we leave behind
> Is not to die.

Swords and heroes don't ordinarily provide the context for a lost child, but with assemblage, a fragment of a text, in this case of a

poem appreciating soldiers in war, is employed in a new context—in another country in another time—to memorialize not a soldier fallen in war, but rather a child, now lost. And this instance isn't unique: the same inscription appears on at least one other contemporaneous tombstone in Emigrant Cemetery.[2] Through assemblage, then, we learn about a child's innocence, about her being beloved, and about her "liv[ing] in hearts [left] behind."

In the case of Jeffrey Daniel Counts, a child who died some six decades later, visual assemblage, made more prominent through layout and juxtaposition, represents the child's identities. Jeffrey's tombstone is a multicolored gray, not a standing tombstone but rather a plaque, not quite flush to the ground but mounted on a slab. Nearly the full surface of its rectangular tablet is used, both for identification and for visual allusion; a square, like a card, anchors the tombstone elements, a sun on the right-hand upper corner, a small visual assemblage of children's objects—a sleeping puppy, a rattle, a block with the letters A and J on it—extending out from the lower left corner. At the top of the tablet, the familial identity of Jeffrey is highlighted in sans serif capital letters: "OUR BELOVED SON." On the next line Jeffrey's full name follows, also centered. The next two lines, the font smaller, parallel the dates of birth and death—June 29, 1975, and June 28, 1976—but they begin at the center of the tablet, including and drawing attention to the vi-

sual assemblage on the left. Just under the card-tablet is a unique personal sentiment, in white sans serif lettering, providing another view of Jeffrey as a guiding light: "Our little guiding light whom we miss." In this assemblage, language tells us that Jeffrey's life was short of a year by a single day, that he was beloved, that he lives on as a guiding light, the idea of light visualized and emphasized by the sun in the right-hand corner and the fact of childhood illustrated in the puppy, tiny blocks, and rattle.

In the late twentieth century and into the twenty-first, tombstones in Emigrant Cemetery, much like that for Jeffrey, relied almost exclusively on secular visuals; in addition, they began to incorporate onto the tombstone face, the "tablet" of the tombstone, what had earlier been various smaller fragments dispersed across the full tombstone—identity information, epitaphs, expressions of grief, and visuals. As important is the presence of a new visual aesthetic articulating individual, community, and geographical features, as is evident in the tombstone for Joseph Karnes. Currently the most recent tombstone in Emigrant Cemetery, Karnes's tombstone is also the most scenic: the tablet has incorporated all elements of the tombstone, using a mountain range of the kind specific to its geographical area as its chief visual, one dominating the tablet and underscoring the name. Acting together with the name Karnes, in two-color block letters with one color providing an outline, the mountains govern the scene, which includes an assemblage of trees, a river, a couple riding on horseback, and a moose, then two "cards" with identifying information and a banner announcing a marriage date. The scene itself is both generic and specific. A mountain scene, it could likely represent any number of places featuring mountains, a river, and mountain wildlife; at the same time, the Yellowstone River runs adjacent to Emigrant, which itself is located in the Yellowstone River Valley. For both area and tombstone, the river is a defining feature, as are the mountains. The couple on horseback, riding into the mountains as though into an afterlife, is also interesting, evoking but replacing the single riderless horse more common on tombstones, with a visual that is (1) more collective and (2) more oriented to life than to death. The back of the

tombstone includes a rose, a conventional visual icon typically referring to love, in this case probably commenting on the couple's relationship. Seen in this assemblage, Joseph Karnes is a devoted husband with a long marriage, an outdoors enthusiast with a love for the valley and its mountains; the idea, as we saw in Mildred's case, that "To live in hearts we leave behind / Is not to die" appears here as a visual, the two riders traveling together toward the mountains.

The three tombstones just described thus support two observations about assemblage in a particular corner of the world, that is, in the context of tombstones and cemeteries. First, Emigrant Cemetery's assembled tombstones are changing the relationships between modes: they are becoming more visual than verbal. We learn about Mildred chiefly from language, from Jeffrey from language and visuals, from Joseph chiefly from visuals. Second, the visuals themselves draw from a wide range of sources, more conventional visuals like a lamb and a rose, and newer, more literal vernacular visuals like the moose and the mountains. Increasingly, tombstones in Emigrant, like that of Joseph, represent the personal, the symbolic, and the local, each in the contexts of the others. As these examples literally illustrate, tombstones thus are a kind of assemblage—in the language of Johndan Johnson-Eilola and Stuart Selber—"texts built primarily and explicitly from existing texts in order to solve a writing or communication problem in a new context" (381). Like the person being memorialized, each tombstone is unique. Each tombstone is, though, also linked to others—through multiple kinds of multimodality, Scottish poetry, religious icons, and/or conventional layouts. In re-presenting through multiple fragments, tombstones are both personal and public, providing a site representing others (1) in the public context of a cemetery and

(2) through a unique assemblage of smaller fragmented texts often borrowed from elsewhere, and thus linking to that elsewhere, that (3) collectively show the multiple identities of those lost.

TOMBSTONE ASSEMBLAGE AS SANCTIONED PRACTICE

It's also not surprising, of course, that texts like tombstones[3] have relied on assemblage given the many different ways that such borrowing has been encouraged. For example, in the colonial period of the United States, many, perhaps most, cemeteries were connected to churches; the purpose of tombstones in these cemeteries wasn't only to commemorate the dead, but also to caution all who encountered the tombstones about what was the proper way to live—and what was not. In creating a tombstone, there was thus both the influence of other tombstones, which served as models, and of religious institutions, whose symbolic resources—visuals of angels and skulls, fragments of Scripture—could be rendered materially. Likewise, in secular contexts, such borrowing was also encouraged, and instruction and samples provided, for example, in guides like *Hill's Manual of Social and Business Forms*. Contextualized in *Hill's Manual,* such guidance included the advice preceding a list of epitaphs suitable for borrowing and assembling:

> The very inscription on tomb-stones may appropriately be accompanied by an epitaph, which should be expressive yet very brief. Formerly it was customary oftentimes to inscribe several stanzas of poetry upon the headstone. With the improved taste of later years, however, it is considered best to condense the epitaph into a few words, usually not exceeding four lines in length. (299)

Even today, those composing tombstones are advised, as are eulogists, to borrow freely and to adapt:

> Please feel free to use these in any way you like, you may find it useful to pull out certain key terms and phrases which you can then build around, you may also find that you can use whole paragraphs with just some minor alterations and adjustments. (FuneralHelper.com)

Unlike the case in school, then, where "us[ing] whole paragraphs
with some minor alterations and adjustments" is considered plagiarism, here the practice is not only allowed but also encouraged.
Moreover, to encourage such borrowing and assembling, a shared
set of texts, verbal and visual, is provided—in historic guides like
Hill's Manual and more recent guides like online tombstone gen-
erators; the working assumption of these guides is that it is through
such borrowing and assembling that we memorialize the dead. In
sum, assemblage is a central composing practice for tombstones,
one culturally sanctioned and endorsed; one supporting linkages
between the deceased, their loved ones, and multiple religious and
secular communities; and one providing for multiple identities.[4]

A LINE FOR WENDY: LYRICAL ARRANGEMENT
AND THE ISSUE OF AUTHORSHIP

Wendy Bishop—professor at Florida State University, former chair
of the Conference on College Composition and Communication,
and scholar in rhetoric and composition—died on November 21,
2003. In agreeing to memorialize Wendy for *College English,* I understood that this writing task offered both a way to honor a friend
and a means of mourning, and quickly: the text needed to be submitted by the end of the year, in less than a month. The question
for me was how to write such a text, my response to call on an
assemblage-composing process, one I describe here, highlighting
especially three dimensions of the process: (1) the role of multiple
voices in creating a lyrical portrait; (2) the role of layout, white
space, and juxtaposition in the making of meaning; and (3) the role
of multiple authorship as critical to assemblage of all kinds.

During my initial thinking about how to go about writing a
memorial text, I recalled the responses of *Time* magazine to two
similar and yet dissimilar exigencies, the unexpected death of Prin-

PRINCESS DIANA, 1961-1997: THE SADDEST FAIRY TALE (Special Report / PRINCESS DIANA, 1961-1997)

PRINCESS DIANA, 1961-1997: BLOOD ON THEIR HANDS? (Special Report / PRINCESS DIANA, 1961-1997)

HER DEATH IS SURE TO INFLAME THE WAR ON THE PAPARAZZI

PRINCESS DIANA, 1961-1997: DODI AL FAYED: DIANA'S UNLIKELY SUITOR (Special Report / PRINCESS DIANA, 1961-1997)

DODI AL FAYED, SCION TO AN EGYPTIAN FORTUNE, WAS A MAN WITH A PAST

PRINCESS DIANA, 1961-1997: DIANA: THE PRINCESS OF HEARTS (Special Report / PRINCESS DIANA, 1961-1997)

EVEN AFTER SHE LOST THE TITLE, DIANA WAS TRULY HER ROYAL HIGHNESS

PRINCESS DIANA, 1961-1997: AN EVENING OUT WITH DIANA (Special

cess Diana in 1997 and the anticipated death of Mother Teresa a week later. In memorializing the two women, *Time* took very different tacks. In the case of Mother Teresa, it employed what Sinor would call a linear design approach, perceiving the coherence of her life in her missionary work, as narrativized by coauthors Subir Bhaumik, Meenakshi Ganguly, and Tim McGirk: "She was beloved as helper to the lowest of the low. But she protested that she could do no less—since she saw her God in each of them."

Time's response to Princess Di's death also exemplified the world's view of her, which, from a Sinorian perspective, was considerably less linear, more ambiguous than certain. Framing Diana's life in two competing questions exemplifies the kind of conundrum *Time* sought to explore: was Diana the altruistic campaigner for human rights, in contexts varying from AIDS to war, or was she the manipulator that Buckingham Palace rightly sought to distance itself from? Taking up such questions, *Time* offered a suite of authors, each taking a different perspective, collectively creating an assemblaged view of Di.

In Wendy's case, it was easier to make sense of her life than of her death: her life, as those who knew her could attest, was abundant. The question was how that abundance might be expressed and from whose perspective. Would a coherent, linear view, as in the case of Mother Teresa, best serve the rhetorical need? Or, as in the case of Princess Di, would multiple perspectives speak more fully to the life lived? I decided that rather than attempt a linear narrative as memorial text, it would be wiser to speak to the Wendy many knew and to do so in the specific voices of her friends and colleagues, that in such a process these voices would articulate a collective memory and contribute material for a lyrical portrait. With that as my intent, I emailed several people, asking them to send me "a line for Wendy," my aim to compose these lines assemblage-like into a memorial text.

My first task of assemblage composing this print memorial, then, was to identify possible texts, which in this case required me to identify colleagues and friends of Wendy's and contact them, both friends I knew and those, like Lad Tobin, I didn't. Wendy's friends responded quickly, graciously, generously. Given my colleagues' contributions, my next task involved selection, revision, and arrangement: selecting which of those texts to use, possibly trimming or revising them, and then arranging them. In inviting each contributor, I had committed to use at least some of the text he or she had shared; the question was how much. My preference, in the spirit of Sinor's vocal mosaic, was for less rather than more, but also for fragments of about the same size and substance so that all would equally contribute; my preference was also to identify lines that would collectively represent Wendy as fully as possible.

Having selected a set of fragments, I next focused on their arrangement. Likely tacitly influenced by related genres like obituaries and tombstones, I first considered a chronological approach, which the selections supported: memories spanned a wide swath of time. Still, given the intent of this memorial text, its evocation of Wendy from multiple perspectives, chronology didn't seem apt. A second approach was to bring the fragmented memories into dialogue with one another, relying on Sinor's more lyrical, associative logic, and relying as well on meaning-making white space, as Sinor suggests: "Often rendered in chunks of text on the page with white space in between, the lyric form behaves more like poetry, leaping from one image-laden paragraph to the next, asking readers to do the work of navigating the white space." I decided on the second approach and began arranging and rearranging these smaller texts.

Trying to create such an assemblage was not easy.[5] A first step was trying to decide where on the pages fragments would go and how they might articulate with each other. In an early draft, for example, I had placed Carrie Leverenz's contribution adjacent to Lad Tobin's:

Although her contributions to the field of Composition are indisputable, like many in our field, she had to fight for recognition from her own department. And fight she did. She fought against the drastic increase of teaching assistants, from seventy to more than a hundred. She fought to make the directorship of the Reading/ Writing Center a tenure-track position—which became mine. She fought, albeit unsuccessfully, to keep me from being denied tenure.

I used to read Wendy's textbooks, chapbooks, professional books, essays, edited collections, ethnographic studies, keynote presentations, and e-mail messages and ask myself, "How could anyone possibly write this much that is this good?" But as I watched her over the years with her students, friends, and family, I realized the real question: "How could anyone possibly write this much that is this good and still be so available, supportive, and loving to so many other people?"

What was emphasized in this sequence, it seemed to me,[6] was a set of abstractions, important but not juxtapositional, not sufficiently contrastive, too alike. Dissatisfied, I moved Lad's text to later in the assemblage and replaced it with a fragment from Pavel Zemliansky, in part because he was one of Wendy's advisees, echoing Carrie's reference to Wendy's students, in part because of the juxtapositional contrast between Carrie's more philosophical account and Pavel's vivid image of the Ukrainian flag hoisted over Wendy's house at Alligator Point:

Although her contribu-
tions to the field of Composition are indisputable,
like many in our field, she
had to fight for recognition
from her own department.
And fight she did. She
fought against the drastic
increase of teaching assistants, from seventy to more
than a hundred. She fought
to make the directorship of
the Reading/Writing Center
a tenure-track position—
which became mine. She
fought, albeit unsuccess-
fully, to keep me from being
denied tenure.

I always looked forward to
talking with Wendy because
she took such deep interest
in the lives of others, both
professionally and outside
of teaching and writing.
One summer, when I was
going to visit my native
Ukraine, Wendy asked me
to bring her a Ukrainian
flag: little did I know that
she would fly it over her
beach house.

For more than seven drafts, I moved blocks of text from one site on a page to another, from one page to another, important compositional moves in creating a memorial mosaic.

At some point in these processes of selecting, revising, arranging, and rearranging, it occurred to me that we might also include Wendy's voice, that if we incorporated her voice *into* the assemblage, her verbal presence, juxtaposed with those of friends, students, colleagues, and mentees, would counterpoint and resonate with those other voices, that, in fact, this fuller set of voices, including Wendy's, would together compose the textual fabric of the memorial. We would hear her talking to all of us in the context of others' words and, in those verbal moments, hear her living. Choosing Wendy's fragments—reading over her published work and her emails to me to identify them—was yet another part of this composing process, as was weaving each into the composition so that it was made whole.

This assemblage-composing involved three other issues. First, as illustrated above, the arrangement is itself a significant site of meaning making, and it relies on the

> I think what I loved most about Wendy was her passion—the way she embraced a worthwhile argument, her writing, her teaching, her research, and the people she loved.
> Deborah Coxwell Teague

I have this eerie feeling that I'll open my mailbox one day and find an e-mail from her. Probably something to Lad Tobin and me with the title line "hey you two."

She'd be writing, of course, and she'd make some joke about having more time for that now. Then she'd tell us how proud she is of Morgan and Tait and how she can't imagine having gone through this fall without Dean and she'd ask about our lives and joke about when the three of us will get together again.

I hear her voice as easily as I hear Lad's or my own. She's thinking about a new book on writing across the cosmos, and she wants us all to contribute something. Libby Rankin

multimodality of white space and layout; the white space needed both to link blocks of text and to provide space between them. As a consequence, the recursive process of arranging textual fragments, reviewing white space, and rearranging fragments was critical. Second, it wasn't clear whether or not "A Line for Wendy" should have an introduction. On the one hand, providing some context would be useful for the reader, and in an early draft I used the invitation I'd sent to participants as an opening frame to establish the text's purpose. On the other hand, allowing the text to speak for itself, much as does a tombstone, could draw the reader in, and an inviting voice setting the tone and hinting at the larger purpose might be more rhetorical, more invitational. Doug Hesse's "This is how I remember Wendy: writer, teacher, writer, mother . . . " (581), speaking to his own memory but suggesting the larger purpose of commemoration, offered such a lead.

Third was the issue of authorship and attribution. "A Line for Wendy" has no author claiming it, nor did I identify one when I submitted the text for publication. Someone at NCTE decided on authorship for bibliographical purposes: all the contributors are listed. Inside the text, I initially had no names identifying textual fragments, though to designate Wendy's prose I had italicized it. In reading the full text with all the fragments anonymous, however, I found it confusing. Thus to create a collectively voiced memorial text both lyrical and coherent, I (as)signed each fragment an author, a shift that also more clearly established the dialogues.

Intentionally built from textual fragments contributed by many, including Wendy Bishop, "A Line for Wendy" is a textual assemblage memorializing her loss by intermingling her voice and ours in a vocal mosaic.

CODA

As a composing practice, assemblage—which, as memorial texts demonstrate, has a long history—has seemed a contradiction in terms: though often pilloried in sites like the classroom, it is valued in other sites like the workplace. In fact, the view of those contributing to this volume is rooted in a sense that assemblage composing is, increasingly, practiced almost everywhere *except* school. As important, what we see here is that assemblage is a part of everyday writing practices, and more specifically a part of the everyday writing practices we use to remember those we have lost. For centuries, tombstones have included assemblage composing of a linear kind, borrowing freely, remixing the words of loved ones with those of poets and prophets, combining religious visuals with the vernacular. More recently, in another memorial text, "A Line for Wendy," assemblage composing included many authors, including Wendy herself, to create a lyrical commemorative mosaic. In both practices, memory is represented and created through an assemblage speaking to multiple contexts, views, heartaches.

Assemblage composing is the foundation of both kinds of memorial texts.

NOTES

1. Some of the tombstones, especially ones for children in the nineteenth and early twentieth centuries, are quite plain, as two clearly demonstrate, those for Oliver and for Baby Munroe. On Oliver's tombstone, only a year is provided, presumably the year of death; meaning is made through a symmetrical layout, the sans serif lowercase font used for "son," keyed to a relationship with parents, juxtaposed with the serif font in all capital letters identifying the particular son Oliver. In both these

tombstones—son Oliver and Baby Munroe—font style and size matter, as does layout, but no visuals adorn the tombstones, nor is any epitaph or sentiment provided.

2. Its use continues today as well, on television shows as well as on blogs: see Yancey.

3. Other ritualistic texts, like wedding invitations, also rely on assemblage, as *Hill's Manual* makes very clear.

4. Other cemeteries privilege other communities. In Denver's Fairmount Cemetery, an upper-class cemetery hosting more than a hundred thousand tombstones, for example, it's common for the deceased to include markers of professional achievement ranging from PhDs to BSNs and MDs. In San Mateo's St. John's cemetery, the tombstones are richly linguistic, often including English and a second language—Chinese, Japanese, Spanish, or Portuguese—on the tablet; more recent tombstones include visuals keyed to hobbies, among them palettes, golf clubs, and tennis rackets.

5. And I'm not at all sure that I succeeded.

6. Another issue with assemblage composing, as suggested here, is what the logic of a given assemblage is.

WORKS CITED

Bhaumik, Subir, Meenakshi Ganguly, and Tim McGirk. "Seeker of Souls." *Time* 15 Sep. 1997: n. pag. Web. 13 Sep. 2016.

FuneralHelper.org. Web. 13 Sep. 2016.

HeadstonesandMemorials.com. Web. 13 Sep. 2016.

Hill, Thomas E. *Hill's Manual of Social and Business Forms: A Guide to Correct Writing*. Chicago: Warren, 1879. Print.

Johnson-Eilola, Johndan, and Stuart A. Selber. "Plagiarism, Originality, Assemblage." *Computers and Composition* 24.4 (2007): 375–403. http://dx.doi.org/10.1016/j.compcom.2007.08.003.

"A Line for Wendy." *College English* 66.6 (2004): 581–84. *ProQuest*. Web. 23 Oct. 2016.

Sinor, Jennifer. "Deserting the Narrative Line: Teaching the Braided Form." *Teaching English in the Two-Year College* 42.2 (2014): 188–96. *ProQuest*. Web. 23 Oct. 2016.

Yancey, Kathleen Blake. "Tombstones, QR Codes, and the Circulation of Past Present Texts." *Circulation, Rhetoric, and Writing*. Ed. Laurie Gries and Collin Brooke. Logan: Utah State UP, 2018.

11

An Ethics of Assemblage: Creative Repetition and the "Electric Pow Wow"

Kristin L. Arola and Adam Arola

> Q: What is your goal when you sample images or references to indigenous people from Hollywood movies or pop songs?
> Bear Witness: *Reclaim, repurpose, and reuse.*
>
> Q: Is it ever strange to bring music that samples traditional music into a club setting?
> Bear Witness: *I don't think it's strange. . . . As for some people thinking it's disrespectful, we're not remixing any honor songs. I used to be a traditional drummer and understand that the pow wow was meant to be a gathering and showcasing of each other's music. Think of it as traditional 2.0.*
> ("Q&A with Powwowstep Pioneers A Tribe Called Red")

Kristin: IT WASN'T THAT LONG AGO WHEN I FIRST heard traditional powwow music mixed with rap. My brother, my coauthor and also a club DJ, sent me a mix including a portion of the track "Get It Up" by Santigold featuring M.I.A. and Gorilla Zoe. I was jogging when the song hit my ears. A steady rhythm of a powwow drum— tha-thump, tha-thump, tha-thump—crescendoing into Gorilla Zoe's deep bass laugh—mwaa heh heh heh. A group of powwow singers kicks in—aaayaa aaayaa aaayaa hey hey. The drumbeat continues, my pace follows the beat, my heart is happy. Gorilla Zoe's rap kicks in. "Hood nigga, I keep the purp by the pound . . . I keep a bad bitch around . . . " Wait, what?

My jogging nearly comes to a halt. Is this OK? I picture our mother, an Anishinaabe jingle dress powwow dancer. What would she think? What would the tribe think? Is this assemblage OK? I love the sound of the drum at pow wows, the heartbeat that keeps the dancers moving, and in spite of myself I pick up my pace and continue to jog to the beat. Tha-thump, tha-thump, tha-thump.

Adam: As a club DJ I have come to attend to music on an exceptionally pragmatic level: will this song make people dance? What else can I mix it with? How will it facilitate my ability to move between genres or BPMs during my set? I am also always self-serving as a DJ, insofar as I can get away with it, and I have a long-standing love of percussion. Few things are as likely to make me dance as a good dancehall riddim. Just as my sister noted, this has always also included for me traditional tribal drumming of the powwow variety. I experience these rhythmic patterns as tapping into something deeper than the culturally inherited norms of what makes for a good dance record. Accordingly, I am always fast to incorporate any song into my sets that pulls from these musical traditions if I see it fulfilling a necessary function on the dance floor.

As a philosopher who is concerned with issues of culture, I am often at loggerheads with myself when confronted with songs, or even whole subgenres of dance music, that pull from more traditional, culturally specific musical styles—in particular when the music or musical elements being appropriated come from the global South or American Indian musical traditions. The Santigold track my sister referred to earlier is a perfect example. Insofar as the song itself was put together by world-renowned and highly respected DJ and producer Diplo, who as far as global-music connoisseurs go is generally respectful and thoughtful with regard to the traditions he may appear to be plundering, I was initially quite excited about the prospect of incorporating this track into my sets.[1] What I couldn't account for in the particular assemblage that emerged when I first played this song in the club was the response of the clubgoers. Regardless of how thoughtful Diplo may have been in his incorporating traditional powwow music into what is essentially a club rap song, this meant nothing with regard to the response of the crowd. I will never forget playing this track for the first time on a Saturday night at a club with about a thousand patrons. Rather than falling into the rhythm as I had hoped might happen, large swaths of the crowd started mimicking powwow dance, clapping their hands over their mouths to the beat while vaguely hopping around and making mock headdress feathers with their hands. Imagine cultural lowlights such as Don Armando's disco version of "I'm an Indian Too," and you may form a picture of what I witnessed.

∿

Adam is a philosopher interested in philosophical psychology, race, and issues concerning novelty and authenticity in post-Kantian thought. He is also a professional club DJ and producer. Kristin is a compositionist who finds herself often looking to indigenous crafting practices in order to reconsider multimodal production. Through our mother, we are descendants of the Keweenaw Bay Indian Community in Upper Michigan, and we are both what locals often call Finndian—a mix of Ojibwe/Anishinaabe and Finlander, a common mix in our homeland and perhaps an assemblage in its own right. We use this opportunity to suggest that conceiving of composition as assemblage, and assemblage as creative repetition—a process of repeating that pays homage without insisting upon essences—opens spaces for rhetorical sovereignty (Lyons, "Rhetorical"). As such, creative repetition both acknowledges Native people's right to develop notions of their own identity through textual production and helps provide an ethical framework for engaging with assemblage theory.

A BRIEF ATTEMPT AT DEFINITION: CREATIVE REPETITION AND THE ASSEMBLAGE

The objective in this section is twofold. First, we briefly introduce the concept of creative repetition as a key component of assemblage, one that provides a way of adjudicating between good and bad assemblages. Second, we intend to show how the epistemological and ontological framework that undergirds much indigenous culture offers a model for considering good/productive assemblages, a point that the second half of this essay unpacks through the case of A Tribe Called Red, a First Nations electronic music group that blends traditional powwow music with musical elements from hip-hop, dubstep, moombahton, and more.

In an attempt to describe a benchmark for a good/productive assemblage, one that embraces and enacts the creation of novelty, we are using the concept of creative repetition. Creative repetition is simply a more succinct manner of gathering Deleuze's notion that true repetition is "difference without a concept" (*Difference* 13). For our purposes, creative repetition is repetition without an essence. It serves as a measuring stick one can employ to adjudicate between good and bad assemblages. As a concept it helps answer the question: how can one repeat cultural gestures while maintaining the continuity and identity of culture without insisting on an essence to which one is beholden?

The issue of creative repetition is anchored in Deleuze's ontology as presented in *Difference and Repetition*. For Deleuze, human beings' general attitude toward repetition is based on an ontology dominated by a concept of being as self-sameness, wherein to repeat means to replicate in an identical manner. However, insofar as Deleuze creates an ontology wherein being is nothing more than a momentary freezing of the infinite process of becoming, repetition for him can never be repetition of the same as such. Repetition of the same is governed by nostalgia and is what Deleuze calls "bare repetition"; imagine one insisting that the only proper way to honor one's tradition as an Ojibwe is to perform a fancy dance at a pow wow in the exact same way as your ancestors. Here one has become enslaved or subjugated to an image of identity that has frozen time and treats oneself as the instantiation of some preexisting essence.

In contrast with bare repetition (performing a dance the precise same way as your ancestors), creative repetition in this case would be to harness the expressive and disruptive force of the pow wow itself insofar as it creates new prospective territories for becoming. This requires that one repeat consistently, but not dogmatically. To repeat dogmatically would be to try to "get everything right," as if there were a transcendent pow wow in the sky that one must mimic. To repeat creatively but consistently requires that one repeat by attending to the specificities of the current milieu, so as to create new ways of thinking and experiencing in the present circumstance, but disrupt in a manner that resonates with disruptions or deterritorializations caused by pow wows of the past.

To understand how we are using creative repetition, it is important to understand the active nature of Deleuze and Félix Guattari's assemblage, as developed in *A Thousand Plateaus*. An assemblage is not merely a collection of otherwise passive objects being thrown together. Such a definition of assemblage removes the active character of the creation itself while also taking for granted an ontological framework wherein static objects existed and were ripe for the picking. The concept of assemblage for Deleuze and Guattari is understood precisely in juxtaposition to any manner of thinking that posits something (the author, the object) as transcendent. Whereas our traditional tropes of identity assume self-sameness, consistency, permanence, and, most important, essence, an assemblage is alive and active, in flux and flight. It is the permanence of becoming. Moreover, the work of assemblage aims at ridding us of the concept of any subject of action that could be characterized as standing as the lone agent relative to the passive material of experience. There is no agent or subject standing over and against a world of objects that is passive and manipulable as one would see fit.[2]

Creative repetition opens up a new manner of both considering the ethical implications of assemblage and discussing the ontological and epistemological commitments made manifest in indigenous culture. What marks off the space of identity in Ojibwe culture specifically is what Scott Lyons (*X-Marks*) characterizes as the consistency of an "ethnie," which is to be understood as a pattern of behavior, a manner of comportment, a set of habits that are expressions of a particular milieu that may change and grow over time all the while retaining a degree of continuity at the level of function and action (52). As Mark Bonta and John Protevi put it, "[O]ne should look to the openness to novelty of each assemblage, the way it invites new connections with other assemblages" (55). Our contention is that Deleuze and Guattari's concept of assemblage can serve as a conceptual bridge between indigenous concerns and the goals of the composition classroom. This bridge, one built on the

foundation of creative repetition, encourages us to consider experiential novelty, transformational ways of evaluating, tasking, acting,
and living, all the while attending to concerns of appropriation.
Not all assemblages are good assemblages.

RHETORICAL SOVEREIGNTY AND
COMPOSING CREATIVE REPETITION

We believe composition and rhetoric has much to gain from understanding assemblage as creative repetition, yet we want to avoid
an understanding of assemblage where cultural appropriation can
enter under the auspices of a remix ethos. Repurposing a Salish
woodcut print of a salmon into an informational video on salmon restoration is a very different act from repurposing a biologi-
cal drawing of a Pacific salmon—the former runs a high risk of
the negative reappropriation of a culturally specific text. A good
assemblage, one that functions through creative repetition, would
acknowledge this distinction.

Johndan Johnson-Eilola and Stuart Selber's definition of assemblage only works if we understand texts as active entities, inherently relational in nature, *and* if we understand the responsiveness of
the assemblage as one that is innovative and productive. Consider
Geoffrey Sirc's argument that digital literacy calls writing teachers to consider the value of "short, well-chosen bricks of meaning"
(70). In considering what makes for a good/productive assemblage,
we suggest a focus on the "well-chosen." An assemblage in Deleuzian terms is not a collection of passive objects, but instead a purposeful gathering of already active objects within a new neighborhood, a new context. Therefore, assemblage in and of itself isn't
inherently good, for "[n]othing's good in itself, it all depends on
careful systematic use" (*Negotiations* 32). What we want to bring to
the fore within composition's discussion of the assemblage is that
while assemblage can afford students with seemingly exciting new
communication options, not all assemblages are transformative.

Lyons's work on rhetorical sovereignty is useful when we consider the potentials and pitfalls of including assemblage in the composition classroom. Lyons asks, "What do American Indians want
from writing?" His answer is "rhetorical sovereignty," that is, "the

inherent right and ability of *peoples* to determine their own communicative needs and desires in this pursuit, to decide for themselves the goals, modes, styles, and languages of public discourse" ("Rhetorical" 449). In composition studies this concept is often misused to suggest an individual, instead of collective, sense of agency. There are two key points from Lyons often brushed over that are important for thinking about assemblage.

First, Lyons's definition of rhetorical sovereignty specifies that it is the inherent right of *peoples*, plural. For Lyons, the individual's communication acts gain importance as they are understood as furthering, and positively transforming and sustaining, the group's culture (455). We suggest that keeping both the idea of *peoples* and *culturing* in mind when working with the rhetorical potential of assemblages encourages a richer understanding of both purpose and audience. That is, if one chooses to compose an assemblage, a leading question should be, "Why, and whom does this benefit?" There is, then, a collective ethical obligation. "Rather than representing an enclave, sovereignty here is the ability to assert oneself renewed—in the presence of others" (457). In this act of asserting oneself and rebuilding in the presence of others, Lyons says, and we agree, that "[i]t is always the 'we'—not the 'I'—that concerns me most" (461). While students may become excited about remixing texts, they need to move from the "I," that is, in the next cool new zoomy thing they can remix out of preexisting objects, and instead focus on the "we," that is, on the question of whom this cool new thing benefits.

Second, Lyons acknowledges that rhetorical sovereignty works to revive a people's possibilities and continuance. When considering assemblage, his notion of "possibility" is quite important. "Attacks on sovereignty are attacks on what it enables us to pursue; the pursuit of sovereignty is an attempt to revive not our past, but our possibilities" (449). Here, Lyons suggests "the possible" as an outcome of communication, resonating with John Poulakos's definition of rhetoric as an "art that seeks to capture in opportune moments that which is appropriate and attempts to suggest that which is possible" (36).

Through the lens of rhetorical sovereignty, creative repetition necessarily includes a sense of cultur*ing*, one that is done for the "we," and one that suggests a way of moving forward, of producing more culture, more life. There should be, then, qualifiers of what counts as a good representation, a good writing act, and by proxy, a good assemblage. In this spirit, we propose the following criteria for engaging with assemblage as creative repetition:

- A good assemblage is responsive, responding to situations and enacting new functions;
- a good assemblage is innovative and productive;
- a good assemblage is novel, opening up new ways of thinking, seeing, and living; and
- a good assemblage does all of this with a focus on the "we" as opposed to the "I," always considering, "Whom does this assemblage benefit?"

Returning to Lyons's question, "What do American Indians want from writing?" he suggests, "I hope to have identified a few things Indians generally do *not* want from writing: stereotypes, cultural appropriations, exclusion, ignorance, irrelevance, rhetorical imperialism" (462). What is at stake here "are the peoples defined by the writing itself; thus one important tenet of rhetorical sovereignty would be to allow Indians to have some say about the nature of their textual representations. The best way to honor this creed would be to have Indian people themselves do the writing, but it might also be recognized that *some representations are better than others,* whoever the author" (458, emphasis ours).

The world is not full of concepts just waiting to be plucked from their contexts. Concepts carry with them the resonance of their contexts. So while Diplo may have had good intentions remixing the Santigold track with a powwow song, that powwow song carries with it a cultural specificity that, when understood by outsiders to that culture (the clubgoers the night Adam played the track), is lost, the song itself reterritorialized through the lens of a fixed essence of what an Indian is and does. In this way, it is not a creative repetition but a bare repetition, a replication of the same colonized understanding of Native culture. Such bare repetition grants us precisely all the things Native folks *do not want* from writing.

As described earlier, a bare repetition would assume that an identity such as Ojibwe could only be upheld through a precise reenactment of past cultural activities, whereas a creative repetition would attend to the specificities of the current milieu so as to create new ways of thinking and experiencing. In such moments of deterritorialization, no essence is made manifest. Rather a particular tendency of becoming is expressed in a moment of actualization, wherein our culturing—which is always a historical process; we *are* our history after all—is what is made manifest. Our style is what provides consistency, and it is also what permits us to improvise without losing all sense of identity. As Deleuze and Guattari put it, "one launches forth, hazards an improvisation. But to improvise is to join with the World, or meld with it. One ventures from home on the thread of a tune" (*A Thousand Plateaus* 311). We suggest that A Tribe Called Red ventures from home in exactly this manner, through a process of creative repetition that attends to the broad historical circumstances of their milieu. As such, they serve, at least in outline, as an example of what a well-formed assemblage ought to look like and do.

A TRIBE CALLED RED, CREATIVE REPETITION IN ACTION

Compeau took a loop from a pow wow song. Bear Witness put a beat under it. That's when, Bear Witness says, they tapped into cultural identity and power, and it all clicked. "*It was the reaction from the aboriginal people in the crowd, where they'd take over the dance floor. This is us now.*"
—David Sommerstein, "Beats and Politics at A Tribe Called Red's 'Electric Pow Wow'"

A Tribe Called Red (ATCR) is a group of three First Nations men (Bear Witness, DJ NDN, and DJ Shub) with deep ties to their respective communities and a profound concern for issues of identity and propriety. They are explicitly concerned with fans wearing what they refer to as "redface" at performances and have performed at festivals where they ask organizers to ban the wearing of what they refer to as "hipster headdresses" (Risk). They have an explicit concern for the idea that it is possible to exhibit oneself as indigenous in a manner that is not anchored in any form of essentialism, cultural voyeurism, or, as Deleuze and Guattari would call it, transcendence (*What Is Philosophy?* 15–34).

ATCR serves as a nearly perfect example of the nuances at work in understanding assemblage as creative repetition. They are involved in a creative process that pulls its influences from wide and disparate terrains, fusing together seemingly wildly incompatible genres of music, thereby generating novelty through creating connections in light of the "image of thought" that they bring to bear on experience. Further, the fact that they are a popular act, headlining festivals all over the world, brings their creative process and its set of relations into further contact with an audience whose expectations, engagements, and reactions lie outside of their own control. As such, we look to ATCR through the lens of creative repetition, exploring how ATCR's texts attend to the specificities of the current milieu so as to create new ways of thinking and experiencing while also disrupting or deterritorializing. This lens allows us to ask of ATCR's assemblages a multipart question that embodies our criteria for a productive assemblage: "Why this assemblage, what community does it benefit, and how does this act of culturing produce or encourage transformation?"

Indigenous communities are concerned about negative cultural reappropriation. Such acts, as Lyons suggests in describing what American Indians *do not want* from writing, include "stereotypes, cultural appropriations, exclusion, ignorance, irrelevance, rhetorical imperialism" ("Rhetorical" 462). Images such as the Washington Redskins and the Cleveland Indians provide an example of the type of image *not* wanted, particularly when it is composed by and authored for non-Natives. Consider also the hipster headdress worn by concertgoers at large music festivals, or fashion designer Paul Frank's 2012 "Dream Catchin' with Paul Frank" "pow wow," which the *Hollywood Reporter* described as "a neon–Native American powwow theme. Glow-in-the-dark war-painted employees in feather headbands and bow and arrows invited guests to be photographed on a mini-runway holding prop tomahawks" (Garcia). We feel fairly confident saying these are examples of what American Indians *do not want* from assemblage. These assemblages do not enact a creative repetition. They do nothing more than repeat preexisting, essentialized tropes of identity, born of an image of thought that treats indigenous populations not simply as subjugated persons, but more drastically as objects stripped of a world of their own. However, this is not to say that indigenous texts cannot be put into assemblage in a productive way. As opposed to a hipster headdress or Frank's "Dream Catchin'" "pow wow," the assemblages put forth by A Tribe Called Red enact a creative repetition, one worth examining when considering how to foster productive assemblages.

ATCR are recording artists, yet the true force of their project comes to the fore in live performances. In 2013, Adam attended an ATCR performance in Portland, Oregon. While on stage, the group's members all handled different tasks: NDN and Shub took turns on the turntables and midi controllers, playing and reconstructing ATCR originals alongside electronic dance music hits. These hits were remixed live, often while Shub manipulated recordings of traditional indigenous songs over the beats. All the while, Bear Witness mixed movie segments and still photos, twisting and distorting in various ways to accompany the music. These images were projected on multiple walls of the club interior.

The fusion of traditional tribal rhythms with contemporary, bass-heavy beats of multiple genres in and of itself created a novel manner of hearing dance music. Listeners were confronted with the fact that the desire for dance driven by rhythmic propulsion cuts across time, history, and culture. Yet Bear Witness's employment of often explicitly racist visuals from classic Hollywood exhibitions of the Native other brought something more to the fore. It explicitly challenged the audience members to consider their own uptake of the fusion of musical styles being presented. Moreover, the fact that the performers themselves were First Nations people who identified as such multiple times during the performance caused even greater interpretive tension. That ATCR exhibit phenotypical characteristics that one would generally identify as indigenous while attiring themselves as your average urban hip-hop fans in hoodies, jeans, and fitted baseball hats was also a simple marker of the rhetorical force of their performance. Through the fusion of musical styles, the employment of repositioned and repurposed imagery, and their own self-presentation, A Tribe Called Red created an aesthetic assemblage that exhibited their indigeneity while also challenging the audience to confront presumably unconsciously held prejudices regarding what being Native could and should mean.

This performance thus enacted a creative repetition of traditional forms of indigeneity; as the classic American imagery of the noble savage, or cowboys versus Indians, flashes across the screen, engaging the audience with the familiar, ATCR are physically present, actively challenging the audience's conception of indigeneity. Their performance employs sonic and visual elements that are easily recognized as belonging to the purview of the indigenous—e.g., powwow drums and vocals—while recasting those traditional elements alongside musical and visual offerings that few members of the audience are likely to consider "authentically Indian." What truly secures their performance as an act of creative repetition, however, is the fact that through all of this dissonance, ATCR draws no attention to the dissonance itself. Rather they present what they are doing as precisely an exhibition of indigeneity, an exhibition of the living, moving, changing, and constant becoming-Indian.

The creative repetition of ATCR benefits the "we" (one of our key criteria for a productive/good assemblage) insofar as it challenges the audience to consider the force of colonialism and territorialized imagery, and to experience the possibilities of reclaiming, repurposing, and reusing for transformative ends. This is a productive assemblage, one instructive for composition. When considered through the questions, "Why this assemblage, what community does it benefit, and how does this act of culturing produce or encourage transformation?" ATCR provides a site for examining how objects can be placed into new neighborhoods without fixing identity, reterritorializing cultures, or colonizing meaning.

Deleuze and Guattari remind us that reality is not fixed, and therefore that the world is not there waiting to be plucked out of context (*What Is Philosophy?* 163–200). This is not to say the world isn't always already being reassembled, but it is to say that no one object—take the concept of the American Indian for example—is a static being. Instead there is, as ATCR highlight, a lived experience of being indigenous. Bear Witness describes this creative repetition:

> I'm a strong believer in the idea that culture and tradition are living, growing and changing things. We learn to understand our past to guide us into the future. I will always remember going to pow wows when I was a kid in the early '80s, right around the time break dancing was getting really big. There were fancy dancers who were adding break dancing moves in with the pow wow steps and things like checkered bandannas to their regalia. (Keene)

Kristin is reminded of a Nez Perce colleague whose uncle's powwow regalia from the 1980s included an elaborately hand-beaded Space Invaders mural.

Bear Witness, and the Space Invaders regalia, make clear that the conception of *being* Ojibwe or Nez Perce has nothing to do with an essentialized Indian standing still, frozen in time. There is nothing anachronistic about fancy dancers adding break dance moves or novel articles of clothing to their powwow regalia; this is creative repetition, as it attends to the specificities of the current milieu (the cultural expectations and context of the pow wow itself), while creating new ways of thinking through acts of disruption (the break dance or seemingly nontraditional item added to one's regalia, acts that function as a means of culturing, of transforming and fostering the culture). This may seem somewhat startling if pow wows are understood as sites wherein one can observe Indians behaving "authentically," insofar as authenticity is taken to mean comporting oneself in a manner that embraces and exhibits one's supposed nature or essence. However, if "culture and tradition are living, growing and changing things," then the very idea of authentically exhibiting a culture becomes significantly more complex, if not impossible. There is not one authentic model American Indian whom all other American Indians must mimic in order to *be* Indian, yet that is not to say that *being* American Indian has no meaning and can be anything. There is both the neighborhood of existing meaning and the possibility for transformation.

Creative repetition, then, asks composition instructors to consider the materials students use to compose assemblages while also considering how we might conceive of authenticity or propriety differently. In the case of Paul Frank's Dream Catchin' pow wow—which one might argue is an assemblage of modern fashion, club-like visuals, and stereotypes of the Indian—indigeneity is being repurposed for the sake of a fashion statement, one that takes an object out of context and assembles it not for transformation but for reterritorialization. As such, it is not a good/productive assemblage. Similarly, ATCR's pleading with fans not to wear headdresses to their shows also indicates that some objects in some contexts with some intentions are not good/productive assemblages. As Bear Witness says, "[The wearing of headdresses] gives the impression that Natives are something from the past. Not here today. If you were to think of an 'Indian' you certainly aren't going to think of me, tattooed in a hoodie with a Sens cap on. We, as First Nation people, have never had control of our image in colonial media since its birth" (Risk). Reclaim, repurpose, reuse.

Insofar as one tends to think of the indigenous as something past, something essential, the idea that there could be a form of music and art that is indigenous and that has become other than its past while maintaining continuity may be difficult. But by using images of Hollywood Indians from the 1950s, over which is laid a tribal beat and an electronic rhythm, ATCR's assemblage specifically challenges existing styles and stereotypes by incorporating juxtapositional media, media generally considered out of place in the context of indigenous works of art. The usage of stereotypical, clichéd, often racist imagery is a means of rhetorically evoking the sedimented conceptions of the indigenous that may lie in the audience. The performance itself exhibits a new manner of presenting oneself as indigenous, one that is growing and changing, and as a

result it is a good/productive assemblage. It illustrates "the ability to assert oneself renewed—in the presence of others" (Lyons,
"Rhetorical" 457). The assertion of A Tribe Called Red is that they
are still First Nations people, but that First Nations people are in a
perpetual process of becoming.

Returning to the question our opening story raises, is Santigold
and Diplo's "Get It Up" track a worthy assemblage when played by
Adam in the club? Probably not, given the audience's predisposed
comportments and subsequent reactions. Additionally, the track itself was not created by indigenous folks with an explicit intent to
deterritorialize colonial concepts of the Indian. That said, the track
may find itself in context (say, remixed in an ATCR performance)
where the subsequent assemblage may be productive. In the case of
ATCR, they cannot control the manner in which their audiences
may interpret or respond to their activity, but it is possible for them
to attend to this fact in advance and to act with specific intent.
One cannot fully predict or control the outcomes of communicative gestures, yet insofar as the gesture of ATCR is motivated by the
desire to open up new ways of thinking and being while still retaining consistency with the culture from which they emerge, one can
certainly recognize their existence, their songs, their performances
as moments of creative repetition.

For Deleuze and Guattari, a worthy assemblage is one that opens
up new possibilities for thought (*What Is Philosophy?*). Whether it
be through direct confrontation with non-Native fans who wear
headdresses to their performances or through subtler means of re-
appropriating explicitly racist visuals from the colonial (not so far
gone) past, ATCR attempts to shock their audience, breaking down
sedimented notions about indigenous life. Again, Bear Witness:

> [The images work because] we can confront people with mis-
> representations [of Indigenous people] in a different environ-
> ment. Their guards are down, and they get hit with the im-
> agery. [They can] think it's funny or entertaining, [but we're
> still] confronting people with what's racist, stereotypical and
> one-dimensional. Allowing people to make their own con-
> nections from the way they've been exposed, [to the way that

we're exposing them] lets people create a new interpretation [of Indigenous people]. [Our sets] help us to be able to articulate our side of the argument. [Through music], we're able to discuss and have those conversations [about respect for the rights of Indigenous people]. The music helps people come to grips with colonialism. [Ideally], we're a doorway to having [those conversations] happen. (Dowling; bracketed insertions in original)

Insofar as ATCR challenges its audience to think anew and outside of their assumed image of thought without betraying their own "ethnie," their performances, their recordings, their very manner of moving through the world serve as an excellent model of assemblage as creative repetition.

While assemblage as creative repetition is, we believe, a worthwhile pursuit for the composition classroom, we hope the specificities of American Indian composing practices remind us that the world is not full of concepts just waiting to be plucked from their contexts. Even if our objective is to create in such a way as to open up new worlds of possibility in response to a confrontation with problems that we presently lack the resources to resolve, we still must be cautious that our employment of and engagement with the world do not unconsciously repeat and reinforce the world from which we are attempting to find lines of flight. This requires attention, attentiveness not just to individual concepts, ideas, or images, but to the neighborhoods they inhabit and their genesis. Let us proceed with assemblage theory making sure to keep the question "Whom does this assemblage benefit?" at the forefront of our assemblage-making practices.

NOTES

1. For example, in the mid-2000s, when Diplo first began incorporating elements of what is generally referred to as baile funk, funk carioca, or favela funk—a tradition of dance music popular in the favelas of Brazil that in itself fuses elements from Miami bass and freestyle along with West Indian rhythms—into his production, particularly his work with M.I.A., he was constantly insistent that if you were into what he

was making, you really needed to attend to artists such as DJ Marlboro or Edu K from Brazil. And, moreover, he was emphatic that the cultural circumstances of life in a favela was an inextricable element of the music. In a sense, he attempted to bring to light issues of social justice through his incorporation of music from the global South into "First-World" club music.

2. We would be remiss were we not to point out that similar notions of being and becoming are also represented in indigenous thought as represented in tribal stories, as well as in the halls of academe through such Native philosophers as Vine Deloria Jr., Brian Yazzie Burkhart, Anne Waters, and Viola Cordova. We recommend you read these scholars if you are interested in the intersections between indigenous thought and any Western philosophy focused on issues of becoming or relationality, yet for the purposes of this article in this collection, we move forward with a focus on the affordances of Deleuze and Guattari's assemblage.

WORKS CITED

Bonta, Mark, and John Protevi. *Deleuze and Geophilosophy: A Guide and Glossary*. Edinburgh: Edinburgh UP, 2004. Print.

Deleuze, Gilles. *Difference and Repetition*. Trans. Paul Patton. New York: Columbia UP, 1994. Print.

————. *Negotiations, 1972–1990*. Trans. Martin Joughin. New York: Columbia UP, 1995. Print.

Deleuze, Gilles, and Félix Guattari. *A Thousand Plateaus*. Trans. Brian Massumi. Minneapolis: U of Minnesota P, 1987. Print. Vol. 2 of *Capitalism and Schizophrenia*. 2 vols. 1972–80.

————. *What Is Philosophy?* New York: Columbia UP, 1994. Print.

Dowling, Marcus. "A Tribe Called Red Speak on Producing for Angel Haze, Their Live Show, and Representing for Indigenous People." Complex.com. Complex, 20 Feb. 2014. Web. 13 Sep. 2016.

Garcia, Rachel. "Fashion's Night Out Fans Choose Kardashians over Real Designers." *Hollywood Reporter* 7 Sep. 2012: n. pag. Web. 13 Sep. 2016.

Johnson-Eilola, Johndan, and Stuart A. Selber. "Plagiarism, Originality, Assemblage." *Computers and Composition* 24.4 (2007): 375–403. http://dx.doi.org/10.1016/j.compcom.2007.08.003.

Keene, Adrienne. "A Tribe Called Red: Powwow Step and Social Commentary for the Masses." *Native Appropriations.com*. Native Appropriations, 27 Mar. 2012. Web. 13 Oct. 2016.

Lyons, Scott Richard. "Rhetorical Sovereignty: What Do American Indians Want from Writing?" *College Composition and Communication* 51.3 (2000): 447–68. *ProQuest*. Web. 22 Oct. 2016.

———. *X-Marks: Native Signatures of Assent*. Minneapolis: U of Minnesota P, 2010. Print.

Poulakos, John. "Toward a Sophistic Definition of Rhetoric." *Philosophy and Rhetoric* 16.1 (1983): 35–48. Print.

Risk, Trevor. "A Tribe Called Red Want White Fans to 'Please Stop' Wearing Redface 'Indian' Costume to Shows." *HuffPost Canada Music*. Huffington Post Canada, 12 July 2013. Web. 13 Sep. 2016.

Sirc, Geoffrey. "Serial Composition." *Rhetorics and Technologies: New Directions in Writing and Communication*. Ed. Stuart A. Selber. Columbia: U of South Carolina P, 2010. 56–73. Print.

Sommerstein, David. "Beats and Politics at A Tribe Called Red's 'Electric Pow Wow.'" NCPR, Canton, NY, 21 Nov. 2012. Radio. *Northcountrypublicradio.org*. Web. 22 Oct. 2016.

12

Conclusion: Reterritorialization

Johndan Johnson-Eilola and Stuart A. Selber

> In a book, as in all things, there are lines of articulation or seg-
> mentarity, strata and territories; but also lines of flight, move-
> ments of deterritorialization and destratification.
> —Gilles Deleuze and Félix Guattari, *A Thousand Plateaus*

COMING TO THE END, WE LOOP ROUND AGAIN. There is not, as you
may have noticed, a single way to articulate "assemblage." Assemblages, like languages or literacies or texts, are recursive and shifting
networks, taking in and dropping off as they go, articulating and
disarticulating. Assemblages are not novel or new, but a different
way of understanding what we are doing and experiencing. That
difference can reshape and redirect how we read and write.

In reading the chapters, we identified at least four emergent
themes around which "assemblage" tended, at least briefly: assemblage as connection with other peoples and times, assemblage
as material object, assemblage as performance, and assemblage as
pedagogy. In these final pages, we reterritorialize or rearticulate the
diverging chapters around those themes to weave the text back together. For now.

ASSEMBLAGE AS CONNECTION WITH
OTHER PEOPLES AND TIMES

When we connect the present to the past, we necessarily decontextualize and recontextualize: We take ourselves back by bringing
something else forward. A text travels forward in time and brings a
chunk of its present always with it, "the infinite process of becom-

ing," as Kristin Arola and Adam Arola, drawing on Gilles Deleuze, phrase it. All of the texts within this text explicitly and implicitly decontextualize and recontextualize the texts that came before them.

On Oliver's tombstone, only a year is provided, presumably the year of death; meaning is made through a symmetrical layout, the sans serif lowercase font used for "son," keyed to a relationship with parents, juxtaposed with the serif font in all capital letters identifying the particular son Oliver. In both these tombstones—son Oliver and Baby Munroe—font style and size matter, as does layout, but no visuals adorn the tombstones, nor is any epitaph or sentiment provided.

> Kathleen Blake Yancey, "Multimodal Assemblage, Compositions, and Composing: The Corresponding Cases of Emigrant Cemetery Tombstones and 'A Line for Wendy'"

When we think and write history, we cannot capture a hidden past; we can only, as Brian Massumi says, "experimentally perturb it as we walk our life's path and see what comes" (68). A physical object hurtles into the future and sparks in us ideas. Meanings are made as we take the object within our networks.

The ribbon appears to have been free-drawn, and the letters within it seem to have been inked by hand as well. Some physical evidence speaks to this inking process: the now seventy-year-old adhesive that was used to hold the elements of the design together is failing, and consequently we can see that the first attempt to ink the word *message* was considered unsatisfactory and was replaced with a second attempt that was affixed in its place. Similar adhesive-related evidence can be seen in the first letter in the word *Colorado*. From the portion of the letter that has come loose, we can see that photographic copies of each of the existing texts were made, portions of them were cut out in the shapes of the letters' faces, and those portions were affixed to the design, which could then be sent on for colorization and printing. We can see from this example, then, the ways in which material assemblage was vital to the process of designing and producing large-letter postcards.

Stephen J. McElroy, "Assemblages of Asbury Park:
The Persistent Legacy of the Large-Letter Postcard"

The historical object is not timeless. Like us, it ages, decays, crumbles. The "Colorado" of the seventy-year-old postcard is not the "Colorado" of today. There is, indeed, no one "Colorado," only many "Colorados," multiple ongoing and interconnected assemblages.

However, insofar as Deleuze creates an ontology wherein being is nothing more than a momentary freezing of the infinite process of becoming, repetition for him can never be repetition of the same as such. Repetition of the same is governed by nostalgia and is what Deleuze calls "bare repetition"; imagine one insisting that the only proper way to honor one's tradition as an Ojibwe is to perform a fancy dance at a pow wow in the exact same way as your ancestors. Here one has become enslaved or subjugated to an image of identity that has frozen time and treats oneself as the instantiation of some preexisting essence; in other words, to return to Scott Lyons, such bare repetition grants us precisely all the things Native folks *do not want* from writing. On the other hand, creative repetition would be to harness the expressive and disruptive force of the pow wow itself insofar as it creates new prospective territories for becoming just as all well-performed pow wows always have, which requires that one repeat consistently, but not dogmatically. To repeat dogmatically would be to try to "get everything right," as if there were a transcendent pow wow in the sky that one must mimic. To repeat creatively but consistently requires that one repeat by attending to the specificities of the current milieu, so as to create new ways of thinking and experiencing in the present circumstance, but disrupt in a manner that resonates with disruptions or deter-ritorializations caused by pow wows of the past.

> Kristin L. Arola and Adam Arola, "An Ethics of Assemblage:
> Creative Repetition and the 'Electric Pow Wow'"

Any dance is an ongoing assemblage. Connecting with other peo-ples and other times necessarily involves deterritorializing and re-territorializing. To "get everything right" would be to consign our-selves to dusty museum exhibits.

ASSEMBLAGE AS MATERIAL OBJECT

Assemblages are temporal but they are also material, the ongoing construction of objects over time. Material objects are, literally, meaningless without our assembling them, over and over again, in our own meaning systems.

> The cemetery itself is a kind of assemblage, hosting a four-part set of multilayered compositions—first, the composi-tion of the cemetery itself (in its layout, foliage, and so on); second, the tombstone compositions, which are richly mul-timodal assemblages; third, what I am calling tombstones extended, sites for improvisational compositions including flowers, flags, beer bottles, stickers, and children's toys; and fourth, the collective composition of the cemetery itself, the portrait it makes of the community which created it and which it represents.

> Kathleen Blake Yancey, "Multimodal Assemblage,
> Compositions, and Composing: The Corresponding
> Cases of Emigrant Cemetery Tombstones and
> 'A Line for Wendy'"

The tombstone becomes enmeshed into the "tombstone extended" into the "Colorado" of the past into the "Colorado" of the present (ongoing) into the community of us (whoever we are, whenever we are).

Again, with Karp's words in mind—collecting is "all about what you choose to be responsible for"—it proves helpful to think about academic, pedagogical, and/or scholarly collections (or collecting practices) in terms of care, choice, commitment, and responsibility. Whether I am creating a print-based linear text, a piece of video scholarship, an assignment, or an in-class activity, I can consider the ways in which, and the degree to which, I have committed to and assume responsibility for the experience or product I share with others.

Jody Shipka, "To Gather, Assemble, and
Display: Composition as [Re]Collection"

An ethics of assemblage, then, would ask us to consider carefully not only the material object, but how that object will be deterritorialized and reterritorialized by those around us. Everything we make will be taken apart and put back together in new ways. We must attend to ourselves and what we make as historical assemblages that will be taken up by others (or ourselves), remade, put together in other contexts. An ethics of assemblages requires that we not oversimplify (or undersimplify) those possibilities (even if we cannot, ultimately, control them).

"One must do much more as a designer [of assemblages]," write Johnson-Eilola and Selber, "than download templates and replace their placeholder items with real content" (391). This is undoubtedly true and yet templates seem deceptively simple to use, sending an implicit message that writing with them is basically an exercise in filling in the blanks. Even selecting a template, as Anders Fagerjord argues, involves a complex decision-making process in which one considers interface, design, and genre precepts that will shape one's composing experience. When assembling compositions, students thus will need opportunities to experiment with different templates in order to discover the affordances and constraints each makes available. This process of experimentation, when combined with discussion and reflection, can further develop students' rhetorical skill.

> Michael J. Michaud, "Assemblage
> Composing, Reconsidered"

Templates provide a rich resource for helping others see how assemblages operate. We take, we take apart, we put together. We often think of templates as something different from finished texts, but templates can show us, and our students, that no text is ever complete. Texts are only stable when "taken out of context"—a misleading phrase because everything is always taken out of context. It has to be. Every text is taken, taken apart, put together.

> This is a useful starting point. However, assemblage theory
> ultimately cannot be limited to the conceptual, linguistic,
> and sociopolitical. It is, more broadly, an ontological theory,
> describing the processes by which objects emerge, maintain
> their identity, relate with others, and mutate. In short, as-
> semblage theory is a theory of composition conceived in the
> broadest possible sense.

> Alex Reid, "Big-Data Assemblies:
> Composing's Nonhuman Ecology"[1]

Indeed. Assemblage theory is not only "a theory of composition conceived in the broadest possible sense." *Living* is a theory of composition conceived in the broadest possible sense.

ASSEMBLAGE AS PERFORMANCE

Once we start to see assemblages as both temporal and material, we start to see assemblage in its verb form: An assemblage is a performance. A performance that never ends, that is continually taken up and reperformed. An ongoing becoming.

> A successful reflection will show both awareness of exigence
> and an appropriate selection of audience(s) and an awareness
> of the fittingness of the assembled texts, medium, and genre

for the selected audience. It will also speak to the process of assemblage: which texts were copied, how they were transformed, and how those texts serve their rhetorical purpose.

Stephen J. McElroy and Travis Maynard,
"Copy, Combine, Transform: Assemblage
in First-Year Composition"

When we take up texts—our own or others'—we are, in many senses, reperforming texts, reassembling texts. It becomes difficult to separate what is *my* text from what is *your* text. We cite, we quote, we set up boundaries and fences to maintain our identities, but they fall apart as fast as we can build them.

Right-click-steal. From where I sat as a teacher of college writing, it was a phrase that made me nervous.

Michael J. Michaud, "Assemblage
Composing, Reconsidered"

Performing assemblage makes us nervous. How many syllabi contain sections on plagiarism that are plagiarized from our institution's plagiarism policies? (We think we've heard this idea before—maybe Jim Porter? Perhaps someone else, but it has his keen perception.) Plagiarism happens everywhere, and we should not be surprised: Our institutions and our students collaborate with us on reassembling us as teachers. That process raises issues both interesting and troubling.

Assemblage, as I shall thus stress throughout this chapter, is not only about the process of combining digital artifacts for a professional portfolio, but also—and perhaps even more significantly—about the process of representing stages of identity formation. For graduate students, this is a liminal process—from being to becoming and back again—as they experiment with multiple tools and genres, even when the larger disciplinary culture encourages a more stable sense of self and academic ethos through genres such as the alphabetic cover letter and *curriculum vitae* intended to meet the expectations of hiring committees.

> Kristine L. Blair, "ePortfolio Artifacts as Graduate
> Student Multimodal Identity Assemblages"

So our students, just as much as do we and our institutions, all collaborate in the endless remaking of identities. Never static. Never isolated. We like to think of ourselves as having some stability—"unstable" used as shorthand for psychologically dysfunctional and dangerous—but it's always a stumbling process searching for a moving center of gravity. Which is a good thing.

> Link sharing functions as a type of response; I read something, believe it has meaning, and in order to respond to that meaning share the link with others who I believe will find meaning in it as well. The other members within my social network, in turn, may share that link. In doing so, we believe that the pieces of information we engage with are, following Karine Nahon and Jeff Hemsley, *remarkable*. "By this we mean that they exhibit qualities such that people want to make a remark about them."

> Jeff Rice, "They Eat Horses, Don't They?"

Language, as William Burroughs famously said, is a virus; signatures, as Jacques Derrida illustrated, prove nothing. The link, any text that gestures at another text, is a material trace of something becoming something else. That original something is never recoverable because that trace always changes it, reassembles it into something related. Not completely new but not unchanged, even if we can't tell what has changed.

> Is this OK? I picture our mother, an Anishinaabe jingle dress powwow dancer. What would she think? What would the tribe think? Is this assemblage OK? I love the sound of the drum at pow wows, the heartbeat that keeps the dancers moving,

and in spite of myself I pick up my pace and continue to jog
to the beat. Tha-thump, tha-thump, tha-thump.

Kristin L. Arola and Adam Arola, "An Ethics of Assemblage:
Creative Repetition and the 'Electric Pow Wow'"

History, then, is also a performance, a reterritorialization in the ongoing moment. We have to continually ask ourselves, "Is this OK?"
because we have a responsibility to ourselves and to others, even as
both "ourselves" and "others" are simultaneously fictional and real.
The walls break down if we look at them too long, but they also
help us function. A "habit," as Deleuze and Guattari implied (3),
but one that's helpful. The habit pushes us to think about, among
other things, what we are asking when we ask others to read our
texts. What are we asking them to reassemble? To learn?

ASSEMBLAGE AS PEDAGOGY

We are asking that people recognize that what they are doing is
disassembling and reassembling. Not that any of us has a choice
about disassembling and reassembling, only about recognition. (All
cognition is re-cognition.) Even if we don't try to help students see
texts as assemblages, we are always teaching them how to make
assemblages. Writing has always been assemblage, even if the texts
looked seamless.

This course in FYC was conceived among a constellation of
several factors and events.

Stephen J. McElroy and Travis Maynard, "Copy, Combine,
Transform: Assemblage in First-Year Composition"

When we and our students begin to recognize everything as a constellation, we can recognize that the question is not whether we
should teach assemblage but how we teach assemblage.

Further, because assemblages in digital environments usually
remix visual and textual elements, students must attend not
just to the words they are producing, but also to the texts and

images they are borrowing and the interaction between the textual and visual elements of their assemblages.

Michael J. Michaud, "Assemblage
Composing, Reconsidered"

But if we can highlight those seams, locate the cracks, we can illuminate how assemblages are constructed. Cracks, Leonard Cohen told us, are "how the light gets in."

What I did realize, however, was that creating texts in such an environment was nothing like the writing I did as a student. To create a webpage in this environment, students had to learn bits and pieces of lots of different disciplines, lots of different software. Instead of the page as a unitary object with words (and sometimes pictures), students had to conceptualize the page as an assemblage composed of lots of little bits and pieces of text, images, videos, etc., potentially stored on servers across the world. Similarly, they had to deconstruct their identity as writers into lots of little pieces of identity and then manage those pieces.[2]

James Kalmbach, "Beyond the Object to the Making
of the Object: Understanding the Process of
Multimodal Composition as Assemblage"

Assemblage feels weird to those of us trained (as we were) in traditional composition: sitting in front of a blank page or screen, waiting for the words to flow. From ourselves, not from elsewhere. New types of texts—the website, the Twitter feed—we can also look back to traditional composition and see that it's always been thus: We do not create unique, original texts in isolation. We've known that at one level for a very long time, but these new forms of text, concrete assemblages—populated with cracks, seams, stitches—ask us to rethink and reassemble how we approach all forms of text. We are all students now.

This lens allows us to ask of ATCR's assemblages a multipart question that embodies our criteria for a productive assemblage: "Why this assemblage, what community does it benefit, and how does this act of culturing produce or encourage transformation?"

Kristin L. Arola and Adam Arola, "An Ethics of Assemblage:
Creative Repetition and the 'Electric Pow Wow'"

We return (always) to the ethics of assemblage: What are we asking people to become when they learn from us? What are they reassembling when they are in our classrooms? When they read the texts we assemble with and from them? Questions that do not have stable answers, which is a good thing. Instead, a constant performance: disassemblage and reassemblage, call and response, writing and rewriting.

NOTES
1. From an earlier draft.
2. From an earlier draft.

WORKS CITED

Deleuze, Gilles, and Félix Guattari. *A Thousand Plateaus.* Trans. Brian Massumi. Minneapolis: U of Minnesota P, 1987. Print. Vol. 2 of *Capitalism and Schizophrenia.* 2 vols. 1972–80.

Massumi, Brian. *A User's Guide to Capitalism and Schizophrenia: Deviations from Deleuze and Guattari.* Cambridge: MIT P, 1992. Print.

INDEX

Note: An *n* following a page number indicates a note; an *f* indicates a figure.

233

EDITORS

Kathleen Blake Yancey is Kellogg W. Hunt Professor of English and Distinguished Research Professor at Florida State University. She has served in several elected leadership positions: as president of the National Council of Teachers of English (NCTE); chair of the Conference on College Composition and Communication (CCCC); president of the Council of Writing Program Administrators (CWPA); and president of the South Atlantic Modern Language Association (SAMLA). Immediate past editor of *College Composition and Communication,* she co-founded the journal *Assessing Writing* and coedited it for seven years: she also co-founded and co-directs the Inter/National Coalition for Electronic Portfolio Research; and she is the lead investigator for the Transfer of Transfer Project, a cross-institutional research study of the efficacy of the Teaching for Transfer (TFT) writing curriculum. In addition, she serves on the boards of several groups, including of the Association for Authentic, Experiential and Evidence-Based Learning. Author or coauthor of over one hundred articles and chapters, Yancey has also authored, coauthored, edited, or coedited thirteen scholarly books, including *Reflection in the Writing Classroom; Assessing Writing Across the Curriculum: Diverse Approaches and Practices; Electronic Portfolios 2.0: Emergent Research on Implementation and Impact; Delivering College Composition: The Fifth Canon; A Rhetoric of Reflection;* and *Writing across Contexts: Transfer, Composition, and Sites of Writing.* She is the recipient of several awards, among them both the CCCC Research Impact Award and the Council of Writing Program Administrators Best Book Award for *Writing across Contexts;* the Purdue Distinguished Women Scholars Award; the FSU Graduate Faculty Mentor Award; and the Donald Murray Prize.

Stephen J. McElroy, PhD, is director of the Reading-Writing Center and Digital Studio at Florida State University. He has pursued his broad interest in visual rhetoric, multimodal design, and digital composing—in terms of both theory and practice as well as both past and present—recently in the *Computers and Composition* article "Assemblage by Design: The Postcards of Curt Teich & Company," which examines the design and production of picture postcards in the early twentieth century, focusing specifically on cards produced by Teich & Company and depicting scenes of Key West, Florida. Examining microhistories of design and production through the lens of assemblage, he argues, helps us better attend to and better theorize our current composing practices. In connection with this work, Stephen is a co-founder, along with Michael Neal and Katherine Bridgman, of the FSU Card Archive <http://fsucardarchive.org/>, a digital archive of around five thousand postcards with scans of both the fronts and the backs of cards, enabling researchers and enthusiasts to explore the imagery of the postcard fronts and the writing on the backs. With Neal and Bridgman, he also coauthored the *Kairos* webtext "Making Meaning at the Intersections: Developing a Digital Archive for Multimodal Research," which won the 2014 *Computers and Composition* Michelle Kendrick Outstanding Digital Production/Scholarship Award. His current projects include developing, in collaboration with Matt Davis and Rory Lee, a set of videographic interviews with prominent scholars on "Ways of Knowing and Doing in Digital Rhetoric." Stephen currently lives in downtown Tallahassee with his wife Gloria, their baby daughter Viola, and their three cats.

CONTRIBUTORS

Adam Arola holds a PhD in philosophy from the University of Oregon and currently works as a strategic planner at Wieden+Kennedy in Portland. He has taught at numerous institutions around the Pacific Northwest and published widely on issues in phenomenology, the history of philosophy, and critical theory and mass culture, as well as indigenous philosophy—including the entry on Native American Philosophy in the *Oxford Handbook of World Philosophy*. Arola also maintains a career as a nationally recognized club DJ under the name Doc Adam.

Kristin L. Arola is associate professor of rhetoric, composition, and technology at Washington State University, where she also serves as director of graduate studies for the Department of English. Her research focuses on the intersections between indigenous rhetoric and multimodal pedagogy. Along with numerous articles and book chapters, she is coauthor of *Writer/Designer: A Guide to Making Multimodal Projects* and coeditor of both *Cross-Talk in Comp Theory: A Reader* and *Composing (Media) = Composing (Embodiment): Bodies, Technologies, Writing, the Teaching of Writing*.

Kristine L. Blair is professor of English and dean of the College of Liberal Arts and Social Sciences at Youngstown State University. She taught courses in digital composing and scholarly publication in the rhetoric and writing doctoral program at Bowling Green State University from 1996 to 2016, where she also served as English department chair from 2005 to 2014. In addition to publishing in the areas of gender and technology, online learning, electronic portfolios, and faculty development, Blair currently serves as editor of both the international print journal *Computers and Composition* and its separate companion journal *Computers and Composition Online*. She is a recipient of the CCCC Technology Innovator Award and the Computers and Composition Charles Moran Award for Distinguished Contributions to the Field.

Johndan Johnson-Eilola works at Clarkson University, where he teaches courses in information design, typography, and audio production. In addition to nearly fifty book chapters and journal articles, he has written, cowritten, or coedited books including *Changing Writing: A Guide with Scenarios*; *Datacloud: Toward a New Theory of Online Work*; *Writing New Media: Theory and Applications for Expanding the Teaching of Composition* (cowritten with Anne Frances Wysocki, Cynthia Selfe, and Geoffrey Sirc); and *Central Works in Technical Communication* and *Solving Problems in Technical Communication* (both coedited with Stuart A. Selber). His work has won awards from NCTE, *Computers and Composition*, *Technical Communication Quarterly*, *Kairos*, and the Council of Writing Program Administrators.

James Kalmbach is the author of *The Computer and the Page: Publishing, Technology and the Classroom* and coeditor (with Cheryl Ball) of *RAW: (Reading and Writing) New Media*. From his first job at Michigan Technological University to his last at Illinois State University, he spent his career exploring the intersections between teaching, technology, and literacy. He is now happily retired and living in Normal, Illinois, where he continues to work with graduate students and direct the English department's internship program.

Travis Maynard is a graduate instructor at Florida State University, where he teaches in the college composition and Editing, Writing, and Media (EWM) programs. A native of eastern Kentucky, he received his BA in writing, rhetoric, and communication from Lexington's Transylvania University; his MA thesis at Florida State examined the use of Kuhnian scientific rhetoric in young-Earth creationist textbooks. His interests beyond assemblage include media studies and the undergraduate major in writing and rhetoric, topics locating his presentations at the Conference on College Composition and Communication and the Rhetoric Society of America. When he's not teaching or writing, you can find him experimenting with video projects, collecting vinyl records, or hunting for treasure at thrift stores.

Michael J. Michaud is associate professor of English and chair of the campus Writing Board at Rhode Island College in Providence, Rhode Island. He teaches courses in digital and multimedia writing, professional writing, composition, and rhetoric. His research interests include approaches to teaching writing, archival research, Writing about Writing

(WAW), and, most recently, the multimajor professional writing course. His work has appeared in *College Composition and Communication*, *Writing and Pedagogy*, *Writing on the Edge*, and is forthcoming in *Intermezzo*. His current book project investigates the history of the writing-process movement as it unfolded at the University of New Hampshire, twice his alma mater.

Alex Reid is associate professor and director of composition and teaching fellows in the English department at the University at Buffalo, where he studies digital rhetoric. He is the author of *The Two Virtuals: New Media and Composition*; the coeditor of *Design Discourse: Composing and Revising Professional Writing Programs*; and the author of "Exposing Assemblages: Unlikely Communities of Digital Scholarship, Video, and Social Networks," published in *enculturation* and selected for *The Best of the Independent Rhetoric and Composition Journals 2011*. He blogs at Digital Digs (alex-reid.net).

Jeff Rice is department chair and Martha B. Reynolds Professor of Writing, Rhetoric, and Digital Studies at the University of Kentucky. The author of more than twenty articles and chapters on rhetoric, composition, and new media, he has also authored or coedited several books, including *The Rhetoric of Cool: Composition Studies and New Media*; *Digital Detroit: Rhetoric and Space in the Age of the Network*; *New Media/New Methods: The Academic Turn from Literacy to Electracy*; and *Craft Obsession: The Social Rhetorics of Beer*.

Stuart A. Selber is associate professor of English at Penn State University, where he directs the Penn State Digital English Studio and works in the rhetoric program. Selber is the author of *Multiliteracies for a Digital Age* and the coeditor, with Johndan Johnson-Eilola, of *Solving Problems in Technical Communication* and *Central Works in Technical Communication*. Selber is a past president of the Association of Teachers of Technical Writing and the Council for Programs in Technical and Scientific Communication and a past chair of the CCCC Committee on Technical Communication. He has won several disciplinary awards for his research publications.

Jody Shipka is associate professor of English at the University of Maryland, Baltimore County, where she teaches courses in the communication and technology track. She is the author of *Toward a Composition Made*

Whole and the editor of *Play! A Collection of Sixty-three Toy Camera Photographs Made by Thirty-six Photographers in Twelve Countries*. Her work has appeared in *College Composition and Communication*, *College English*, *Computers and Composition*, *enculturation*, *Itineration*, *Kairos*, *Text and Talk*, and a number of edited collections, including *Writing Selves, Writing Societies: Research from Activity Perspectives*; *Exploring Semiotic Remediation as Discourse Practice*; *Multimodal Literacies and Emerging Genres*; *First-Year Composition: From Theory to Practice*; and *Provocations: Reconstructing the Archive*.

BOOKS IN THE CCCC STUDIES IN WRITING & RHETORIC SERIES

Whistlin' and Crowin' Women of Appalachia: Literacy Practices since College
Katherine Kelleher Sohn

Sexuality and the Politics of Ethos in the Writing Classroom
Zan Meyer Gonçalves

African American Literacies Unleashed: Vernacular English and the Composition Classroom
Arnetha F. Ball and Ted Lardner

Revisionary Rhetoric, Feminist Pedagogy, and Multigenre Texts
Julie Jung

Archives of Instruction: Nineteenth-Century Rhetorics, Readers, and Composition Books in the United States
Jean Ferguson Carr, Stephen L. Carr, and Lucille M. Schultz

Response to Reform: Composition and the Professionalization of Teaching
Margaret J. Marshall

Multiliteracies for a Digital Age
Stuart A. Selber

Personally Speaking: Experience as Evidence in Academic Discourse
Candace Spigelman

Self-Development and College Writing
Nick Tingle

Minor Re/Visions: Asian American Literacy Narratives as a Rhetoric of Citizenship
Morris Young

A Communion of Friendship: Literacy, Spiritual Practice, and Women in Recovery
Beth Daniell

Embodied Literacies: Imageword and a Poetics of Teaching
Kristie S. Fleckenstein

Language Diversity in the Classroom: From Intention to Practice
edited by Geneva Smitherman and Victor Villanueva

Rehearsing New Roles: How College Students Develop as Writers
Lee Ann Carroll

Across Property Lines: Textual Ownership in Writing Groups
Candace Spigelman

Mutuality in the Rhetoric and Composition Classroom
David L. Wallace and Helen Rothschild Ewald

The Young Composers: Composition's Beginnings in Nineteenth-Century Schools
Lucille M. Schultz

Technology and Literacy in the Twenty-First Century: The Importance of Paying Attention
Cynthia L. Selfe

Women Writing the Academy: Audience, Authority, and Transformation
Gesa E. Kirsch

Gender Influences: Reading Student Texts
Donnalee Rubin

Something Old, Something New: College Writing Teachers and Classroom Change
Wendy Bishop

Dialogue, Dialectic, and Conversation: A Social Perspective on the Function of Writing
Gregory Clark

Audience Expectations and Teacher Demands
Robert Brooke and John Hendricks

Toward a Grammar of Passages
Richard M. Coe

This book was typeset in Garamond and Frutiger by Barbara Frazier.
Typefaces used on the cover include Adobe Garamond and Formata.
The book was printed on 55-lb. Natural Offset paper
by King Printing Company, Inc.